To Dan Coll
with best wishes for
a great 87!

Bill
12-1-86

Significant Trends In Agency Management

Significant Trends In Agency Management

Eleven directions that will determine survival and success

By Robert L. Utne, CLU

FARNSWORTH PUBLISHING COMPANY, INC.
(a Longman Group USA company)
Rockville Centre, New York 11570

© 1985, Robert L. Utne.
All rights reserved.
Published by Farnsworth Publishing Co., Inc.
(a Longman Group USA company)
78 Randall Avenue
Rockville Centre, New York 11570.
Library of Congress Catalog Card No. 85-70594.
ISBN 0-87863-239-5.
Manufactured in the United States of America.
No part of this book may be reproduced
without the written permission of the publisher.

To Edith, with love and gratitude. And also to Bob Jr., Eric, Mary, Phil, Greg, and sorely missed Tom. Special acknowledgements, and thanks too, to Dan Chabot and Larry Wilson.

Finally and importantly, this book is dedicated to general agents and managers everywhere. As they help others to grow, they themselves grow. What a wonderful way to live!

Contents

Introduction

In October of 1982, near the end of my 13 years as part of the Wilson Learning Corporation, the company held a Clients' Conference that featured an impressive array of guest speakers.

One was Warren Bennis, distinguished author, educator and university administrator, currently the Dubell Distinguished Professor at the University of Southern California. He told of having just completed what he called his "Odyssey" of four and a half years during which he held in-depth interviews with 90 outstanding leaders/achievers in an effort to learn what significant common traits, abilities, skills, philosophies, and attitudes might be revealed. Sixty were Chief Executive Officers of Fortune 1000 companies. The others came from various fields and included educators, artists, entrepreneurs, and even a preeminently successful basketball coach. Dr. Bennis told of the book he was preparing and shared with us observations he'd made to date.

I was fascinated. First, because it's a fascinating subject. But even more because I had a feeling of kinship with the speaker. It occurred to me that my credentials for making observations about the leaders in the art and science of agency management were every bit as good as Warren Bennis' for his chosen assignment. He interviewed 90 people in four and a half years. Why, as Bob Turner, the itinerant GAMC interviewer for the Legacy of Learning audiocassette series, I had interviewed more than 150 leading agency heads in six years! And worked intimately in and with their industry for more than four decades. I had recently given talks to meetings of agency heads in Toronto, New Orleans and Minneapolis in which I shared some of my observations, and it was evident that I could serve as a channel of communication to agency managers, present and future, who were eager to learn what their outstanding peers were currently doing and thinking.

I had more than 3,000 pages of transcripts of those interviews, a veritable treasure-trove of agency management lore. Why not put together a book, based upon those interviews, presenting in organized fashion the most timely ideas and methods of the best agency heads anywhere?

One reason why not: it would take a lot of time and work. One reason why: I was about to retire. I'd have the time, and certainly it would be a labor of love, for these are the people, and theirs is the calling, that intrigue me above all others.

So I laid the idea before some leading general agents and managers at the annual Life Agency Management Program (LAMP) in Phoenix, and was heartened by their encouragement. Prospective publishers encountered there were keenly interested too.

And then my wife and I read John Naisbitt's best seller, *Megatrends: Ten New Directions Transforming Our Lives.* That cinched it. Where his organization tracked significant trends in our total society by monitoring the space accorded them in the press, perhaps now I could identify significant trends in agency management by reviewing the emphases given them in these many, many interviews over the most dynamic six-year period in the history of a great industry!

By going through the transcript of every single interview, and by noting every time the interviewee cited a given area of his responsibilities, and then putting that observation together with every other observation in that specific area by every other interviewee who touched on it (a formidable undertaking—just how formidable I had no idea!), then the truly significant trends in agency management should emerge with crystal clarity. They could be identified and stated. They could be exemplified with illustrations from specific and real agencies, and could be described in the very words of those being quoted.

Each chapter of this volume is devoted to one of those trends. It will be noted that there is but incidental mention of the product revolution, of financial planning on a fee basis, or the entry into the multiple-line world by so many companies and agencies, important as those and similar developments may be.

That is because the 11 trends cited apply across the industry. Timely recognition of the trends will enable alert agency heads to put themselves in positions of leadership in the field of agency management. For, as John Naisbitt says, "Leadership involves finding a parade and getting in front of it."

While specific products and services will continue to change and evolve and new ones will be introduced as conditions dictate, these significant trends will be discernible in the better agencies, irrespective of what combination of products they sell and markets they serve.

Now let me tell you how I feel about those people whose words really are the guts of this book, and all their peers, general agents and managers everywhere, for whom this book is intended.

Years ago my good friend and life insurance client Bill Gove, famous speaker to sales groups in all industries, called me and said, "Bob, Billy is thinking about going into the life insurance business. You know all the companies. You know who has good products and good training. That's why I'm calling you."

My response was, "Bill, many companies have good products and good training programs. The important thing is the guy—the manager or general agent there where Billy wants to live. What's he like? What is his track record? You see, Bill, *he* will have more to do with Billy's success than any other factor—products, training, financing or whatever. So the question is, how does Billy relate with *him*? It's the guy. He's the key."

Although today, because of some outstanding women who are blazing trails in agency management, I would say it's the "person," the principle remains the same. The success of any life insurance company in any location is largely determined by the person in charge of its sales outlet there.

If someone predicted that General Motors would sell more cars in Birmingham, Alabama than in Chicago, or that Coca-Cola sales in Denver would exceed those in Philadelphia, or that more Campbell soup would be bought in Boise, Idaho, than in Los Angeles, you'd send him to a shrink.

But the Birmingham agency often led all the giant Equitable Society's agencies in life insurance sales because of a guy, a guy named J.B. Conway.

The Denver agency was Number One in the largest company of all, The Prudential, because of a guy, a guy named Jim Smallwood.

And in sparsely populated Idaho the MONY (Mutual of New York) agency, headed by a guy named Aldin Porter, consistently outperforms its peers in great metropolitan centers with far more people and buying power.

In the whole hierarchy of a life insurance company—from the Chairman of the Board to the lowliest shipping clerk—the key persons are the agency heads. In my experience it's easy to get a company's president to concede that when his agency heads are meeting their objectives, the company will meet its objectives. Quantitative and qualitative company goals, whether in sales, mortality, persistency or profits, are directly influenced by the performance of its field management corps.

When I was a general agent I often said, and meant, that the agents were key. And of course it's true that without those agents doing the creative job of finding persons to talk with, helping them fix their objectives, understand their needs and *do* something about them, nothing would happen. The Home Office would have nothing to do—no applications to review, no money to invest nor claims to pay. But, without the agency heads there would be no agents recruited, trained, supervised, led, inspired, worked with, counseled with, cried with, and all the other thousand and one things general agents and managers do with and for their producers.

A college coach can't produce a winning record without good athletes to develop, competent assistants and real support from the institution, the alumni and community. But winning coaches have a way of developing those things. At a GAMC Board of Directors meeting a few years ago, I challenged those present to name any member of the current championship Alabama football team. None could. They all knew, though, that the coach was Bear Bryant!

So, too, a winning agency head finds ways to "turn a program around." Norman Levine moved across the continent, changed companies, and "turned the program around" in San Francisco.

Many wonderful but less well-known managers and general agents are doing the same thing—although not always as dramatically. Daily, they are helping men and women to higher achievements and rewards than they have ever dreamed of. They are doing so all over North America. I've met them in Florida, in Canada, in sophisticated population centers, in suburbs, in smaller cities and towns. I respect them. I admire them. I want this volume to honor them.

It's frustrating to me that only their peers can really understand and appreciate the significance of the careers of successful agency heads. Others don't. They can't. All they can do is observe the outer symbols of success.

I'm retired now. These words are being written at a golfing mecca full of oldsters like me. To a few of them I have confided that I'm working on a book about agency management in the life insurance business. That probably sounds like pretty pallid stuff to the man who built a business from nothing and sold it for several million dollars. I can't really explain to him while riding in a golf cart to the next tee that these top-flight agency heads I'm writing about are truly exciting people who make important and enduring contributions to the communities and the society of which they are a part.

But that really isn't important. The audience for this project is today's and tomorrow's agency heads—as well as all those in Home Offices and educational institutions who can benefit from a better understanding of the significant role of the agency head in this most significant industry.

I hope they will make many, many trips to this volume for the ideas and inspiration (as well as confirmation of their present sound practices) that I know await them, thanks to the greats we have been able to quote on every aspect of agency management.

1 | You Don't Have To Reinvent The Wheel

The Agency Head as a Learner

> **SIGNIFICANT TREND:** More agency
> heads will make a conscious effort to
> learn from the experience of their suc-
> cessful peers.

Remember the philosophy of the confirmed gambler? He
says, "Y'know, you really ought to shoot a little craps every
day—else you might be walking around lucky and not even
know it!"

The same philosopher might well subscribe to the cliché
that "it's better to be lucky than smart." But it's the major
premise of this volume that everyone in the agency end of the
life insurance business is lucky—lucky to be in a business
where seeming competitors, agents and managers alike, are
quite willing to share their ideas and methods with one
another.

Those who are smart take advantage of this phenomenon.
Those who are less than smart don't. They're dumb. They are
walking around lucky and don't even know it.

Current "new age" writers such as Marilyn Ferguson and
John Naisbitt have called our attention to the "networking"
phenomenon. Naisbitt says that "networks are people talking
to each other, sharing ideas, information and resources."
One of his 10 megatrends is the giving up of hierarchal structure in favor of informal networks. Ferguson, in her book
The Aquarian Conspiracy, says that networking is done by
"conferences, phone calls, air travel, books, phantom organizations, papers, pamphleteering, photocopying, lectures,
workshops, parties, grapevines, mutual friends, summit
meetings, coalitions, tapes, newsletters."

Well! Now we know what to call it. Life insurance people
have been way ahead of the rest of the world in this area. We
were "networking" all the time, and didn't even know it. We
just called it sharing.

Agents found out long ago that they could learn more from one another than from their managers or the Home Office, so they formed associations and study groups and the Million Dollar Round Table in order to do so. Agency heads did the same thing. That's why the General Agents and Managers Conference (GAMC) and LIMAC (Life Insurance Managers Association of Canada) came into being. It's why annual LAMP sessions are held. It's why the Legacy of Learning series and AMTC (Agency Management Training Course) were created.

So why, then, do we see this learning-from-each-other phenomenon as a "trend" when it has been going on all the time? It's because far too many agency heads have failed to take real advantage of these opportunities in the past, and also because the need for these networks of agency heads is now greater than ever. The time was, not so long ago, when it was possible to learn by trial and error. But today it's doubtful (probably impossible) that any agency head can survive long enough to learn enough, fast enough, from his or her own personal experience. It's essential therefore to learn, and quickly, from the relevant experience of others. Another reason is that change in the world of agency management takes place at such a rapid rate that much of the experience of Home Office people is no longer relevant. They operated in a different world when they were in the field. That's why so many of them are so supportive of the networking activity of their agency heads.

We asked Norman Levine what he might do differently if he were starting in management all over again. Here is part of his reply:

> I think the first thing I might do if I had to do it again is not wait for years of experience to teach me what I perhaps evolved into. But I might go out and pick a lot of people's brains and visit different kinds of agencies and get to see how other people are doing things.

Here is what Bill Wallace said:

> Nothing, perhaps, helped me more than my expo-
> sure to some truly great agency heads that I had the
> opportunity of meeting through attendance at each
> LAMP meeting. I've never missed one. They raised
> my sights. They convinced me that rather normal
> but wonderful people were able to accomplish
> these results if they used the ideas that were work-
> ing for other people. And I made it my mission to
> seek out the ideas of successful people and to
> associate with some of them.

When asked about the agency head's responsibility to keep
growing, Walter Vreeland responded:

> He's out in front. Could be doing a lot of things.
> He's probably teaching LUTC. He's going through
> the chairs in GAMA, which is suggesting to all of
> his associates that they make a commitment to
> their local life underwriter's association. He's go-
> ing out to LAMP every year, which is telling his
> agents that they should be going to all Million
> Dollar Round Table meetings. He's probably in a
> study group. I'm in a couple of study groups. I
> encourage and help develop study groups for my
> associates.

Jim Harding in the Pacific Northwest said this:

> I've made it a practice, and I think every successful
> agent and manager that I've seen has also made it a
> practice, to go to every company meeting regard-
> less of how much inconvenience it may seem to of-
> fer at the time. Every seminar that's available. One
> of the things that's been particularly valuable to me
> is study groups. We have a group of 12 general
> agents that's met now for 13 years. For a while it
> was a sharing of ideas only. And now it's a sharing
> of feelings, it's a support group. And as we get into

the new era that we're in now, we're able to share together some of the world that we're venturing out into to try and grow and to be better general agents. Some general agents ask me why I also go to a sales study group. I think that even though maybe we're less technicians as we get into bigger and bigger agencies and more involved with strategy and counseling, nevertheless we still have to be cognizant of what's going on in that area. The more we can be attuned to the things that our agents are dealing with on a day-to-day basis, the more we can be attuned to the marketplace, the better off we are. Obviously there are meetings and seminars on management skills, understanding people and that sort of thing.

Tom Bray was a manager in Hartford when he said these things about learning from others:

My first two-and-a-half years back in Cleveland and Akron were pretty miserable in terms of results. I asked myself if I really was dedicated to this idea in my mind that some day I wanted to be great, and if so, maybe I should quit letting these years go by without doing anything about it. So I went around and visited some really prime people in the industry in the area: Bill Earls' organization in Cincinnati, Frank Sullivan's in South Bend, and Clare Webber right in Cleveland, and I came to some conclusions about hard work and systems management. And using the information there with some things I'd gotten from some other really great men in our business, I was able to turn my performance around.

When we came upon the above quotation we called Tom up. He's now back in Cleveland heading another outstanding agency. We asked him if he still felt the same way about the importance of learning from others. Here was his reply:

I now require the head of each of our financial service companies to be in a network of six or more in other parts of the country and to report to me each month something of value he's picked up through his network. Our system has evolved and improved as a result of our national network involvement.

Wayne LeNeave provided another reason for exposure to successful peers—to help crystallize the mental picture of where and what the agency can become:

It's important that one be able to visualize the type of agency operation he'd like to have come into being one day. To say it another way: If I attend a LAMP meeting or listen to a Legacy of Learning cassette where successful people are describing their agencies and methods, if I can't even imagine myself in their position the chances are that I'm not ever going to get there. So I suggest we stimulate our vision by visiting successful agencies, attending LAMP meetings and listening often to the Legacy tapes.

Maurice L. Stewart told of going to see people like Al Granum and Bill Wallace, as well as how he spent a week with the leading general agent of his company when he was starting out as an agency head:

I had an opportunity to follow Coop Curry and his associates around and to see what they did do and what they didn't do. Then I brought back those ideas that would fit into our agency.

In a unit of Legacy devoted to Study Groups, four agency heads told of their value. Former American Society of CLU's president Jack Nix described the LIMRA-sponsored Research Agencies Group comprised of 18 to 20 general agents and managers, with no more than two from a company.

Bill Olson told of his involvement in an all-Prudential

study group of six members from different parts of the country. He said:

> We have a simple goal. The goal is to become more expert as managers. Not to try to run the company. Not to get together to play golf. Not to bitch, but to be positive, concerned managers. We represent no one but ourselves as managers. We take no stand as a group. We are peers in fact. Being associated with these peers has helped me greatly to feel constantly challenged and excited about my job. We're friends. We really root for each other. But when we get together, we get together as professional business people, as managers. Our meetings are structured. We work from a preprinted and precirculated agenda. The chairmanship revolves with each meeting. Each person comes with a specific responsibility that's agreed upon in advance. By touching me with their ideas and thinking, they have helped me to grow as a manager.

Paul Oliver, a former MDRT chairman, told of the formation of "GAS Group II," modeled after the already existing General Agents Symposium (a study group that such leaders as Earl Jordan, Gus Hansch, Des Lizzotte and others have given so much credit to for their own success). Like its distinguished model, this was an inter-company group, and one in which each of the eight members valued highly the objective counsel of the other seven.

George Ellison told of the help he got in personal production through membership in an inter-company study group of personal producers, and then described his intra-company study group of fellow New England Life general agents:

> It's helped control our costs in the three basic areas of rent, supervision and clerical. They can really get out of line. We can ask, "Why do you pay your cashier that much money?" or "How did you get your supervisor for that much?"

Jack Nix added:

> I'd define a study group as a group of individuals
> voluntarily joined together. They are compatible.
> They share common goals, common requirements
> and experiences; and they join together to help
> each other towards a better professional accom-
> plishment. This means that you really can have all
> kinds of study groups. You can have one where
> they are all with the same company, all general
> agents. Or there could be a sharing of inter-com-
> pany experiences, part general agents, part man-
> agers. Legacy of Learning actually causes a study
> group within my own agency. As I conduct Legacy
> of Learning classes, my own management team is a
> study group.

C.A. "Cy" Pick, a recent GAMC president, told of the
value of not only study groups but also "mentors" when he
said:

> We have seven general agents in our organization
> who meet once a year for three days. The reinforce-
> ment, ideas and camaraderie that I get in these
> three days is just unparalleled.
>
> Some companies have set up a mentor situation,
> too. When they appoint a new general agent, they
> assign an older general agent to him. They try to set
> up that relationship early in the new agency head's
> career to enable the new appointee to grow under
> the counsel and auspices of the mentor.
>
> GAMC's annual LAMP provides a great opportu-
> nity to find that mentor, because they're all at that
> great meeting. If you don't find a mentor in that
> group, you never will.

One unit of Legacy featured five St. Paul women from different companies. Each is a secretary or administrative assis-

tant to one to three producers. They formed a study group to exchange ideas, and also put on a meeting for 46 of their peers in the Twin Cities (in some industries we suspect they'd be putting their jobs in jeopardy by this kind of sharing!). The subjects they covered were:

1. The nomenclature of the various associations and organizations in the industry
2. Career opportunities for the insurance secretary
3. How to get along with office managers and other office personnel
4. How to teach an agent to efficiently utilize a secretary.
5. Delegation of work
6. Communication
7. Job awareness
8. Time control and how to set priorities.

Although General Agents and Managers Associations and the industry's new Agency Management Training Course (AMTC) afford splendid and valuable opportunities for communion with one's professional peers locally, it appears that the study group kind of sharing is most profitable when the members come from different cities, regardless of whether it is an inter- or intra-company group. There seems to be something about traveling to another place, spending money, and taking the time to get away from the daily routine that serves to insure that such investments will pay off.

However, for most agency heads there is a problem when it comes to getting involved with an inter-company study group. Unless they are invited to join an existing group, they don't know how to align themselves with appropriate, compatible agency heads from other companies in other parts of the country. At one point in my role as Bob Turner, the itinerant interviewer for Legacy, I invited subscribers to let me play matchmaker, suggesting that if they wanted to start a study group they write me and tell me about themselves and their agency and I, in turn, would get them in touch with others of similar bent. It worked, and several outstanding groups are off and running.

But I can't keep on doing that, and the need for and value of these kinds of associations was never greater. As Bill Millar said in asking for help in the formulation of an inter-company group:

> I think there's a danger that we can get too inbred without some opportunity for cross-fertilization with peers from outside our own companies.

So I'd like to suggest a solution (it's really two): (1) ask agency heads of other companies in your own town to nominate someone in their company in another city who, in their opinion, would have a real contribution to make to such a group and whose situation is comparable in some respects to your own, or (2) ask agency heads in your own company to suggest someone in their community, but with another company, who might meet those criteria. Better yet, do both, and you can match individuals nominated by one method with the appropriate individual from the other.

In a time when industrial espionage is big business world-wide, the willingness of life insurance people to share through formal and informal networks offers a tremendous advantage and opportunity to those who take advantage of it. They're smart to do so, and foolish if they don't.

However, sharing with their peers is not a ticket to heaven. After hearing so many speakers say things like, "Does Macy's tell Gimbel's? Does Ford tell General Motors? Of course not. Only in our great business do we share like this," it occurred to me one day that our Creator probably had not ordained that life insurance people should be more generous and noble, and less selfish, than other people. As we learned early in Wilson Learning's Counselor Selling program, "People do things for their reasons, not ours." So what might the reason(s) be?

Finally it dawned on me—we share because we realize, consciously or unconsciously, that our real competition is not with each other. Seldom is the prospect asking, "Shall I buy from A or B?'' No, he's wondering, "Should I buy this much or that much? Should I buy now, or can I put it off?''

If you as a manager learn that another manager in your town has had a great year and led his company in production, you are delighted. You know that his team's success has in no way diminished the opportunities for you and your people. On the contrary, it has enhanced them. If every agency in your town was a company leader, that would be a great place to start a new scratch agency. The appreciation of life insurance and the services of those who sell it would benefit every agent and every recruiter.

Not so in the property-casualty lines. Whereas a life agent would prefer to call on a prospect who already has a life insurance program under way over one who has no life insurance (he's already manifested his appreciation of the *product* and its importance), if you already have an auto policy or a homeowner's, you're not a prospect for another, let alone several more. The "pie" of those coverages in your town is only so big. It's just a question of how it will be sliced up each year. But if you could clone each of your life agents, the chances are that you'd sell about twice as much life insurance.

Those are the facts of life that underlie our willingness to share with our colleagues (rarely competitors) in the business. We should be thankful that our business is like it is, and that our real competitors (aside from inertia and indolence) are all the others who are after our clients' disposable income and, perhaps, those who'd seek to demonstrate that the agency system is something less than the best way to serve the financial security needs of the public.

The real purpose of this volume is to provide a useful, readily available facility by which you, the reader, can at any time tune in on the thinking, ideas, and methods of people with the best credentials in agency management.

That will be another way to take advantage of the fact that you are lucky to be in a business that shares and smart enough to profit from that fact.

You have probably had the experience of urging another person to join your GAMA or attend its meetings more regularly or enroll in AMTC and had him respond with the chestnut: "I'm like the farmer who said, 'Why should I buy a book about farming? I'm not farming now as well as I know how!' Haw! Haw!"

We can only feel sorry for that kind of agency manager. If he were a farmer, he'd still be producing 30 bushels per acre while his neighbor produced 100. The many industry leaders we've encountered are eagerly seeking to learn from each other.

Al Granum, a model for many, has told us several times that "I listened to that last tape three or four times. Gee, that was great." And he'd write notes or call people whose sharing was especially meaningful to him.

Bill Wallace, after hearing New Yorker Joe Casale on Legacy, called Joe up and said, "Can my partner and I come up from Washington and spend a day with you?" And of course they did.

When invited to be an interviewee on Volume Six of Legacy, Charlie Smith, nominated for this distinction because of his outstanding record of agency development in West Palm Beach, said, "Oh, I'm so flattered to be asked. You see, Legacy of Learning has been my mentor for the last five years."

Similarly, Gordon F. Stovel, a shining light for his company in Ontario, said, "Our branch is leagues ahead of where we'd have been without Legacy." In his actual interview he talked about planning for the future in these words:

At the present time we're sort of rethinking the next five years; and with that thought in mind I'm going to isolate myself in Florida for a period of time with my plan books. But far more important, I'm going to take all of the basic planning tapes from Legacy of Learning that have been produced over the last five years, the philosophy tapes, and so forth, to rethink where we're going—with very valuable input from some managers that I wouldn't normally have the opportunity to sit down and chat with. I'm really looking forward to it.'

For all these and many more reasons that will occur to the alert agency heads who read this, "Trend One" tells us that as never before:

More agency heads will make a conscious effort to learn from the experience of their successful peers.

May this volume help you to do so.

2 | *Why Are You Needed?*

The Agency Head as a Philosopher

SIGNIFICANT TREND: Successful agencies will be built upon a foundation or philosophy about the agency's role in facilitating the growth and development of its members.

In a very real sense each quotation in this volume is an expression of the philosophy of the agency head being quoted. It may reveal an attitude about the role of the agent *vis-a-vis* the manager's or the role of the manager with respect to the agent. It may indicate convictions about the importance of the services and products sold by the agency.

A number of agencies have put together formal statements of agency philosophy (examples will be found in this section). If you have never done so, we'd suggest you interrupt your reading of this chapter whenever a thought occurs to you as being relevant to your own situation. Make a note of it before reading on. In the pages following are quotations that reveal much about how those quoted feel about their jobs.

For example, Blaine Sprout said:

> I look at the agency as totally a support system. I see myself as working for the agent. I try to instill in our staff people that they are working for the agents, and that our total reason for being is to provide a total support system for them to be more successful—both to help them be personally successful and to assure that they are looking at our organization as the place where they can best fulfill their future goals.

Billy Mixon put it similarly:

> My concept of a general agent is simply one who makes it possible for an individual to achieve his or

her goals. My entire reason for existence, I believe, is to identify talent and to create an atmosphere in which it can flourish, and provide the means for it to grow and maximize this benefit. And then I think it's my job to get the hell out of the way. Certainly it's not to impose my scheme of things on anyone else.

In the very first unit of the first volume of Legacy of Learning, Ken Sadler said:

We talk about the people in the agency as associates, and we really feel that way, that we're associated—that I as general agent am a consultant to them in their career. They certainly don't work for me. I feel that I work for them.

If we drew an organizational chart for the agency, at the top of the chart are the associates, the sales agents. Coming down beneath them and in support of them are the supervisor and the general agent and the staff, and then all the resources in the community that the general agent can draw on to be of service to associates in the field, such as the Home Office and outside consultants, psychologists and other professionals.

A strikingly similar viewpoint was expressed in these words by Dave Smith:

A view of management that I try to stress is that we work for the agent, he doesn't work for us. That's the most important thing I would try to get through to a young manager who is recruiting people. Is he working for the agent and does the agent really feel that? If he drew a management chart and put himself on that management chart, where would he appear? At the top or at the bottom? Well, if he's going to be good, he ought to appear at the bottom, in my opinion. I feel I honestly work for the agents. They don't work for me. This doesn't mean being subservient. I just mean that we know where our bread is buttered. Unless the agent makes a sale, I don't make any money. He should know I feel that way and want to help him make a sale in any way I can. If the younger manager comes into the business and feels that and exudes that and recruits to that and then builds all the other things that evolve from his style, he's going to build a successful agency.

We asked him what he meant by style, and he said:

I think it's really important to have the agent know you feel this way. I don't mean you put a sign on your door or that you tell him every day. You do it through your actions and the kind of person you are on a day-to-day basis. Just something as simple as the way your desk is turned in your office. Does it face the person when he or she comes in or is it sideways? Is your door open 95 percent of the time? Do you answer your own phone calls? Do you have your secretary make your phone calls for you or do you make them? I realize the time control experts would say I'm crazy, but I make all my own phone calls whether I'm calling a client or I'm calling an agent. We're dealing with people on a one-on-one basis about very personal things. What you do really lets the agent know who you are.

Wayne LeNeave's convictions proved just as relevant in Minneapolis as they had earlier in Detroit:

I concluded long ago that successful agencies become so only when they are helping their associates succeed as individuals, building their own successful insurance practice or business. To this end we have committed ourselves, and to it we attribute the high ratio of retention results we've achieved. '

The late Harvey Rogers was an outstanding student of the art and science of management—as well-informed on the subject as anyone we've met. These words of his reveal much about him:

> We have an agency philosophy. Management as we see it is a helping function. So often we try to needle and poke and cajole and persuade and convince people to do what we want them to do. If we merely listen to them and find out what they're trying to do, out of that can be developed a goal. And it's really important that we help them develop these goals. All we're there to do is to facilitate their thinking. Help them think where it is they're trying to go. These goals become standards. Now we focus any tension that might arise between a manager and one of his people, any relationship tension on the task, and cause the standard to be the place for that focus. What happens is that rather than our working on each other, I trying to convince him what to do and he trying to convince me that he can't do it, or is doing it, or whatever, now all the energy goes toward exceeding the standard. So rather than facing each other, now we're side by side, both going in the same direction.

Certainly any philosophy about the role of the agency and the agency head must include some sense of mission about the business and the life insurance product. It would be hard to find two more eloquent statements than these from Frank Sullivan and Bernie Rosen. Frank said:

> What is the base of our business? What is the base of a life insurance business? It is one person persuading, perhaps helping, another person to make a decision, and it doesn't matter whether you're the chairman of the board of the biggest life insurance company in the world or whether you're the newest agent starting out tomorrow. The basis of this business is it's a one-on-one business in which a single

person, an agent, persuades or helps another person, a prospect, to make the right decision. The title of a talk I used at the LUTC luncheon at the NALU meeting in Atlanta in 1972 was "Life Insurance Still Has To Be Sold" and yes, in the '80s life insurance still has to be sold. Because the day will never come when all of the populace who need life insurance will take time to determine how much it is they need, what kind they need, what kind of service they need unless they are helped in the decision by a competent agent.

Bernie Rosen's words will stiffen many backbones:

> I think any general agent, or any agent, who doesn't feel a mission in the work he does is missing the most delightful part. We get people to sit down and think through their responsibilities to themselves, to their spouses, to their kids, to their businesses, to their employees. We're valuable people that way. Also, we sort of insist people make decisions. We're decision requirers. We make people think through important responsibilities, and kind of push people to make decisions. I think these are marvelous missions that we have.

How you spend your time is a pretty good indication of what you feel is really important, what your philosophy of agency management really is. These words from J.D. Surber may make some readers uncomfortable:

> The second key after planning, which is number one for success as an agency manager, is to assign a priority to our business. I think there are so many agency heads who really fail to assign a proper priority to building their organizations. They have all the talent and knowledge they need, but somehow they seem to get caught up in becoming real estate tycoons, or they become heavily involved in community or industry activities. We really fail to re-

cognize that our primary task in almost all companies is to build a sales organization that's going to produce high volumes of life insurance that stay on the books and therefore become profitable. We spread ourselves too thin and building our organization slips down to a "C" priority many times. We can't shut out all outside involvement, but in the early stages we must not overcommit ourselves. Later on when we have a strong backup team we can look forward to paying back the industry that has given us such a fine opportunity. I think most of us really want an outstanding sales organization, and to me that takes an "A" priority and commitment.

These few words from Norbert Siegfried tell volumes about how he feels about his job:

I've encouraged two of my own sons into the business. They're both in the agency. I don't want to sound mushy about it, but each year that I live now, I think I become more appreciative of the fine opportunities that exist in management in the life insurance business.

Charlie Drimal in New York and I were young general agents in the same company a long time ago. He said this:

After 29 years as a general agent, instead of being burned out I'm excited about the future because I see people are excited around me. And it's actually more fun than ever. Where I see the big change in my own life is my ability now to delegate authority more and more and not get uptight about thinking I have to do everything. The longer I'm in the business, the more I realize that in order to be successful and to be very big, you can't do it by yourself. It's impossible to carry out all the assignments. Management to me is leading the way. And as one person once said, the speed of the boss is the speed of the shop. You set the pace and set the tone of that operation. And how you behave determines where you go as a manager or a general agent.

Don Heatherington's philosophy was built from a base of broad experience and intelligent observation. Here's what he said:

> I was an agency officer for 10 years, and I had the opportunity of visiting 45 different branch managers all over the United States. I saw how the successful ones operated, and also the not-so-successful ones. I had the opportunity of meeting many successful people with other companies as well. It became apparent to me that the ones who were building the great agencies were doing it, in effect, through building great agents within the agency.

Mel Hebert manages a sophisticated Southern California agency that provides advanced financial planning services and products to an affluent clientele. But these observations of his show that his philosophy of the business is anything but a narrow one (multiple-line and home service type agencies are equally as important as those serving the economic elite):

> There are more people today making more money than ever before. Which means that we have more people to serve. We have more people to sell more life insurance to than we would ever have dreamed of several years back. But I do have a concern for the people who have not grown financially—that we not ignore them and thereby allow the government to take over handling their needs. They still have needs. And one of the great lessons for me in working with the Life Underwriters Association has been to learn that we have a cadre of agents out there still working those marketplaces and they should be encouraged to do so. We have a tendency to look at the multimillion dollar producer and the super agency as the ideal and what everyone

should work for. That's good, that's proper, but the people that are out knocking door to door selling your small policies are providing a vital service to the rest of us because if they weren't out there, I think we'd see far more government encroachment than we have.

Martin Polhemus gave this reply when asked how he managed to maintain his enthusiasm for the job:

To me it's just part of the zest for all parts of life. Our work to me is extremely exciting in terms of its social meaning, the depth with which we get into other people's lives, of the wide open opportunities for growth, both personal and financial. I've searched far and wide and I don't believe I would trade positions or occupations with any single person in any job I've ever seen. I think I've got the best thing on earth. And if I believe that, it isn't hard to be zestful about it.

Jim Gurley explained his philosophy in very specific terms. One part of it is related to the sales situation and the other part to the recruiting area. Here's what he said:

One of the things a manager can really establish in his agency is the attitude and atmosphere that prevail. This philosophy that he has or he is perceived by his agents to have is probably the big factor in helping to establish the attitude and atmosphere. What do I mean by philosophy? We say that when an agent makes a sale, in that environment and under those circumstances, the client buying the policy has to have the need for the insurance more than the agent needs to earn a commission—or it's an invalid sale.

I don't judge my managers on how many people they hire a year but how many they hire that are successful. They're told that this is a very heavy re-

sponsibility to have someone come and be interviewed by them. Those being interviewed look at
these managers and say, "I would like to have his
lifestyle. I'd like to belong to his club. I'd like to
drive his kind of car. I'd like to work in that kind
of an office." We're asking them to change what
they may have been doing, and what they may have
been doing successfully, in order to come into the
life insurance business—a business they don't
know anything about. They're trusting us with
their entire lives and the livelihood of their families. As managers we must be willing to take that
responsibility and must realize the weight of the responsibility we're taking; otherwise, the manager
shouldn't hire that person nor encourage him or
her to come into the business. Those are two pieces
of philosophy that we have. They've stood us well
for a long period of time.

Past GAMC president Vincent Bowhers is a statesman and
philosopher of the life insurance business. Consider this
example:

One of the oldest principles that I've ever paid real
attention to, yet one that is critically important to
all of us, is the concept that our rewards and our
punishments in the life insurance business tend to
be delayed. We gain our pay later for what we do
or don't do today. This is true of essentially every
field position in our business and especially so with
a general agent or a manager. The general agent
has to interview people today so that he can test
some of these people tomorrow and select from
those people the day after tomorrow. Ultimately he
will contract some of them. That whole process
takes a very long time and there is still further time
delay before any business results. Then of course
there is attrition and substantial further delay before we see the kind of solid flow of business that
comes from the established survivor. Everyone

who looks back over a career as a manager or general agent, if that career extends any real length of time, will spot certain years where he didn't do those things. You'll hear him refer to that year as sort of being a washout. That time factor becomes even more protracted when we look at the development of the managing team. It is these sorts of principles that we do not want to lose sight of as we find ourselves preoccupied with change.

Mr. Bowhers also told about having been at a meeting of general agents in his company where they were discussing the agency of the future. They took one day to do so in little study groups and their subject was to talk about those things that would influence the agency of the future and what steps they might take to develop their agency so they could be more effective when that future came. He said:

> We took a coffee break about mid-afternoon that day and I sat down with a piece of paper and wrote out those things from that discussion that I wanted to be sure to remember, and here they are:
>
> 1. People who come into the agency office to discuss career opportunities from direct contact with a general agent, the supervisor or an agent are substantially better in every way than those people who come in from any other source.
>
> 2. The more truly successful role models that we have in our agencies, the better everything is going to be. And we should be careful to house these role models somewhere in the agency where everyone else can see them.
>
> 3. Adequate activity control is critical. We're referring to everything from preapproach mailings and direct mail to phoning, to face-to-face interviews, to the completion of facts on prospective new clients, the whole area of activity and proper management of that activity.

4. The final key issue has to do with precontract training.

Now isn't it amazing that it would be those basic elements of agency management that stood out from our discussion?

Outside expert Dr. Martin Seldman put his finger on one aspect of the agency head's job that must be especially meaningful to general agents and managers as they contemplate the effect their efforts can have on the lives of hundreds, even thousands, of people—most of whom they never will meet:

A characteristic to look for in management people is that they get excited about the multiplier effect. I can give you an example from my career, being a counselor, a psychologist versus being a consultant. If I were an individual therapist, over the course of a year I might help 20 or 30 people and get some satisfaction out of it; but I wanted to perhaps train 50 or 100 therapists a year. They in turn would help 20 or 30 people each and this is what we mean by the multiplier effect. People who move into consulting or managing get a great deal of inner satisfaction, whether it's ego or altruism doesn't really matter. They get turned on. They get excited by that idea. They have some sense of their whole life span, of what they will contribute in a lifetime.

The eloquent Norman Levine revealed much about his philosophy of agency management when he said:

I think this business is like a marathon with a thousand people all starting in one blob of humanity when that gun goes off, and all kinds of people in that pack. Some of them haven't taken the time or trouble to prepare or train, and they won't make it for the 26 miles; they'll fade at the five- or 10-mile marker. There are others that take off like a bat and want to show off. They run as fast as they can run, and it's no trick in a marathon to take the lead for five miles, but then they're going to run out of gas and they're going to fail. But there will be a significant number in there that rehearsed and prepared and trained and know that their objective is to finish. People who enter a marathon are winners if they just finish. In order to finish, they have to be persistent. They've got to go at it. They've got to prepare. They don't have to worry about what everyone else is doing—only themselves. They've got to pace themselves.

Now our business is like that. It's a marathon. It doesn't matter what other general agents or managers and their companies are doing. It doesn't matter whether they're going to finish first or tenth or twentieth or fiftieth or three hundredth. What does matter is that they get the pleasure and pride of knowing that every year they're growing. Every year they're doing better than they did the year before. Every year they've got a plan, and they're contributing to their own agency and the industry and the company growth. And then whether you're first or tenth or twentieth in the company, you're a winner. But you're going to have to do it over a lifetime, not over five years. You're going to have to do it not with sprints or spurts or lightning in a bottle. You're going to have to do it with growth. You're going to have to learn and you're going to have to study, you're going to have to build an organization. You're going to have to do things for the long run. So, I guess what it boils down to is any new general agent or manager, in my opinion, ought to sit down and decide it's forever. It's for the rest of their lives that every year they're going to be better than the year before. And that they're not going to care very much about what anyone else does because that's their problem or that's their opportunity. The one thing they've got to worry about is how they do themselves. They've got to beat themselves consistently and persistently over the rest of their lives. And that's a good, happy way to live and a great way to build an agency.

What Bill Wallace described as a statement of agency objectives was just as truly a statement of his own agency philosophy. He told of taking over the Washington agency of his company in 1966, with 15 agents, at a time when only one agency in the company was doing $10 million of volume:

> I announced that we would be doing $50 million of business in 10 years, which we were able to do.
>
> I put into writing a statement of agency objectives in January, 1966, my first month as an agency manager. I defined these objectives in six different ways:
>
> 1. I felt it was essential if I was to be happy in management to work toward being an aggressive, quality, growing life insurance agency.
>
> 2. I felt we had to offer our clientele continuing and understanding service in solving their personal, business and financial problems through the adequate use of life insurance. We would use the CLU creed to spell out our responsibilities to our clients.
>
> 3. We would recognize the importance of continued self-development of each member of the organization.
>
> 4. We would provide the services and facilities needed for a proper business atmosphere for our associates.
>
> 5. We would recognize the importance and necessity for the growth of our organization, both individually and collectively.

6. We would recognize that we were an association of individuals who were primarily in business for themselves, and in order for such an association to be a happy and beneficial one, each of us must recognize our responsibilities and obligations to each other and the company we represent.

We make reference to them each year in an annual planning meeting, and we include them in writing in our annual agency report. We also provide each new recruit with a statement of these objectives.

Here's how Tom O'Haren "puts it in writing" in setting up an agreement between new agents and his agency. It's really a statement of the agency philosophy to which the new associate is asked to subscribe.

1. The most important aspect of keeping career agents is a clear understanding on each party's part as to what are the terms of the agreement. "What's the deal—the philosophy?"

   A. Training second to none.

   B. Product wrapped in our service; best buy in the marketplace.

   C. Professional surroundings.

   D. Associates you will be proud to work with.

   E. Professional support in administrative handling of business.

   F. Business allowances based on production on a formula basis—no special deals.

   G. You will never lose a piece of business because

we are not competitive or do not have the product or for medical reasons. We will find a product for you.

H. You must offer all of your business to C.G. If you don't, we assume that you do not want to be part of our team—placing business outside is equivalent to resigning.

I. You must conduct your business on a legal, ethical, and moral basis.

J. We expect you to buy into making our agency the highest quality agency in our marketplace.

(With that as a basis of understanding, there is then only one other thing that you must do in order not to lose career agents and that is communicate with them.)

Dr. Hugh Russell—Georgia State University—says that we are "responsible to people, not for them," and that as managers we are responsible for creating an environment which encourages people to motivate themselves. If you create that environment and then communicate with your agents, there really is no reason for them to go anyplace else. If you recognize that you have got to hang in and not give up, you will find that people's attitudes change and you are found with different degrees of favor by your agents at different times. Just hang in there with your career agents; recognize their attitudes are a function of many things.

2. Keeping career agents is also a function of support systems. A good agency has them; a bad agency doesn't. They include:

A. Formal Training program on a continuing basis.
B. Weekly classroom activities.

(Formal training program with weekly class-room sessions—offers security to the career agent. He is continually made aware of the commitment made to him by the agency to keep him the best trained agent possible.)

C. Weekly supervision sessions.
(Weekly planning sessions are invaluable—even the biggest producer wants the attention of his manager and each of us needs to be held accountable for our actions.)

D. Advanced underwriting training.
E. Pension and profit-sharing support.
(Advanced underwriting and pension and profit-sharing support make the career agent feel that he is special—knows more than competitors and allows him to enter areas that others won't get into because they feel they don't have the knowledge.)

F. New product and new market development.
(New product and new market development—change is the most difficult thing we deal with in our business lives. Career agents want to feel that they have leadership equal to dealing with that kind of a task. Taking advantage of change to market new ideas and products again makes him feel superior to his competitors.)

3. I have been convinced that it is impossible to be too demanding from a career agent as long as he or she becomes successful. As I look around our industry, the people who are most successful expect more than others. When that breeds success, the career agent doesn't want to go elsewhere because he knows why he became successful. In our agency, the "agent is king." Both the management staff and the administrative staff are reminded of that constantly. The agent is the reason that we exist;

there is no need for us without them. Sometimes it gets easy for our egos to convince us that we are the bosses. When that happens, we have lost our perspective and stand a chance of losing some top-notch people. I view my organization as a partnership with me as the managing partner but nonetheless answerable to my partners. Make no mistake, the partners with the greatest production have the most influence. I must continually work to keep that perspective because it is easy to convince yourself that you are the most important; when that happens you have trouble brewing.

After rereading the quotations included in this chapter, it occurred to this observer that they spoke eloquently of the agency's (and the agency head's) responsibilities to and relationships with the agents.

But with a few exceptions they didn't say a lot about the agency head's largest responsibility, that of continuing to bring aboard new blood. Of course, it was there by implication, for without new associates to offset normal attrition (let alone to allow growth), the noblest of philosophies would have little meaning.

In our next chapter we'll see just how important top agency heads consider the recruiting/selection function to be.

But first, let's acknowledge this significant trend:

Successful agencies will be built upon a foundation or philosophy about the agency's role in facilitating the growth and development of its members.

Such agencies answer every day, with their deeds and spirit, the question all agency heads must answer: Why are YOU needed?

3 | You Can't Teach A Duck To Chase Mice

The Agency Head
as a Recruiter/Selector

> **SIGNIFICANT TREND:** Agency heads will recruit higher quality people than ever before.

No one who ever heard J.B. Conway say the following will need to have his name cited as the source:

> The big problem, the big waste in our business today, is trying to make people, trying to teach people, to be something or do something they aren't cut out to be or do in the first place. You can't teach a duck to chase mice, and you can't teach a turkey to sell life insurance. . . . You can't motivate a meatball. . . . First-rate people hire first-rate people. Second-rate people hire third-rate people.

This chapter is likely to be the largest in the book. That's not just because each volume of the Legacy of Learning series had a chapter dealing with the recruiting and/or selection area. It's also because so many of these superb agency builders, no matter what the topic of their Legacy interview may have been, made important observations about one or another aspect of this subject.

The quotations selected seem to fall into several categories:

1. Those suggesting the importance of the recruiting function.

2. Those dealing with the importance of careful selection.

3. Those about the "how" of recruiting.

4. Those about the "how" of selecting.

THE IMPORTANCE OF RECRUITING

Naturally some of the quotes are equally applicable to more than one of those four classifications. But before we quote any of these life insurance people, let's quote two college basketball coaches. As these words were being written, DePaul's famous Ray Meyer had just coached his last game. A few days earlier we had cut out this statement by him from the sports page:

> We had had three bad years and there were no scholarships. Then the university decided to give us some money, a full-time assistant and a recruiting budget. Joey [his son and assistant] went out and got some great players, and that's how I became a good coach!

The University of Minnesota's Jim Dutcher made such a fine contribution as guest expert on an early recruiting unit of **Legacy of Learning** that he was asked to appear at LAMP on the same subject. Here's what he said:

> Basketball coaches at major universities—well, at any level really—will tell you that it's impossible to be a successful coach without talented performers. There are the coaches who can pull an occasional upset; but to be a consistent winner you have to have talent. And so the game of recruiting is vital to any kind of success in college coaching. And the search for talent is really never-ending.

Los Angeles' Robert B. Hanseen made the analogy totally clear with these words:

> To be successful in recruiting you have to think that that's the most important thing that you are hired to do. And if you want your agency to grow and to succeed, you've got to have a successful recruiting program. Look at the major universities who have major football teams or basketball

teams. It's not the coaching. The coaching is important. But it's the recruiting that's really important. In the life insurance business it is exactly like recruiting top-notch basketball players or top-notch football players. You've got to go find them and hire them and bring them in. And then as a manager you look awfully good if you've hired a lot of good people, just as many of the great coaches look good because they've recruited a lot of successful people.

However, there's a big difference between the life insurance business and the coaching profession because the coaching profession has the high schools to train and determine which are the good prospects to play in each sport. Unfortunately, we don't have a farm team to find out who's a good candidate for the life insurance business. So we have to do a lot of selecting before we get to the right prospect. But the concept is exactly the same. So when I'm saying recruiting is an attitude, it's the basis of our business. Unless you are really aggressively out on a consistent basis doing recruiting each and every week, you're not going to have enough people to select from.

Chicago's Earl Jordan, a past GAMC president, put it succinctly when he said:

I think the number one job of a general agent or a manager is recruiting, recruiting, recruiting. If we're going to maintain a strong agency, we must recruit.

Norbert Siegfried made the recruiting priority very clear with these words:

A very wise management person said, "If you will become an outstanding recruiter, it won't guarantee success; but not being able to recruit, for whatever reason, will guarantee failure.'' I believe that most of the problems that most of us have in management are because we have not established a self-disciplined program of obtaining names on a daily basis.

These words from Tom O'Haren would have been equally appropriate for Chapter Two when we were dealing with agency philosophy:

> The most important thing that you could do on a continuing basis within your agency is to recruit. In a family situation the dynamics of a family expand, I think, geometrically, every time a child is born. And I think it's tremendously supportive to everybody in the agency that you're bringing along new blood all the time. I think it does a number of things. First of all, to my own thinking, it energizes me. I love to see that new individual, man or woman, come along who's going to bring some new production, new energy into the agency. I think it helps the associates who are aboard, because they see that I'm doing my job. They feel challenged by the newcomer coming aboard. And if we have done our job in selection properly and have upgraded the average of the agency in bringing that person aboard, we've made it a more interesting place to work. The most important thing people ever do in building and keeping career agents is to recruit new agents.

Tom O'Haren was, by implication, pointing out one of the most delightful aspects of the agency head's job—the fact that he or she is able to *choose* those with whom to work. Few people have that privilege.

Wayne LeNeave used the words "most critical" to refer to the recruiting function by saying:

> The most critical aspect of agency building is that

of having a profile of the kind of person you want
to be associated with and want to attract, and then
to have an idea of how many of these people it
would be reasonable—not what would sound
good, but really would be reasonable—to try to attract each year, and that you can work closely with
in their individual growth and development.

Al Granum, the most systematic and organized of agency
heads, made this confession:

A mistake I made was trusting to luck too long on
the recruiting side. But the luck ran out. When I
wakened and got back on the system, it still took a
while to work out of that. Now I'm absolutely
dedicated to the unconditional necessity for any
general agent or agent who is not getting ready to
retire, to be conscious of the flow—that input
flow.

THE IMPORTANCE OF SELECTION

The foregoing quotations dealt with the importance of the
recruiting function. The next series of statements have been
selected as reminders of the importance of selection. It's not
enough to recruit. We must recruit those with high potential
for success.

In many Legacy interviews we asked distinguished agency
heads: "What's the most important counsel you could give a
young agency builder?"

The responses, expressed in different ways, were like this:
"Decide what you want. Set your standards high. Don't set-
tle for the expedient. Don't deviate."

When asked what they might do differently if they had it to
do all over again, the typical reply was: "I'd refuse to make
exceptions. Every time I've made exceptions to my own game
plan I've been burned. It's cost me money."

Predictions about the future of the industry frequently include mention of the trend toward larger agencies. To maintain a large agency, and especially to build one, requires much recruiting activity and regular new appointments. In the face of a planned schedule for new appointments to fill waiting empty desks, with a scheduled precontract training class having but one enrollee, the temptation to put just anyone in that class is difficult to resist. But if that single enrollee is a superbly qualified candidate and we have to introduce to him or her another person of minimal qualifications, what message are we sending to the first person, the one we really want? People like to feel they have been selected, that they have been picked out, as opposed to being one of many who can meet minimal requirements. An invitation to join an agency that follows a reasonable and consistent selection process conveys to the successful candidate a sincere compliment that is seen as such. However, when the invitation is cheapened by indiscriminate use, well, one is reminded of Groucho's famous line: "I refuse to belong to any organization that has such low standards that it would accept me as a member."

Burt Bauernfeind, in the first unit of the Legacy of Learning series, looked back at his distinguished record and said that if he had it to do all over again:

> I would be selective in my recruiting and bring in people who have the potential and the capacity. This may take a little more time and a little more work and may cost you a little more money in the beginning. I am confident that it will pay off greatly in the end, so I would be more selective in my recruiting process.

In our interview with Jim Smallwood we said to him, "You've won all the awards your company can bestow. You have a superb agency. What's the biggest lesson your experience has taught you about selection?" Jim said:

> The selection is so very, very important. To start

with, we do have to have enough recruits so that we can exercise selection. We can't select one-on-one. We need to have enough for comparison.

Bernie Rosen said the following:

My goal, and really my plan of operation, was to recruit only a very few people a year, but put everything I had into them, and make sure that at the end of each year I would end up with two more people I felt were absolutely the kinds of people I wanted to be associated with, who were on their way and would be with me on a relatively permanent basis. Recruiting is selling. Selection is buying. And too often we forget the importance of depth of selection. Sometimes we sell the person into the industry, rather than let that person fundamentally select himself or herself in.

In Grand Rapids, John Wiener had this to say:

I'm known as being a pretty tough taskmaster with the staff people who work for me, but I'm pretty soft at heart too. And I've made exceptions throughout the years when maybe everything is perfect on this recruit, except there's just one thing where I don't think he's going to be a winner, and through pressures or whatever, we hire him or her. But I sort of knew down deep that it was wrong. Well, those exceptions have never worked. I have never yet, and I've been hiring people for 15 years, had an exception come through.

We asked Jim Cameron what advice he'd give to a new young manager who asked him for counsel, and he said:

I think there's a tendency when you become the new young manager to try to get the job done very quickly, and I would counsel him against doing that. Bernie Rosen said in one of the Legacy of

Learning tapes that the president of his company had advised him to try to recruit one man each year that he thought would be with him for the rest of his life. And of course Bernie decided to do two a year and we know what kind of job he did. Too often we try to bring somebody in that we're not sure is the right type and we find out pretty soon that he isn't the right type and we've wasted the time. After all, the name of the game is not how many you hire in a year, but how many you keep. We have to come up at the end of the year with a net gain in manpower and the only way you can do that is by hiring quality people. The second thing I'd like to pass on to him would be that he should keep his standards high. He should start immediately and decide what kind of agency he wants and what kind of people he wants in it and make people measure up to that standard. I would also like to suggest to him that he shouldn't try to be the most popular man in the office. If he tries to be the fairest person in the office, he'd be much more respected for it.

John Snow was most candid when he said:

I think that maybe if I would have put together a more specific picture in terms of the kind of people I wanted, perhaps I would not have made some of the recruiting mistakes. Some of those mistakes were made by hiring people with too many negative problems, problems I was aware they had. Making mistakes is part of growing and learning, and we can only hope that as we progress the mistakes are fewer and smaller.

Toronto's Tony Lawes said it this way:

The agency will be only as good as the people selected for it. Manpower selection has certainly got to rank in the top echelon of priorities. My dear mother always said, "You can't make a silk purse out of a sow's ear." That should be engraved on every manager's doorstep. . .

You cannot change anybody. All that you can hope to do as a manager is create an environment in which people can change themselves. But if you start out with a person who is recruited because of your needs rather than his desire, you're going to have some real problems. Having lived through that myself, I tend to be hyper-selective. Now I think that a manager should strive to make his branch a difficult place to join.

Stan Eason pointed out that today's recruiters must force themselves to seek people who may be far less compliant than we were when we came in the business, people who will stretch us:

I remember a statement I heard many, many years ago. Basically it was that if you've got a lamb in the office, you've probably got a lamb in the field. And if you've got a tiger in the office, why maybe you've got one in the field. Young people today are smarter. They've seen much more of the world than we have. They have a much broader outlook. I think we have to hire people that we can guide perhaps, but we sure can't dictate how they do things. They've got to be free spirits to a certain degree. You know they're getting some financing money so they have to do some things. But those are only until they can learn their own limits so they can supervise themselves.

Bill Millar said that life insurance people have every right to shoot high and seek the best of people for their career opportunities:

Most reasonably well-equipped individuals today, let's say having gone through college and presenting themselves well, could qualify to work for IBM or RCA or Ford or General Motors or many of the large corporations. However, few of them could qualify to be in the life insurance business. In my judgment we're entitled to ask for and receive our fair share of the super talent around today. After all, the life insurance business is the best business in the United States of America today for the right person.

THE HOW OF RECRUITING

Successful recruiters give top priority to the recruiting/ selection part of the job. In northern California Dave White has developed ratios based upon experience that show the importance of processing many to obtain a few associates:

During the first quarter of this year in our recruiting and selection activity, we've had over 100 people come through the front door. We have tested 57 and contracted six individuals. Our experience is that we have to have 20 come through the front door to test 12 to have six pass and have three what we call career days and, by the time we end up with a precontract training process, one recruit.

Legacy of Learning interviewees shared many recruiting methods and sources. For example, Don Edwards introduced the idea of recruiting to "schools" as opposed to hiring a single person. He also uttered some thought-provoking philosophy with this observation:

In my opinion there are three kinds of managers: the builders, the caretakers and the liquidators. I hate to say it, but I have been both a caretaker and a liquidator in the past; and I almost got liquidated myself. In our company we must be builders. And this led us to realize that we can conserve much of our time by recruiting to schools rather than hiring every hot prospect that comes along each week. We

run a highly intensive induction school. Our entire
state is involved in it, and so we've had to go to a
class schedule. We currently have six schools a
year, and our objective is to get this to only four
schools a year.

Tony Lawes identified a specific source of recruits (one
also cited by George Ellison when he spoke at the GAMC day
of an NALU meeting):

A new manager should select very carefully, and he
should keep a weather eye open for new ideas, new
systems, new procedures, support services, training
staff to do things, putting in internal dictating systems. So what better place to recruit good men
than a business equipment show where he can go
and see the kinds of things he can use in his branch,
and engage in conversation with young IBM and
Xerox salesmen. These are potential recruits too,
so you can kill two birds with one stone.

Gus Hansch believes that the service concept and the full financial service approach are effective with the outstanding
prospective recruits he seeks. Here's what he said:

For all of our selection techniques in the life insurance industry, we're still not doing a good job because the man we should be hiring for processing
never applies to our agency for a job and never
takes an aptitude index or any form of test, so how
can we select him?

By that I mean the man who comes out of Stanford
and looks at the job market. . . he's rather adequately trained, but he doesn't have the answer to
the prospecting situation. He wouldn't be able to
answer "yes" if the general agent said, "Do you
know 200 people in your community who make
over X?" And so he probably could be (1) looked
at and turned down, but (2) he doesn't want to go

into a field where he's being measured in the selection process by how many people he knows. And so he winds up with IBM, or sometimes, in the old days, with Merrill Lynch and people who generate a lot of training and ways for him to grow up in that field. Unfortunately, we never saw him in the past.

I must say that with this concept of service, objective and diagnostic service, with the concept of building a clientele slowly around many, many services, we are starting to get a crack at some outstanding young men.

Does it work? Well, we have two young men in our organization who are only 32 now, who have been with us three years, who are earning in excess of $200,000 a year in first year commissions.

After explaining that getting established agents to adopt the financial planning concept has been an unsuccessful effort, Gus went on to say:

But the young person coming out of school has a service drive, in my opinion, greater than a dollar drive. More and more in our recruiting we're talking about service and about objectivity and empathy. And that fits the young fellow a lot more than "Hey, let me show you how to make a buck." Sure, he wants the house on the hill and to be a big shot. But between him and that accomplishment are a lot of pluses and a lot of minuses. The minuses primarily are, "I don't want to buy life insurance." "I don't want to contemplate death." "I don't have the money."

We've dedicated ourselves to help ordinary fellows like you and me try to fight that job, that opening of doors, by giving them an approach. It causes the other fellow to say, "Hey, come on in. Tell me about that." In business insurance, it's based on tax-oriented methods of saving money. Individual insurance is based on "tell me how and what your concerns are, and we'll show you how well you're doing."

We said to Bob Hanseen, "Let's pretend I'm 28 years old and you got my name from somebody in the course of the kind of work you've been doing with nominators. You call me on the telephone. What might you say?"

I'd just say, "Bob, your name has been given to me by someone who thinks you're a very successful person and has said a lot of nice things about you. I'd just like to put a name and face together and would like to have you come into my office so that I could talk to you about what I think is a great opportunity to be either a salesman or be in sales management. I know you don't know much about what I'm talking about and I don't want you to have any preconceived ideas about it. But I'd like you to just come in and let me give you a little information so that you could determine whether or not I've got something worthwhile for you. And all I can promise you is that if you spend an hour with me it will be one of the most stimulating hours that you've had. And whether you come into the life insurance business or whether you don't, the worst thing that could result from it is that we could be friends. Could I see you Friday, maybe at three in the afternoon? I have an opening. Could you come in and see me then?"

Bob Hanseen would be the first to say that no magic is inherent in those words. The magic is in the results that follow their frequent and continuing use!

We asked Lynn Prewitt a question about how he found today's conditions affecting recruiting. He said:

We believe we must work harder attracting a greater number of better recruits. Basically we're using the same sources. We're just working harder. Good people still want an opportunity to cope with the problems of inflation. They don't want their future tied to somebody else's evaluation of their worth. So we're finding that we can locate and attract good people. We just have to work at the job harder. When it comes to financing them into the business, actually these people we're talking to have to be financed at a higher level because we're in competition with other industries for these people. These high financing levels are hard for some of us old timers to adjust to, but we have to adjust.

Early in his management career Irving Katz read a New York Life study indicating that "the greatest number of successful new agents have been recommended by current agents. Irv said:

This gave me the idea for our Matchmaker program. Retention of people appointed through our Matchmaker program is more than twice that of all other sources, roughly 70 percent versus 30 percent.

In the Matchmaker program our present sales force is recruiting and prescreening candidates for us. We wind up with a wonderful banquet each year, normally on a Saturday evening in a first-class restaurant with a cocktail hour, full sit-down dinner, and band and entertainment. Only "Matchmakers" (nominators in the agency) and their nominee recruits (and spouses or dates) can attend.

As result of this program we've had our sales reps bring us their brothers, cousins, nieces, nephews, classmates, clients, brothers-in-law, fraternity brothers, and so on. Each Matchmaker receives a Matchmaker plaque, and everyone can join.

Probably one of the biggest advantages of it is the way it ties people together, the way it makes people concerned about more than themselves. If I as an agent bring you into the business, then I have a stake in your success. I'm going to be watching very closely because, after all, you are a reflection of me. Therefore, I'm going to have to set the pace for you. There's a little pressure on me to perform, because you're going to be watching, and you're my friend.

Irving also pointed out that the sponsoring agent is going to make sure that the training of his nominee is all that it should be—another benefit of the program.

Just like any other part of the agency head's job, recruiting can be a system. Tom Bray told about the system he was using in his Hartford agency:

It's a 90-day recruiting cycle in which we gather names for 30 days. Then we have a series of selection interviews over a 30-day period. And in the final 30 days we run a precontract school. We have four contract dates a year: January, April, July and October. We stick very, very closely to our system.

The precontract school consists of six to eight classes of two hours on Tuesday and Thursday evenings. We meet at 7:00 and we go to 9:00 on the dot. These classes are designed to provide a competitive educational environment where we can overview our candidates in an extremely good selection climate. In our last two recruiting cycles we've had 14 and 15 candidates enter the first precontract class. Basically, they all want the job. We want to find out who are the best two or three, so we put them through a rather competitive experience and let them show us who is best.

Tom is now in Cleveland with another company. We called him there to ask if he is still using the system. He said he is, but now is recruiting among CPAs, JDs, and MBAs with good experience. In that week and the following one he had scheduled 41 interviews with CPAs. He is still using the quarterly system described above.

We asked Cameron MacIntosh, a Vancouver, British Columbia, manager, about his sources of recruits. Like Irving Katz, he said the major sources would have to be "present associates," adding:

> I've got the best recruiting team in the industry right in our agency. They don't all bear the title of sales manager or manager. They are people who've been involved with us for some time and see the advantages of being actively involved in helping get the quality of people that we want to have associated with us.

We asked what those advantages might be as perceived by his associates. He said:

> I guess it starts with me and the people on the management team associated with me. We all see very clearly that there are some very, very tangible advantages for the people associated with us in the marketing function. It's just a fact of life that one of the prime responsibilities that those of us in management have is that of recruiting. If there is some way that we can best utilize our time by eliminating a lot of prescreening of recruits using cold nominators and those kinds of things and getting instead well-qualified prospects from the people associated with us, then they recognize that we on the management team will have a lot more time to devote to helping them reach their goals. I suppose too that we've been able to demonstrate that as our agency has grown and become more effective, we do have more clout. We have better premises. We

have better backup as far as tax and estate planning and group services. And these are very, very tangible things that they can see as being an advantage to being associated in the top agency. And they recognize that that only happens through adding new blood to the agency.

LIMRA has referred to Glenn Martin as the builder of a "billion dollar agency." Obviously Glenn has had to find shortcuts to enable his organization to grow so dramatically. He said:

We do a lot of recruiting in groups. We may have four or five agents in one group and that's how I started recruiting. I knew in 1970 that if I was going to continue to sell life insurance and that's what I really wanted to do, I didn't have time for one-on-one recruiting. So I would get involved. I mean I would go to communities and bring people in and recruit four or five at one time, or interview four or five at one time. The selection was the same. We went through all the same pains. We spent three or four months with them. We did everything, but we started five at one time instead of one.

Norbert Siegfried, like Irving Katz, relies on his present people as a prime source of new ones. But he makes sure they know this help to the agency is in their own interest. He's also discovered another way to multiply the potential for each nominee:

Our number one source, the largest number, and maybe the highest quality of new associates come from our own established associates. You see, each time that we do something new—when we added our pension company, when we brought an attorney with a masters in tax law into the agency to work with our existing agents, when we take new space, when we upgrade the quality of our staff people, when we put in a new computer, I always spend a lot of time making sure that every associate in our agency realizes that those great things are there to help them increase their own individual personal production, and are only possible because of the addition of new quality associates each year.

Our second source comes from getting recruit names from the prospective recruits we interview. We indoctrinate the new field underwriter that in order to survive, he must get three recommendations on his initial call in his two-interview sales process. Well, a year or so ago, it seemed sensible to me that rather than drive across town and spend three hours calling on a so-called center of influence that probably didn't want to see me and would give me a name that was questionable, it would make a lot more sense to get two quality new recruit names from the recruits sitting before me. So we simply ask the new recruit who he considers to be the two best salesmen in town. I want to know for two reasons: I want an idea of his image of what a good salesman is and what his life is like. Secondly, I'm going to ask him to permit me to contact these two people if they sound like candidates later in the interview.

Never in recent years have so many quality people been available for us to interview. There are a lot of entrepreneurial people out there who want to make over $50,000 a year. They want to have the independence that we have, and, finally, I believe our business has more excitement to offer than it ever had before.

Interestingly, Cam MacIntosh uses the same technique in Canada that Norb Siegfried employs in St. Louis. Cam said it this way:

In our in-depth interview with a potential recruit in the selection process, we asked him to list the names of two or three people he feels are top sales-people and the reasons why. This is a genuine part of the selection process. But also whether or not he ultimately joins us, he is a potential source of new recruits. Because if he doesn't come with us in the final interview, I'll go through those people with him and say, "We initially decided that this is not the right spot for you at this time, and I think it's been a wise decision, but how do you feel about what you've seen?" And the normal reaction is a reasonably positive one. And then I say, "Now you remember when we were having our in-depth dis-cussion together, we talked about two or three peo-ple whose names you jotted down as being top salespeople in your opinion. How do you see them as potentially fitting into this agency? For instance, there's Joe Doe. How do you feel about that?" It's just the Granum prospecting method turned over and used in the recruiting process.

Charlie Smith's great results reflect how well organized and planned his recruiting system really is. He shared these thoughts:

We have to ask ourselves as marketing managers and general agents the same questions the industry is asking; that is, who am I as a general agent and manager in the distribution system in my com-pany? What marketing delivery system am I com-mitted to and what type of agent will I have to re-cruit in order to function successfully in that kind of system? What are the clues to finding that kind of agent? Now I find myself in a company that is committed to multi-line marketing, but I'm in a branch of that company that focuses on the upper inccme market.

I find that I have three sources available to me where I can find that type of person more often. First, personal observation by the manager and his division manager. Second, agent referral. And in the history of our agency, by far the largest number of recruits have come from that source. And third, through the use of well-placed nominators. As our agency has become more visible in the community because of its success and the contacts we've had, we've been able to develop successful nominators who have now become interested as supporters in our success.

He then told about one of the early units of Legacy in which Clair Strommen told about the fact that the highly qualified candidate will not reveal that he or she is occupationally disturbed until presented with another opportunity. Mr. Smith said:

I believe that is a cardinal principle of recruiting. It's been at the base of a recruiting piece which we developed in our organization that we call a "prospectus on a career." What we try to do is recognize the people we spot in the business community who in our opinion should be in our industry who are not likely to respond favorably to either a direct approach to stop what they're doing or even the implication that they're occupationally disturbed. And we send the prospectus to them. We asked ourselves what questions we would have about the insurance business if we were considering it and then attempted to answer those questions in our prospectus for a career.

I asked Mr. Smith what those questions were, and he said:

In a nutshell the questions are these: "What is the Prudential?" "Who is the Prudential in Palm Beach?" "What would I sell?" "How do I earn money?" "How can I know if this career is right for me?" "How would I get started?" "What training would I receive?" "Would I always sell insurance?" "What company benefits do you provide?'' And certainly the last and one of the most important questions: ''Aren't there too many insurance persons in this industry already?''

Jim Gurley, like others, knows his ratios. He said:

> If you hire quality people, you will do quality business. The hiring portion is probably at least 75 percent of the success formula. In that respect there is no shortcut to just plain hard work and lots of it. But first you probably need to give the needed quality an exact definition. To us that translates into being a person who first is a college graduate or has the experience equivalency and scores at least 12 on the AIB. We work off a hiring formula of 30, 20, 10 to 1. What that means is that it takes the names of 30 prospective recruits to find 20 who will listen to a brief career presentation. Of these, 10 will take the AIB. Of those who pass, you can hire 1. We have kept good records over the past five years and the formula is pretty accurate. If a manager secures the names of his prospective recruits from newspapers or college interviews, he would need more than 30. If the names are from his agents or from policyholders or from nominators or personal observation, then initially he can put less than 30 names into the hopper. Also the AIBs per hire is closer to 8 than it is to 10. But we figure 30, 20, 10, 1 is close enough to meet the exact ratio. We put it in our computer and we mark each district manager through a monthly recruiting log.

We asked Ted Santon to trace the progression of the typical new associate in his or her early years. He told of a novel ''internship'' for law students:

> Let me tell you what we're doing right now. We're recruiting law students who have finished their second year on the three-year program. And we're hiring them for the summer and will continue on

through the fall—as much time as they can give us. For lack of a better word, we call them runners. We teach them all of our product lines and we teach them the sales course. Then we introduce them to all of our agents and all of our partnerships [he has a lot of partnerships in his agency that specialize in one or another area]. And then we spend time with them through a one-week span giving them an idea about the business and about us. The purpose, of course, is to recruit them and have them come with us on a full-time basis when they've finished law school. We've gotten to know them and they've gotten to know us during what we call this intern or precontract training period. They're put on a basic sales course just like anybody else.

We asked if they were licensed during the summer. He said:

Yes, they're licensed and we have orphan policyholders as one part of our program where they will call on them and just describe each one of our products and services to find out what the policyholder might not now be getting and what they might be interested in. They will bring that information back to one of the specialists. We have them on a salary of $1,000 a month, plus we give them a commission for each fact-finding interview that they do. That interview is the one where they talk about the products and services that we now have. They fill out a form and bring it back and we check it and pay them for it. I think maybe we could always have done this, recruited better people; we just sometimes didn't think we could.

Gerald F. Twigg spoke of target recruiting in a way not unlike what target marketing has come to mean in the sales arena, when he said this:

We're trying to make a more concentrated effort to

recruit from certain occupational fields: coaching, CPA or law, and salesmen. A coach is well disciplined for the transition period. He probably has known defeat, but he's also known what it is like to shake off the loss and get right back in the victory column. The CPA has a keen sense of the needs of the businessman and will have tremendous credibility with the prospective client or his advisers because of his CPA status. And the professional salesman is used to selling, used to quotas, sales objectives and goals. He may be in a commission situation where he can relate to the peaks and valleys of all commission salespeople.

Many general agents and managers are using the recruiting videocassettes in the GAMC New Horizons series to attract the interest of coaches and teachers, public accountants, women, salespeople, college graduates, and attorneys (women, obviously, can be in any of the other categories as well). It was our privilege to produce these as companions to Legacy, and we were totally captivated by the outstanding men and women agents who told, with obvious sincerity and conviction, how they have found "new horizons" of opportunity in the life insurance business.

J.D. Surber responded to our question about sources of recruits for his agency with a whole list. Here is how he put it:

What we begin doing at one stage in building an agency may not be the process three years down the road. Today's solutions may get boring if repeated in an agency year in and year out. It's okay to go to new sources if you recognize why you're doing it. I think there are nine places to get new people. First, I'd list referred leads from agents. I think we'd all like to have them come from that source. Second, I think the college campuses are a fantastic source. Third, good results can be obtained with employment agencies. Fourth, newspaper ads have been effective for many companies and agencies. Teachers are a fine source of new candidates. State employment services in major cities are a good source, and a free source, by the way. Salespeople from other industries represent an outstanding source. And I think another source could well be the result of the growing reputation of your agency and company that in turn causes people to walk in the door because they've heard about you. And last would be the "all others" category.

I think that an agency manager ought to try to become an expert with three of these sources, and the three that you used one year might not be the three that your agency uses three years later. I can tell you that in our case of the 52 hires in the last three years, 36 had been referrals originally from our agency force. That source has been growing each year and I'm very proud of that. I came direct from the college campus, and I suppose that's why I see that source as a primary one. I'd urge agency managers to consider their own source as one of the three in which they would develop special expertise. Certainly they can do so with real conviction.

When we interviewed Neal Campbell, whose office is in Corpus Christi, we asked him how he recruited in towns away from the agency base where he has a large territory, including the Rio Grande Valley which is 150 miles from his office. This was his reply:

We have centers of influence in those areas, Bob, and what we're doing is talking to these centers of influence and telling them that we now need one more man in their particular community, asking from them the names of the young outstanding businessmen in the community. And if we get several people that are saying that Joe Brown is one of the outstanding young men in the community, that's the person we want.

We then asked him how he developed those centers of influence in the first place, and he responded:

> We do it through our agency force. We have agents in most of the small communities, as well as the larger towns. And through our agents we have met these people, their clients over the years—the presidents of banks, the owners of different firms. We go with the agent first. We encourage it in our agents to help us recruit.

Before going to Texas, Mr. Campbell had opened up the state of Arizona. We reminded him that he was not able to get centers of influence there through his agents because he didn't have any agents, so he told us how he did establish centers of influence:

> When I first got to Phoenix, I cross-indexed all of the civic clubs in the communities, found out who the leading business people were in each community, and wrote them letters asking for an appointment, telling them I would call. Then I called and visited with them and gradually developed, over a period of time, about 600 centers of influence in Arizona.

We asked if he really meant 600 and his reply was:

> Yes, 600, Bob. That started out from a group of about 1900 people which was a lot of work of course, but fun. It was fun because we had an opportunity of meeting new people, finding out what makes them tick, and had an opportunity to sell them on what our company could do.

I responded that it sounded as though the care and feeding, nurturing and developing of centers of influence was a key element in his recruiting process.

It sure is and we put out a quarterly report down

there in Phoenix telling the progress of the agency and telling them that we had an opportunity for one person at this time. And after I got that developed, I could normally get 50 to 75 referrals from a quarterly letter.

Harry Hoopis has charted the course of his agency's growth to billion dollar production by the end of the decade. His comments are encouraging to every agency builder when he says:

I like to talk in terms of statements of opportunities for the '80s. One of these is in regard to recruiting. The most basic aspect of this is the demographic aspect in the '80s. And that is that more and more people who are in the prime recruiting age between 25 and, say, 35 will become the greatest segment of American population. They also are the biggest buyers of life insurance in that same demographic breakdown. So now we have more people in our prime age and more buyers. So we obviously need more people to service that market. In my day-to-day recruiting activity, more and more people come to me and say, "I know that salaried positions won't keep up with inflation. As a result, I am in tune with the commission aspect of your business." So for the first time in the 12 years that I've been involved in recruiting and managing agents, I find that we have a greater receptivity to the sales profession than we've ever had before. This is exciting to me because it means that now I can have a greater base from which to select the quality high caliber agent we need during the '80s.

THE HOW OF SELECTION

In Volume Five of Legacy, the unit on Selection begins with the narrator saying the following:

"Many are called, but few are chosen." Matthew

22:21. That familiar quotation seems appropriate for the subject of picking or selecting career agents. To the busy manager or general agent with formidable recruiting objectives that are being measured against a calendar whose weeks and months seem to be racing by, there are times when any candidate can look like a potential Rookie of the Year. But those are the very times when more effort must be expended; not just to recruit this candidate but to assure that the suitability of every candidate will be measured against standards, as well as by comparison with other candidates.

As agents we are told a Prospect is one with a need who can pass and can pay. We sought those who appeared to have needs and to be able to pay. The underwriters in the Home Offices did the selecting. They told us whether the applicants could pass or if an extra premium would be required. But as recruiters we have to be our own underwriters. No one else is going to assess a Table D rating because of this candidate's deficiencies. It's our responsibility at the agency management level to predict the life expectancy, so to speak, of each prospective associate we consider for our agency. That's both a sobering and exciting responsibility. You see, few people have a comparable opportunity to choose, which is another word for select, those with whom they will work.

In Volume One of Legacy, Minnesota's Clair Strommen became known throughout the industry when he gave this recruiting advice:

It's important to talk to people who are already successful, because it takes successful people to really change your agency operation. And your agency philosophy and concept must seek these people. Maybe I should just back up and say, people change—but seldom. So get your nominator to recommend successful people.

So in reality, Clair was saying that the selection process really begins before we even see the candidate. The methods we use to produce candidates can be geared to finding people with higher-than-average qualifications. Here's how he made that discovery (one which an agency officer called worth the whole price of the Legacy of Learning series):

> The first three years that I really used the nominator system, we were always asking the nominator to recommend someone he thought would be interested in the insurance business. In other words, the nominator was controlling the situation. And most of the time he was referring people who generally had unsuccessful track records. In other words, I felt he controlled the nominations. So we started using a different system and a different style to prompt the nominator to suggest not someone he thought should go into the business, but someone who is a successful person. For example, I wouldn't say, "I'm in the process of expanding our organization. Who do you know that I might contact?" I would say, "Ron, I'd like to ask you a question, and I'd like to ask you to think about it for a few seconds before answering. Who are the one or two most successful people you know?" or "Who are the one or two most successful attorneys or CPAs between the ages of 27 and 35?" People seldom change, so get your nominator to recommend successful people. And the nominator must be successful. If I talk to unsuccessful nominators, I'm going to get unsuccessful nominees.

He had this to say about his other great discovery:

> A successful person never shares his vocational disturbance publicly until he's given another opportunity. For example, many times when I've sat down with a really high class nominee and I tell him he's been spoken of so highly, he will respond by saying, "How did you know I was unhappy?"

And I'd say, "I didn't. I just knew you were successful. I've heard so many great things about you that I wanted to share some ideas with you over a cup of coffee."

Bill Millar has made a large agency one of the very biggest. He said this:

Successful people seem to have a track that you can trace. Don't hire unsuccessful people because you'll get exactly what you hire—and that is an unsuccessful person. You don't have the time. You don't have the money. . . so you've got to search out and seek the successful person who is yet to bloom.

We asked James Smallwood how he started the selection process in terms of his objectives for the candidate's first visit to his office. He said:

I would arrange a time to meet and devote full attention to the interview. I would, of course, stop all phone calls and interruptions. I would want the office to appear businesslike and to have some evidence of a successful look to it. I'd put the candidate at ease by offering him coffee and engage in some small talk for a brief period. I keep in mind that my immediate objective is to determine as early as possible in this new relationship whether we have enough in common to pursue the steps involved in our selection procedure that would lead to the candidate's employment. Early in our relationship I mentally apply a brief evaluation formula. I call it the CAP (Character, Ambition and Potential). I watch for evidence of the ingredients to support these characteristics as we progress through the interview.

Auburn Lambeth quoted the owner of the Dallas Cowboys football team as follows:

"Our philosophy when hiring a coach or anybody is to get intelligent and capable people. We assume that if they're intelligent and capable one day, they aren't going to be incapable and dumb the next. That goes especially for football coaches."

Mr. Lambeth went on to say:

> I think it goes especially for career life insurance agents as well. This business gets more difficult. It gets tougher. It takes somebody that's exceptionally intelligent and creative. At least one of the judgment questions I ask myself is, "Can I see this person standing up in front of the board of directors at the largest bank in our state and making a capable presentation?"

Bernie Rosen has made many, many contributions to his industry. Here is another—his outline of the selection procedure he uses. It's a track that many will want to emulate. Notice, too, how Bernie has made a verb of action out of the word "reference." A reference is not something you get. It's something you do!

> Our selection procedure is a track, and we follow that track carefully. We use six interviews. The first interview is fundamentally a get-acquainted sort of thing. We have some chit-chat, become comfortable with each other. I want to know a little about his or her background. Then we tour the facilities in our office, trying to explain how we're organized, and letting the prospective agent know some of the facts about our company, about our agency, and then lead into the description of the job of the agent. Really, a life insurance agent starting in our business is a brand new business start. A new proprietorship is being formed and capitalized. We then explain what our selection process is about. We tell how we'll interview in succeeding interviews, how we'll use tests and refer-

ence forms and anything else involved in trying to come to this mutual decision. We explain at this point that we must not shortcut the full selection process.

The second interview is a demonstration of how we sell. We literally role-play an interview. We describe in detail how we get prospects and demonstrate, for example, how we ask for referred leads.

Third interview: how we train people into all markets and into all the products that we have. We demonstrate the specific materials and go through some of them. We give them some of the books to take home and peruse. We describe our training process. We have an immense amount of emphasis on continuing education in our agency. We want our people to know in advance that we expect them to take courses every year, CLU or LUTC or certain company courses or anything else that's available in the industry to keep them current and growing and able to serve their clients better.

Fourth interview: how we finance. Any new business that starts needs to be capitalized. We talk about the capital grants, the financial help that both the company and the agency provide to help a person in those early months and years before there's enough cash flow coming in just from the profit and loss of their new business.

Fifth interview: if that prospective agent is married, we like to have the prospect and spouse come into the office but not because we're trying to interview the spouse to see whether he or she 'fits' our agency. One's spouse is one's business, but how critical it is that the two of them understand what it is that they're getting involved in. We also brief the two of them on the fact that there are contractual relationships, that this is a limited proprietorship to be started. I give a set of contracts to the two of them, asking that they take some time, and go to any advisers they want to for help in understanding the contracts in detail before we go over them in final detail and ask for signatures.

The sixth interview is the one in which we go through contracts in whatever detail the prospective agent wants. It's crucial that they understand what they're signing. The more you can anticipate any later disillusionment, the less turnover will result.

We believe tests are best used as merely one more reference source. So far as interviews are concerned, after enough interviews, perhaps I begin to get the feel of the person. But certainly in the early interviews people are on best behavior. Perhaps I see things that remind me of others I like or don't like. I'm a mass of prejudices, just as everybody else is.

Well, if tests and interviewing aren't the key way of doing it, what might be? I think referencing is the most valid, by far the most valuable, of all the selection tools. After all, people don't change quickly or dramatically. Hopefully, people mature or sometimes they de-mature; but if you can find out what a person has done in recent years, and find out in detail about that, I think you have your best fix on whether the person can make it or not. The point is, though, you really have to reference, and not make a pass at it. You have to go in person and see the person giving the information. It's the only way you can get truly accurate information.

After explaining that his good recruits had no common background or age characteristics, Bernie said:

Perhaps there's only one common quality among

almost all of the people we have in our agency and that is an ability to persevere. When I reference, I keep trying to determine whether this person has indicated perseverance in prior things. Did they finish up what they had started?

H.J. "Jay" Quinn also detailed his selection procedure as follows:

We start with the initial interview of the candidate. At this interview we merchandise the career, establish a good relationship, and attempt to set a time to visit the office for the aptitude index. Step two involves his first visit to the agency. If time permits, we show a 15-minute recruiting film developed by our company. He then completes the aptitude index and an experience record similar to most personal history forms. We spend a few minutes discussing some industry and company brochures we'd like him to look over and share with his wife.

Step three involves a meeting with the candidate to discuss his test results. Assuming they were satisfactory, we give him the "perceiver" interview. This is a structured, taped interview that can be evaluated later with greater objectivity. If this step is satisfactory, we then order an inspection report, and make an appointment for the next visit to the agency office.

During this visit we have our selection interview using LIMRA's Selection Blueprint. At this meeting we schedule visits for him with some of our agency associates, attempting to have him spend some time with both our new and established agents. Before he leaves this meeting, we give him 12 market surveys to complete, and a target date for fulfilling this assignment. With these market surveys, he contacts six individuals by himself, and the unit manager goes with him on six. It is very helpful to watch him perform in front of other people. It also gives us an insight into the caliber of people he calls his friends.

He is also assigned a market inventory to develop, listing relevant information on each of at least 100 people. This list represents his early potential buyers. At this time we request permission to check his references. No less than 10 reference checks are made, and at least five of these are face-to-face. They include friends, neighbors, co-workers, and former employers.

Our next step involves a joint interview with the prospect's wife, normally in their home. Before this we have sent her an industry brochure to read with information about the agency and company. This interview gives the manager the opportunity to determine the wife's attitude and to make sure she understands the job of the agent. Time is spent also in discussing the candidate's probable work and study schedule as well as a family budget and the uniqueness of our plan of compensation.

Our next step involves our career presentation. We do this in the office, utilizing training aids. We go into an in-depth review of our company's financing plan and also our career agent's contract. Then we give illustrations of the weekly sales activity required to achieve production and income objectives we feel appropriate for this person.

Following this interview, the division manager and I are ready for final appraisal and recommendation for selection or rejection. To help us tie all the loose ends together, we use an appraisal form. We systematically grade the candidate on financial stability, overall stability (including time in our setting), time in his last job, family changes. We look closely at his market potential, social mobility, community activities. We look for success patterns and past earnings and advancements and achievements. We look for preparatory strengths, educational background, sales background, if any. We also look at his precontract training results. We individually list his weaknesses and strengths. Then we compare our analyses and make a selection decision. We then have our final meeting with the candidate in the selection flow and extend an invitation to join our agency. Of course, the selection process continues to be a factor throughout precontract training.

We asked Jay if he'd learned anything about selection the hard way. Here's how he replied:

One of my greatest mistakes in my earlier years in field management was allowing my ego to make me believe I was a giant builder. I would occasionally compromise the standards I knew were correct with the honest belief that I could overlook these missing qualities in a candidate. This is not the case at all. I am not a giant-builder. The candidates themselves either possess or do not possess the qualities needed for success.

The sophistication of many of today's marketing methods and products has a real impact on selection criteria, as Roland Hymel explains:

We concentrate a little more in the accounting and the business background of the candidate. When he comes in for his interview with me, I'll hand him a financial statement, and I'll ask him questions about that statement just to see if he can understand it. If he has not been able to understand a basic balance sheet or P&L statement, the chances of his moving quite rapidly into the employee benefit field is going to be small. We feel that we don't wait in our office until three, four, or five years to move him into the business market. We feel that the personal market under $35,000-$40,000 is drying up. We feel that the employee benefits market is growing and that only 15-20 percent of it has been tapped. But in order to get into that market a person must be educated in that subject matter, and he's got to have the support services to know how to deal with the businessman.

This statement from Bob Szeyller is another case in point:

I used to believe that the best agent to recruit was a prospective agent who knew the most people. Today I'm not quite sure that's as true as it used to be. We're trying to look for agents whom we can put into markets that we've already identified. If we recruit a young attorney or an accountant with some experience, somebody that we could train with all of the techniques necessary to operate in a given marketplace, then we have the management tool to open those market doors for him.

Bill Topkis succinctly described the very specific and demanding selection process used in his agency:

For us to consider anybody today, they must have two years minimum in the work force, pass successfully the aptitude index battery test of LIMRA, successfully complete our selection process of several interviews and calls on proactive centers of influence, and have made three sales, paid and approved, before contract. This entire process takes between a month to two months.

I know no other way to find out if somebody wants to pay the price or if they have the "can do." If we want to have good people in this industry and we want to increase our retention, we've got to have good selection.

And Jerry Nigro reminded us that the stakes are high when he said:

> When you're recruiting, you want to see a lot of people within a certain profile. You're doing a lot of selling and prospecting. However, in the selecting area you've got to be very, very cautious. You want to look for things in a person that you don't even want to find, but you've got to do it and it's got to be done fairly. Selection is just the devil's advocate. You've got to look at that person with a different eye. Because if you make a mistake, it's going to be very costly to you. You're going to measure two things. How much might it cost me and will we come out making money for the company if I hire this person? So it must be very thorough.

We asked Jerry, "What was the biggest lesson you've learned about selection?" This was his reponse:

> Don't be too hasty. Don't hire under a stress situation because you'll compound your problems. You must be patient. He may look like the greatest recruit in the world on interview one, two, and three, but all of a sudden in the spouse interview you find out that he's not the same person you saw in the office. You must take the time that you need to ascertain that all these things you think are right are really there. If you don't, you're going to make a lot of mistakes. I don't think it's proper to go against the odds.

Dick Larson was talking about his agency's selection process when he said:

> I will not call any candidate after the original interview. I let them know that the next step is the aptitude index test, which is a requirement of our agen-

cy and company. If they wish to take it, they can tell me on the first interview. That would be fine and we'll set it up. But if they have some things to think about first, it's up to them to call the office and make an appointment. Of course, after the aptitude test I need to call them to let them know what the score is. But if we don't hear from them, they'll not hear from us. Everything that we ask them to do beyond that is done on that basis, so that every time they go away from us with a task that must be accomplished, it is up to them to call us when they are done. I will not call them.

Once the AIB is out of the way, assuming it's positive, the next step is to complete 20 confidential inventory surveys that are like the Norm Levine Surveys that I learned about at the Atlanta LAMP meeting. We ask them to call us when the first 10 are completed. Then they come in and we review them. What we're trying to find out is, "How did it feel?" We like to find out how people feel about the job itself before we go into the contract. And that's what the confidential survey helps us to do. We review the first 10 when they come back. They go away and come back after the next 10 are completed, assuming there has been a positive kind of response.

We next put them through a class in what we call professional selling skills. If they stammer and stutter and turn red and get embarrassed and their eyes don't sparkle, we know that we've got someone that we should direct into another area. If, however, the person is able to improvise, take factual situations and make an approach or a presentation or answer a question or close a sale, depending on the segment that we are working on, then we have someone we need to go further with. At that point, we will begin licensing and serious study because we don't think it makes much sense to have someone do that work until the decision has been a little farther along as to whether he or she is coming with us. We also begin to do some joint field work as soon as the application for the license has been sent in. We require the completion of the test and $850 of first-year commissions in the pot before contract date. Along the way, as we're moving to that final handshake and the signing of the contracts, we are dealing with workbook exercises and all the different kinds of things they need to begin to be exposed to.

I know Marvin Blair and his record too well to deprecate in any way a selection tool that is working very well for him. Here is what he told me:

Seventy-five to 80 percent of management time can be spent working with unsuccessful agents. Many prospective agents are well versed in how to pass a standard inventory test and how to look pretty good on interviews because they study what it takes to get hired. I wanted to find a way to select agents who had the right personality dynamics to succeed. That is when I started using handwriting analysis reports. This has proven to be a profitable factor in my sales and management selection. I feel I am now working with the right raw material. When an individual has a natural talent and drive to succeed, the training and management task is more than half accomplished. By far the greatest part of successful selling must come from within the person. Management can train in sales techniques, but cannot give the basic selling skills and persuasiveness and assertiveness. Management may coax and threaten but cannot give the person the natural drives of determination, initiative, and ability to overcome discouragement. Management can instruct and preach but can never instill a positive attitude, confidence or enthusiasm. These critical qualities must come from within the person.

Whereupon I said, "Are you saying you learned about those qualities solely through handwriting analysis?" His answer:

> Yes, Bob. Everybody in the agency has gone through handwriting analysis. The biggest part of our growth is due to finding and having the right people.

Philip Kessler, as part of his selection procedure, likes to challenge the candidate:

> I will challenge him by saying, "This is what you told me you want. This business will provide what you want." And then I challenge him from that point. Either you're not telling me the truth or you don't really want what you said you want. I hired one fellow 23 years old. He finished high school, did not go on to college because he wanted to get a job and make money, and he's now been out of high school about six years. He'd done well on his jobs but he really hadn't found the right situation. He was the most mature 23-year-old I'd ever met. I challenged him in the way I just indicated. He did join the agency, made the Million Dollar Round Table his first year, and couldn't be happier.

Speaking of challenging the candidate will inevitably remind me of Mike Edison. Mike and I were talking about recruiting and how he would present the life insurance career and he said:

> Well, let's role play for a minute, Bob. I might ask you this question. "What is it that you want to achieve, that you want to accomplish?"

Whereupon I replied, "Let's say I'm 28 years old and I have a wife and baby. I have a pretty decent job in the marketing department of a large corporation, but I'd like a little more freedom to do things my way and I'd like to move ahead faster. I want to do work that's worthwhile. I don't expect to be a millionaire, but I'd like to live comfortably. I like golf and would like to be able to afford the country club. I want my son to have a good education. Those are the primary things.''

This was Mike's reply:

Well, Bob, you've told me all the things that everybody likes to hear. You've walked through all of the nice buzz words that all of us want. What you haven't told me is where is your comfort level? In other words, there's a burner inside you that's either on a high flame, a medium flame, or a low flame. What's important to understand is where that little Bunsen burner is inside you. And if the reason you want to change is because there's something gnawing at the inside of you so that you can't stand to put up with what's going on, then we should continue to talk. If it's because you want to have a little money, but you're basically content, you find yourself pretty pleased with what's going on in general, then you should stay where you're at. You have a low burner and that doesn't make you bad. Everyone should know where theirs is. To move out of the protection of that corporation, to come into a rough, tough, entrepreneur business is a bad thing for you. One of the most frustrating things for me as a manager is to attract a real attractive guy like you who has all the right things, who has all the reasons to succeed, and the only problem is his burner is low. He's got a low agitation point. He has a low desire. And you know what? This business is an absolute disaster for that kind of person. I see so many managers tear their guts out working with Mr. Blueblood, nice kid, good guy, tremendous potential and can't understand why the guy just never gets it done. This is the wrong business. You should go work for some big corporation or stay where you're at. Because you know what? You're going to be happy and you're going to get all those things that you just said you wanted there. But if you're in the situation where somebody's asking for a high flame and you're a low flame, it's going to cost you all of the things you wanted in your family. It's going to cost you all the things in your outside life that you want because you are going to be mismatched.

But if you are the high flame guy, and you come into the place where we are running with other high flame guys, you are going to be able to give your family all those things because you are going to be happy at what you do. I can show you how to turn the flame on, but I can't keep it going. Give me the guy with the broken leg and a patch over his eye and a high flame who grew up in Harlem. He'll be a great life insurance man because we are in a high flame business. We are in an entrepreneurial, high flame business. Give me a guy from M.I.T. who would really rather be a professor (there is nothing wrong with professors; we need them), and he's going to be miscast. We do ourselves a disservice hiring people and then thinking that because I'm a great manager I'm going to make this guy great. You know what? I don't make anybody good, I don't turn anybody's flame on. All the people are good; they just have different motivation levels and they motivate themselves. I don't do that for them.

Whereupon I replied, "Wow, if I were that candidate I think I'd say, 'Look I've got a high flame, really I have!' "

Mike said:

I'll try to find out if you've got a high flame, but you can't fake that. Whether you sell me on a high flame or not, 90 days from now, six months from now, we're going to know, aren't we? So you know deep down inside. Don't sell me. You don't even have to answer because I'm going to hire you based on your track record and your external appearance. But if you don't show the high flame and the high desire, I'm not going to continue to work with you because that is a breach of confidence with our other people. So if you want help and you want our work, you've got to meet a certain expectation. And the flame is the only thing that will get you there because that's when training starts—after you've proved that you have a right to demand training from our organization.

"What's the right age for a new recruit?" Walter Downing in Boston has had splendid results with mature men who had their own businesses before coming with him. Phil Kessler spoke of his star 23-year-old. Joe Casale in New York City told of having recruited a number of ex-stockbrokers when the market was having bad times in the early half of the '70s and having very poor experience with them. He said:

When we got over that and lost so many of those people, I was determined to follow something that I think I learned in the Marine Corps on the rifle range. That was that people who had never fired a rifle before were the best shots because they did exactly what the drill instructor told them—either out of a healthy fear of the drill instructor, or just because they didn't know any better, or some happy combination of both. I fired "expert" in the Marine Corps, and I had never fired a rifle in my life. And some of the other recruits from out west or down south who had grown up with a shotgun or a .22 in their hands, shooting rabbits or whatever, just wouldn't pay attention. They had been firing a rifle so long they couldn't believe that anybody else could tell them a better way to do it. Well, they wound up with a lot of sore heads and also with low scores.

I had a chance to reflect upon that and I decided we'd follow the same principle. We would hire people who had no previous business experience to look back on. People who couldn't say, "Well, on my job we did it this way." So we hired people right out of college. I mean, people 21 years old, 22 years old. That was in 1975. I can safely say that everyone that we kept for 30 days or more in '75 is still with me. I have everybody that I hired that year who was not terminated in the first 30 days for immediate post-selection reasons. I was so impressed with our success that we adopted that as the official recruiting policy in the agency—that we would only hire young people and preferably those with no experience. We have hired a couple of guys that were 24 or 25 and had a job or two for a year or so before, but strangely enough they are not our most successful people. Our most successful guys are those who never had a job of any kind, other than going to school or working summers during college, until they got to us.

Elliot Rothstein, on the other hand, said this:

I'm not looking for people that are in a certain age category; I'm looking for the kind of candidate who is money-motivated, somebody who is aggressive, ambitious, and somebody who can speak well, somebody who wants to make a lot of money and wants to do a service. I want to hire the kind of candidate that I would buy from myself.

The "right age" for one situation might be the wrong age for another. Each of these successful agency heads takes pains to assure recruits are qualified to handle the training and move gracefully in the markets the agency has chosen to serve.

From all the quotations in this unit it should be safe to conclude that a very significant trend is distinctly evident:

Agency heads will recruit higher quality people than ever before.

After all, "You can't teach a duck to chase mice!"

4 | *Where Are We Going?*

The Agency Head as a Planner

> **SIGNIFICANT TREND:** Agencies will grow and progress to the degree that such growth and progress is planned and the plan is bought by those who will execute it.

Warren Bennis said that a key common characteristic of the 90 outstanding leader-achievers whom he interviewed in his "Odyssey" of over four years was that they had what he called a "vision" of what could be, of where they wanted to go, of what they wanted to bring about.

He also said that a second characteristic was "communication and alignment." They could make their vision clear and meaningful to their associates and cause them to "align" themselves with their leader in a common effort to bring the vision to reality.

Mr. Bennis was speaking about those he had interviewed, but his words could apply as well to those general agents and managers who were interviewed for the Legacy of Learning series. Everyone in every agency—agents, staff, clerks, everyone—wants to know, "Where are we going and how will that affect me?"

To me there is something both romantic and dramatic when pragmatic, no-nonsense business people like Bill Millar and Tom Hogan say, in almost identical words, "It all starts with a dream." Agency heads form mental pictures of what their agencies can be. Those pictures get translated into goals and objectives. Plans are laid for their attainment. Checkpoints are established along the way.

Most people are work processors. For them the job itself provides tasks for them to perform. Underwriters in the Home Office will have their work schedule determined by the flow of applications sent in by the field force. The investment department can invest only the money available from premiums.

But agency heads (and agents too) are involved in truly creative roles. They must first visualize where they are going, for "if you don't know where you're going, any road will take you there!" That visualizing and the determination of how they will "get there," is called planning. Here is how Mr. Millar says he does it:

> Most of my planning I do in my office from 6:30 in the morning until about 9:00. And I use typical yellow pads to plan. It all begins with a dream. It all begins with seeing something in the distant future, and then seeing that something become more and more vivid all the time. Crystallizing the vision into increments that are now becoming understandable and increments that are workable so that you can implement the dream. So as you can imagine, many pads are used before you can come down to the final plan. But you really cannot determine where you are going in this or any other business unless you can see yourself there quite clearly. And that is seeing the surroundings, the circumstances, the people, and the rewards and all the implications and all the prices that must be paid to get there. All these things you have to see before you take a pragmatic approach to communicating them to other people.

These are Tom Hogan's words:

> I think planning starts with a dream. Unless you have a long-term idea of where you want to go, what kind of an agency you want to build, the type of producers you want to build, then planning probably doesn't have a whole lot of meaning or direction for you. So I think it all starts with an image of where you ultimately want to be. Then you start the process of figuring out what do I do today? This year? Next year and the year after? . . .

to ultimately get me to where I would like to be with the agency some years down the road.

We asked Mr. Hogan what was the most important thing he'd learned about planning. This was his reply:

> You'd better do it. If you don't do it, you end up with nothing but problems. The less you plan the more you react to things rather than causing things to happen, the more you spend your time chasing around putting out brush fires. If you want to avoid those things, just do a better job of planning. The biggest problem I have with planning is not spending enough time doing it. I still find myself caught up in the day-to-day routine of things as opposed to closing the door and getting out by myself and spending enough time just thinking and planning. An hour spent there will probably save 10 hours elsewhere in the job. One way to make the hours stretch, one way to get more accomplished and to have more time to do the things that need doing is to spend a little more time planning so you don't spend so much of your time doing the unnecessary things that probably didn't need to done in the first place.

In Michigan, not far from Bill Millar, young Terry Knight is implementing his well-considered dreams/plans. He quoted his company president Jim Luhrs (a former general agent himself) as saying:

 "There are more Horatio Alger stories in this business than any other business that is now or has ever been in existence."

Bob Hemmick observed that the need for planning by general agents and managers wasn't always as great as it has now become. And then he made an important observation, one not cited nearly often enough, about a most important reward for good planning:

It used to be that you could run an agency by being a pretty fair sales manager, but that's not true today. You have to be involved in planning and marketing and research and merchandising and personnel work and all the other things that go along with it. And all these things have to be planned!

The first reward for good planning is peace of mind.

Years ago I had a bright and personable young agent who was well into his second, quite productive year in the business whom I endeavored to persuade to fill out an annual plan book. He could see no reason for doing so, saying, "I know what my job is, it's to sell life insurance. If I work hard at it and see all the people I can and sell as many as I can, I don't see how messing around with that plan book, which I don't like to do, will help me do any more."

I was reminded of him by these words from Bob Duncan:

Every year I go to a national meeting, and I'll have several managers come up and tell me they've worked about as hard as they could but they seem to have a lot of problems during the year. Had bad recruiting, bad retention, didn't have any growth, and just seemed to have an overall bad attitude and a lot of excuses why nothing happened. Yet they were the same people who often said, "I don't need to plan, I know what I'm doing, all I've got to do is go out and work hard." Others that I know at these meetings are good planners and they always seem to have had a great year, a lot of growth. And they always have a good attitude. I consider the difference being that those people are the best planners. Dr. Covey says that change creates problems and then problems create more change. And then more change creates more problems. It's an endless cycle. I think through planning we can change that word "problems" to "opportunity" and so say

change creates opportunity. More opportunity
creates more change, more change creates more opportunity. Then we're going to have a lot more fun
in the business and not be as frustrated and at the
same time be better planners.

But how should we go about the planning job? Here are
some tips from some outstanding people: Bob Duncan,
George Joseph, Frank Sullivan, and J.D. Surber.

Bob Duncan said this about his approach to planning:

I think five years is too long; I'm now down to
three years. I look at what I think's going to happen in the next three years and what I want to plan
to achieve in terms of objectives in that period of
time. I usually do that in the spring. Sometimes in
early fall I'll take a full day by myself and usually
just stay at home and sit by the pool or in the
library in my home and do some thinking. Sometimes I just let my mind soar and have visions of
grandeur of what I want to do. But I really do a lot
of thinking and I'll plan an agenda for our annual
planning. That will include what I'm going to do as
far as the agency is concerned. I'll write the agents
letters. I'll write the agency team that I have as well
as the staff members. And I'll tell them about the
agenda. We'll take the entire staff, the assistant
managers, the training supervisors, the advanced
underwriting consultants, the office managers, and
my administrative assistant and go out of town for
about three and one-half days. We go to a resort.
After a formal day of agenda planning, we'll sit
around and discuss some of the real meat later in
the evening. This is usually in December, sometimes as early as November. And we'll plan out our
whole year. One of the best ways to establish a
good attitude for this occasion is to review where
you were last year, what your plans were then,
what your systems were. And sort of check on

yourself and see where you are. Because of good planning, you're ahead of where you plan to be and so have a good opinion about your planning the previous year as well as confidence in your systems. Then it becomes more a matter of improving them, rather than trying to reinvent the wheel again every year.

George Joseph started out with a plan of his own making, but then took an interesting and important step to assure himself that it was a sound one:

> When I became a general agent I wrote down a plan. I tried very hard to keep the rose-colored glasses out of the way and be as hard-nosed and realistic as I could possibly be. And then I was given some good advice, and I followed it. I took my agency plan to two of the great general agents in my company and asked them if they thought I had a plan that was workable, and if I had methods that made some sense to them. They gave me a lot of very good practical advice on how to take my plan and adjust it so that it could work out.
>
> I based the plan on the concept of the amount of premium that was in the agency at the time, and the amount of premium I wanted to build up year by year over five years. I based it on the kind of agents that I wanted in the agency, and the manner in which we were going to market the company products. And so when I left those general agents, I had a feeling of confidence that at least I had a plan that a couple of real solid professionals said was a plan that could work if I would make it work.

Frank Sullivan shared his formula, one of classic simplicity and effectiveness, saying:

> I don't know really where I stumbled into it, but I used it at my talk at the MDRT in 1960. It's so sim-

ple it embarrasses me when I get up, and yet every single year when I start my planning, it's the keystone from which I operate. The formula has four simple points.

The first is to decide what you want to make of yourself. Write it all out. Just daydream to your heart's content. Say, "If I owned the world this is what I would want to be."

Point number two brings you back down to earth because that decides how you're going to do it. And once you get into that you have to get more realistic. I like to use a silly little example. Many of you know I'm a jogging nut, and in my wildest dreams I can see myself winning the Boston Marathon. I can see myself crossing the finish line in front of the Prudential Building and tipping my hat to the Prudential people saying, "I won the Marathon!" Every December when I start my planning, I say, "Okay, you say you'd like to run in a marathon. How are you going to do it?" I have to write down that I would have to train 65 miles a week every week from the first of January to the middle of April in order to be able to finish a marathon. And then I have to say realistically, "I am not willing to pay that kind of price." So I have to scratch that item off.

The third point is to develop a checklist on yourself. I think perhaps one of the things insurance agents do best is to make promises. And the second is to break the promises because they don't develop a checklist on how to get the job done. It's a simple thing—you write it down. Have your wife or secretary or somebody check you once a month and once a quarter to see if you do it.

And that leads me to the fourth point in the formula. Do it. Don't talk about it anymore. Don't write about it anymore. Once you've agreed on the first three points, just start and do it. And it'll work for you every single day for the rest of your life.

J.D. Surber's words on this subject include a suggestion for company officers who work with agency heads:

> One of the very first things I was asked to do by my company was to put my thoughts on paper as to what the needs were in the agency and how I felt an organization could be developed in the future. I zeroed in on what I dubbed an 85-125 theme. I thought our organization could grow to 85 agents producing at least $125 million of ordinary life insurance volume in addition to our other product lines. This I wanted to accomplish by 1981. Out of this whole experience I've come to really agree with those behavioral scientists who tell us that the way to reach objectives is, first of all, to commit them to paper and, secondly, to put down a date as to when we expect to meet those objectives. I think it's a big secret in recruiting and that perhaps we overlook it as agency managers. When company executives begin to help new agency managers become whatever it is they want to become, I think the odds will improve if they begin together by following this process of committing to paper and sharing goals.

Bill Millar reminded us that our limitations are usually self-imposed, when he said:

> In 1973 when I dreamt that someday we would have a million dollar agency, meaning a million dollars in first-year commissions, I don't know whether I really believed it myself the day that I dreamt it. However, as the day crept nearer and nearer, I could see the million dollar agency as very much on the drawing board. And even before it

was achieved, I was planning the two million dollar agency. Counting on a 15 percent growth per year, in five years you imagine yourself then having a two million dollar agency. As it stands now, we'll probably have the two million dollar agency in just three short years. Now that we see the two million dollar agency coming over the horizon in just six short months from now, we're looking very seriously at the four million dollar agency. And occasionally I get the whim that it could even be 10 million some day. The American people today are not served adequately by the life insurance industry, as many of us know. Segments of that market are neglected more than others. I have no hang-ups about going from 120 agents to 140 agents and saturating a new market when perhaps 300 to 400 agents could be a more realistic assumption for decent market penetration. The marketplace is one which is growing continually. There will always be a place for good, competent life insurance counseling.

And Harry Hoopis put himself and his ambitious dream on record, not only with his associates, but with the whole industry, when he said the following:

I've heard recently that the job description of the general agent is to recruit and to plan and to counsel. At this stage in my career, I suppose that I spend about a third of my time in each of those three, and I have consciously tried to de-skill myself of some of the other functions. One of the postures that I enjoy is the planning aspect of my job. When I first came to Evanston, I developed a five-year plan, and that five-year plan said that by 1982 we would do $250 million in business on $5 million of premium. What I had was an agency where in five years the average productivity per man would rise from about $1,800,000 in volume to nearly $4,500,000. I didn't appreciate the impact of that until I watched the reaction of the agent who stood up and said, "This is exciting. Tell us how we'll do the four and one-half million." This led me to do some thinking about the plan, and so now I've developed and broken it down into two phases.

First we have what I like to call the strategic plan, and that is now my 10-year plan. I enjoy the five-year planning and we keep moving that along each year. But I set a plan for the decade. I have a 1989 goal, and that goal is for the agency to do one billion dollars in life insurance sales.

I asked Harry, "Did you say one billion dollars?" And his answer was:

Yes, Bob, I did say a billion, and you'll notice I can even say it with a straight face now. The first several times I presented this it was pretty tough not to smile. This strategic plan, then, is to reach a billion dollars of sales. That's a very impersonal objective. It just says that as an agency that would be our result. Incidentally, that involves some 12 million dollars of premium on 12 thousand lives, and the answer to that agent's question, "Tell me how we'll do this," lies in our annual tactical plan. This involves things like how do we improve productivity per agent which is a breakdown of how do we improve lives per agent or premium per case size, the volume per case size. And on a day-to-day basis we deal with those types of problems. The 10-year plan of reaching a billion dollars of business says that we'll have 125 agents. We currently have 60. So you see there is a substantial factor for horizontal growth.

The second factor would be the inflation factor. If we take an eight percent inflation rate over the next decade, we know that we'll double everything that we have today and more than double it.

The third factor is one of premium per thousand. Anyone in the business knows the trend. And that trend will continue. What many agents and managers have not come to grips with is that a 30 percent reduction in the premium per thousand results in a 43 percent increase in the face amount of insurance you can buy for the same premium dollar. The major impact of this information on my agents was that they now realize they weren't thinking big enough. As a result, I've become known as the resident big thinker in the agency. It's a title I really enjoy and have some fun with. In the one-third of my time that I devote to planning, I am trying to do planning for my agents as well as for the agency. I find agents have trouble understanding that by 1989 the average agent in our agency will produce over eight million dollars per year in volume.

Bob Duncan said, "Sometimes I just let my mind soar." Those words remind me of Bernie Rosen's response to this question: "Do you recall making a conscious decision that you wanted to build a great agency?" He replied:

I make that conscious decision every single year. Although I'm delighted with the agency that we have, nonetheless, every year I make the decision I want to build a big, great agency. And I hope I never lose that feeling, no matter how well we've done the year before. The opportunity to become great is still out there. The challenge is still out there.

What comes through to me in reviewing this chapter is that planning by the agency head and his associates, rather than being an onerous chore, can be exhilarating and satisfying and fun! Sure, companies can assign quotas, but agents and agency heads alike can set their own exciting objectives well beyond those that any Home Office might impose, and then lay out the plans that will assure their attainment.

That's not to say that the plans need not be realistic and sound. In fact, the title of our next chapter is "Don't Kid Yourself." In it we'll examine the need for agency heads to be realistic and practical business persons.

But first, let's acknowledge the significance of the trend observed in the quotations cited:

> *Agencies will grow and progress to the degree that such growth and progress is planned and the plan is bought by those who will execute it.*

Plans of that nature work because they answer this question of every member of the agency, whether voiced or not:

"Where are we going?"

5 | Don't Kid Yourself

The Agency Head as a Business Manager

> **SIGNIFICANT TREND:** Standards of performance in the agency will be higher and more strictly enforced than ever before.

It was in the late '50s at one of the first Agency Officers Schools of LIAMA (now LIMRA) that a well-known actuary was quoted as having said, "You can't ruin a life insurance company without malice. Stupidity alone is not enough!"

At a time when the whole life premium per thousand at age 35, male or female, was over $28.00 (for one thousand or a million) in some of the very largest mutuals, when agents, agencies, and companies had average premiums over $30.00 per thousand, when rents were a fraction of today's, when $1,000 a month financing was highly exceptional, it was not essential that an agency head be a good business person. If he (for he was always male) could recruit agents and help a decent percentage of them survive, he was successful and his company was happy.

Today it's a different kind of a ball game. Some companies have abandoned the agency system as being uneconomic. Volume (face amount) of insurance is a meaningless way of keeping score. Premiums alone tell but a part of the story. Commissions tell a little more. Expenses add another essential dimension. For the first time agency heads now need to be business people with real sensitivity to the importance of the bottom line.

Elliot Rothstein said it very clearly in the course of our interview with him about profitability:

> The economy in the last 10 years has changed dramatically, just as our industry has changed. It has forced the agency manager to become a businessman. No longer is his job just to recruit and

train and supervise full-time field underwriters. His job really is to become a profit center. An agency must be a profit center. For example, we just recently opened a branch office. Until that time we had everything under one roof. Before we opened the branch, we made a projection. How many field underwriters would be housed in that branch office and how much business would they do? And we sat down and asked what is it going to cost to have that office? What is the rent? What are the clerical salaries? What are the telephone charges? What is the postage? What are the sundries? What are the equipment charges? And then how much business does that branch have to do at the end of the year to cover those expenses? Years ago we would just have opened the branch. There would have been no thought as to whether it was going to be profitable or not. Gee, we've got five people, they live in that area, why not open an office for them? Now that branch must be a profit center, just as the main agency must be a profit center. The job of the agency manager has become one of being a businessman as well as a recruiter.

The implications of what Mr. Rothstein was saying are many, and they affect virtually all aspects of the agency's operations. In considering those implications with respect to this chapter, it seemed that several areas must be included— areas that we had earlier anticipated would be separate chapters of this volume.

So we shall look at the agency head as a business manager under each of these broad, often overlapping, categories:

1. Profitability and Business Management
2. Time Control and Personal Efficiency
3. Production Standards, Present Agents
4. Production Standards, New Agents

It will be a big chapter, a chapter that might not even have been included in a book about agency management when you came in the business. Its relevance is attested to by the fact that while some companies have forsaken the career agency system, others have just as decisively strengthened their commitment to it.

PROFITABILITY AND BUSINESS MANAGEMENT

To set the scene for this area, consider these words from Norman Levine:

> . . . another thing I think I should have certainly done early on and didn't is to spend a lot more time on money management. I didn't understand at all when I started as a general agent the fiscal responsibilities of a general agent. I don't think there's enough formal training at the company or field level in the areas of fiscal and administrative management.

Down in Orlando, Glenn Martin's perspective is interesting. He compares the agency head to the Cadillac dealer. As many readers will know, the enterprise Glenn has built would equate to not "a" car dealer, but many! Here's how he said it:

> I think for too long this industry has identified agent as an agent, manager as a manager, instead of saying, well, this agent has really developed into a business. He's got his own business. He's got a very successful business, just like a one-man corporation. What's the difference? An agency head who is now a businessman and has 25 agents and functions in his community, well, he's just as much a business as the guy down the street that owns the Cadillac dealership. There's really no difference. I think for too long we've hindered the insurance man because we've identified him with an insurance company and said, "He's with New York Life." No, New York Life is with him in reality. Or

American Amicable. My company is with him because that's the product he might represent.
They're the manufacturer. He's the distributor.

All the way across the continent in British Columbia, can-
ny Canadian Donald Hart has sound counsel for all agency
heads who want to operate as sound business persons:

We've got to control costs by careful budgeting
and by proper planning. It's much easier to control
costs when we've done a proper planning job. We
know what we want to do, the money we have
available, and what we want to accomplish. I think
a clear concept of what you intend to accomplish in
accurate budgeting is important, particularly in
those areas where you have controllable costs. So
far as noncontrollable costs are concerned, the only answer is to have more units of production.

We asked Mr. Hart how his agency came to enjoy such
good persistency on its business. This was his reply:

I think perhaps it starts with a philosophy and an
attitude. We attempt to tell our people why persistency is important to them as sales representatives,
why it's terribly important to the buyer and of
course to the company.

So we start with an attitude. We also stress the
needs approach to selling, and so in effect people
know why they're buying. They're buying in most
instances because they feel they have the need for
the amount of insurance they purchased. There are
a number of other things we do in addition to that,
however. We're very careful about the method of
premium payment. We will not accept a quarterly
premium, for example, because we found that our
experience with that has been very poor indeed. We
also have a rater which we use. And it then
becomes the responsibility of those of us on the

management team to discuss that application with the representative and to resell the need for quality business. In more cases than one, we have sent the individual back to arrange for the premium on a different settlement basis. It's a waste of time to write poor quality business. It's certainly very demoralizing for the representative to see a high percentage of his business go off the books. It's a disservice to the public and it's not good for the image of life insurance and all we stand for. But from a pure economic standpoint, it's suicide. You're working too hard for too little money. You just can't afford to write poor quality business.

We asked Mr. Hart how he determined whether it was wise and appropriate to invest now for the future of the agency. This, in part, was his reply:

I think the best approach is to take a cost/benefit approach. This is to say I'm going to weigh the cost against the anticipated benefits, and when I've thought that through clearly, I'm usually able to make an intelligent decision.

I'm also in the position to find out how accurate my predictions were because, if the benefit that was anticipated has been clearly defined as not being cheap, then I had better make some changes and I'd better cut something in that budget. Space is a good example. A growing agency frequently finds that they're out of space. This becomes a big ticket item, however. And one had better be able to anticipate and to make the calculations as to how much production is necessary to maintain a proper cost ratio if that space is taken on. It helps make the decision as to how much space he might consider. It allows you to look at alternatives, perhaps a satellite office on the outskirts of the city.

Oklahoma's Bill Branham is highly regarded for his business acumen. These words of his place profits in the perspective they deserve:

> Agency profits are the source of agency services, supports, facilities, atmosphere. The agency without profits or the general agent without profits really can't provide what every really well-motivated, successful agent deserves.

When we asked Mr. Branham what advice he'd give another young agency head about operating a profitable agency, he said:

> Well, a quick summary would be to always predict your production conservatively. Don't have rose-colored glasses on about the human beings involved. So when you're projecting production for budget purposes be conservative, and be realistic in projecting your expenses. They're going to go up with inflation and they may go up for other reasons. Don't leave any of those items out. Two things that seem to really hurt a lot of people are financing losses and their cost of doing business. They can be budgeted and they should be budgeted, and then they don't come with a shock. You need to be realistic here but you can take the number of recruits you're projecting for the next few years. You can take the average that survive either from your own or your company records over the three-year period. You therefore have your number of terminators. So if 33 percent survive three years, and you're going to average six appointments per year, you're going to have four losses. Right? And if in the average loss in the company's finance plan your share is $3,000, then $3,000 times four is $12,000. You therefore should put $1,000 per month aside into an escrow account, a savings account. If you don't do it, you'll some day be paying the bank or Home Office controller because they loaned you the money. You might as

well do it from day one. If you've got to recruit, you're going to have turnover. And with turnover you're going to have some financing loss. These should be budgeted.

I would also say don't be afraid to borrow money when it seems justified, and don't be afraid to finance new or established agents for purposes that are going to produce more business. Another item is to watch your personal budget just as carefully as you watch the agency budget. Don't fool yourself into personal or business expenditures, thinking you have to live like someone on the hill. You're not going to impress anyone if the eventual press release reads that you're "returning to serve your substantial personal clientele." You've got to remember a business can go broke because the owner spent too much at home or he spends too much at his office.

Agency expenses can't be controlled solely by the agency head. Agents and staff alike need to be involved. The amount and quality of business will determine the amount and quality of the services the agency can provide, so everyone has a stake. Leonard Day said:

We monitor each individual agent to make sure that he's operating as a profit center for us.

He explained how agents participate in decisions about who bears what expenses for agency services:

We operate on a branch (agency) steering committee basis. The steering committee is made up of three management people, plus myself and four agents. We talk about virtually anything from a policy standpoint that might affect the agency. Since the agents are part of a decision-making process and policy-setting body, I'm able to enlist their support for changes, for example in the expense area, that may be unpopular. Right now we have a question in front of the committee pertaining to whether or not we should charge an agent for *extraordinary* support in the advanced underwriting area. By extraordinary I mean if our advanced underwriting department is going to get right into the point of sale in helping the agent to close.

Profitability will mean different things to different people. You've got to really get down and look at your general agent's or manager's contract to understand it and the fine points of it. Your contract should really govern your behavior in terms of profitability. Some contracts weigh very highly in terms of production, or conservation. Others will be heavier in terms of agent retention or expense ratios.

Donald Hart feels that the agency's profitability depends to a great degree on the agents' also operating on a sound financial basis. Here's how he puts it:

I believe today one of the greatest missed opportunities is in helping our people to understand personal money management. I have seen so many fine representatives with good potential leave our business because of unsound financial money management practices. We are in the business of helping people build estates. We are in the business of assisting in their financial planning. And I don't see how we can do that job properly unless our own house is in order.

For example, it seems to me that one of the most powerful ways to help people make decisions that are in their own best interest insofar as having an adequate insurance program would go something like this. Let us say that I had made the recommendation to you following an interview during which you have told me what you wanted to do for yourself and your family. And based upon what you have told me, I have made a recommendation and you seem to be hesitating. And I say something like this to you, "Bob, these recommendations were made to you because this is what you say you want for yourself and your family, and I agree those are very sound desires on your part. But let me make one thing clear. Whether you do this or not, it's not going to make any difference to me. It's not going to change my standard of living in any way, shape, or form, but it's going to make a tremendous difference to your family if you don't do it and if you die this afternoon. It's going to make a tremendous difference when you reach retirement age and you don't have the income that you say you want. Whether you do it or not is up to you. It won't affect me to any extent." Now an agent whose financial house is not in order or an agency head whose financial house is not in order can't say that with sincerity because it's not true. And I'm afraid he begins to think about what he wants rather than what the client wants. And that makes for a very difficult sales process as well as poor quality in his business. I think that we have a great challenge and a real responsibility to help our people in financial planning.

Elliot Rothstein gave these practical pieces of counsel:

Many managers expand their office space and their facilities with the idea that they hope to recruit and fill it up. My philosophy has been the exact opposite. If necessary, I will put a third desk in a two-man office. I might even have two people work at one desk while they are in pre-contract training. I won't take additional space until I know that the space can be profitable. Fixed expenses have to be watched very, very carefully. You can always hire another clerical person if you need that person, but you don't hire that person until you have the work for them to do so that they'll be cost effective. You don't sign an additional lease for another 1,000, 1,500, or 2,000 square feet and say, "Well, I hope I'm going to recruit enough people to fill it." You then create the feeling of excitement within the agency. It becomes a positive feeling when the office is crowded. We had an old copying machine and I announced to the agency that when we hit a certain level of production, I would buy a bond paper copier. When we hit that level of production one week later, we had a bond paper copier. The field underwriters begin to feel that the manager has credibility when he says he'll do something and he does it. There should be a carrot for reward as well as a stick for punishment. Agency managers must insist on minimum levels of production for housing. You can't house the $500,000 producer any longer because he is not profitable. He is a cost for the agency. If you ask me to invest $1 in something and you tell me that maybe I'll get back 90¢, I have no interest in that investment. You must spend $1 where it will bring you back at least $1.10 or $1.25. That's the way an agency manager must look at his agents and he must look at the services and facilities that he provides for these agents.

Harry Hoopis provided an interesting perspective when he spoke of the agent's responsibility in his or her own business:

The agents, I think, for the first time will have to consider themselves more like a small business than they ever have before. To date most agents appear to use their expenses under some very strict guidelines—for instance, 20 to 30 percent of their gross earnings. I think that we're going to see more and more agents willing to make greater expenditures to improve the bottom line. Some of our super producers today are spending 50 or 60 percent of their gross income, even 70 percent, but have net incomes of $200,000, $300,000, and $400,000. The concept will be, spend as much as you have to to penetrate the markets that you want to work in and be successful in.

Roland Hymel's father was a general agent whose practical counsel to his son was extended into an unusual and practical modern day application. I asked Roland about how he used video equipment in the office situation, for I'd seen it by a desk of one of his clerical people. He said this:

> My father always taught me, "Make sure you always have a cover-up for every desk. Rotate your girls. Make sure they can handle two or three desks at one time in case one is sick or on vacation. That way you don't become completely dependent." By videotaping each particular desk and job, we now have a lot more confidence, not having to worry about whether everybody knows what so and so does every day and can we get a new person to do it. We not only show it so she can look at it two or three times to be sure she is doing it correctly (all we have to do is just move the little television set and the video equipment right next to her desk), but we also have a training session every week for secretaries. We try to select only people who are marketing-oriented. They come in contact with people every day and we feel that's very important. It also gives them something to move up to from general office secretary to private secretary and eventually to marketing assistant. Two of our leading agents have two marketing assistants who not only are secretaries but also are licensed and take applications. When they enroll a large company in a benefit plan, they actually go out in the field and work with the employees. This produces time for the agent to be doing more valuable work.

Robert Pogue identified three potential problem areas for those endeavoring to operate on a sound financial basis:

Where I see most individuals really get into trouble is with what I call the Big Three: staff, telephone, and usually space or rent. Most of the time when I see that people are excessive in those areas, it's because they are over-anticipating.

About a year ago I did some year-to-year cost studies on our individuals to find out how productive we were or were not in each situation. And the results were kind of startling, because I found in a number of instances, for example, that we were spending more money to support an individual in rent, telephone, secretarial services, etc., than he was actually generating in income. And that is indeed startling when you find the individual you're supporting is a net loss to you. So I encourage someone if he really wants to find out how he's doing or how well he's functioning . . . match your expenses against the productivity of your people.

Sidney De Young in Massachusetts and Mike McAdams in Texas made real contributions to their peers everywhere when they shared their ideas and procedures in the area of building and maintaining good persistency. Each has a splendid record, and it is the direct result of their own philosophies and those of their associates.

We asked Mike McAdams to describe the behavior he'd expect from each of two agents, one with a good persistency record and the other with a record not nearly as good, if each got the news one morning that a key client had lapsed or was about to. This was his response:

The agent who has a persistency problem is likely to say, "Well, I've got a lot of other things to do today; I'll attend to that later if at all." He pushes it on the far side of his desk or under some other papers that are stacked on his desk and basically forgets about it. He's more concerned about today's survival and his other problems that happen to be pressing him at the moment. He just simply doesn't recognize the importance of quality control in his business. On the other side of the coin, and I'm thinking of a particular agent who represents most of the people in our agency, that agent becomes angry when he sees that lapse notice. He feels challenged. He doesn't like the fact that this business is about to lapse. He remembers why it was sold in the first place. The first thing he does is pick up that telephone and contact that client. A pressing appointment or an imminent appointment that he may have to sell a larger case has become secondary in his mind because of this symbolic threat to what the life insurance business represents to him.

I think perhaps the most compelling reason for careful selection of agents lies in the area of persistency. Terminated agents cause a great deal of our persistency problems. If you're going to have an inevitable termination of an agent, then do it as early and as quickly as possible so you don't pile up all these orphans that represent the kind of problem that we're talking about.

Sid De Young is quite clear about where the responsibility for good persistency really lies:

If the general agent or a manager had poor persistency, it would be difficult for him to train other people to have better persistency than he's capable of producing. So I think it starts right at home with the man in charge. Also, quality recruiting and quality selection are very important in establishing good persistency in your agency. An agency that has a lot of turnover in manpower probably will have poor persistency. The agency that tends to keep the manpower that it recruits will probably, in the long run, have much better persistency. In the selling process itself, I believe that need selling probably has the most material effect on the business staying on the books. If the client or the policyholder really understands the need for that insurance and it is continually brought to his attention on a regular basis, which means constant review of insurance programs, then I think you'll find that persistency will be at a much higher level.

I think every agent and every agency ought to make sure that all of the applications that are sold are prepaid. We established that rule in our agency 15 years ago. We don't allow any applications to be turned in unless the money is turned in with them. The exceptions are probably four or five in a year, and those have to be approved through me in order for such applications to be processed. It doesn't make much sense for the office staff to just move paper around if a client isn't serious about what he's trying to accomplish. Needless to say we don't have many policies sent back to the Home Office once they're issued.

Both Sid and Mike, as might be anticipated from their words, have systems in place to deal with possible lapses. Here is how Mike described his:

We have a regular follow-up system on impending lapses. We have follow-up telephone calls from my assistant, from my office manager, and myself. My secretary may even get into the act. We talk about this persistency problem enough and frankly we harass the agents enough that I think sometimes they feel it's easier to go ahead and reinstate a policy than to continue to hear from us because they know they're going to hear from us until something is done about it one way or another. We contact the agent and say, "What can we do to help you?" or, "I noticed that the policy on Mr. Johnson is lapsing. Is there anything at all that we can do to help?" or, "Can you tell us about the problem?'' At the same time, by offering that assistance the agent remains aware of the fact that we are concerned about persistency. After a while they just realize that that's part of the ball game.

And Sid De Young is equally thorough:

We have some systems set up for keeping business on the books. I'm sure most companies have an overdue list to notify the agent of people that are currently overdue. We get a composite list of those every week. In our agency it's my secretary's responsibility to immediately get a report from every agent on the overdue premiums for that week. This composite list continues to grow from week to week. If the person hasn't paid his premium, the following week his name will still be on that list. So there will be another follow-up. Before a person really is in trouble, my secretary has contacted the agent four times. If she feels that there's some problem involved, she brings it to my attention and I personally follow up. When the 30 days are up and the policy is in a lapse condition, then the agent gets a card that he has to fill out telling exactly what he did to conserve that business. When that card is filled out, it's put on my desk and I review it. If it appears that the explanation is not satisfactory, then I talk directly to the agent and ask him perhaps to do a little more work on it before the final disposition of the policy takes place. If there's no way that we can conserve that business for whatever reason, then it goes in our lapse book. Once a month I review all of the lapses for every single agent. On the monthly review, and when we review the sales figures for the month, we also review the business that went off the books that month. So it's really constant vigilance that takes place. Someone said a long time ago that things that get checked are the things that get done.

Both Messrs. McAdams and De Young mentioned that his company has a persistency bonus program, and that in some instances five-figure checks are written to some of the better persistency agents—a very significant incentive!

Two more clues to Mr. De Young's persistency record are these:

> One of the other areas which I think is very, very valuable is the assigning of orphan policyholders. Like other agencies we lose manpower from time to time. When this happens, prior to the agent leaving, I sit down with him and go over every single piece of business that he has on the books. I try to determine in that last interview with him who would best serve that client. Within a week or 10 days we try to have all of his policyholders assigned to a new agent so that immediately they can pick up the service and the follow-up that has to be done on that block of business. That has proven to be very, very valuable.

> Another thing I think has helped with persistency is the automatic monthly deductions from checking accounts. I would say three-quarters of our business is on that basis.

And this last De Young quote is a continuing reminder that we can paraphrase J.B. Conway and say "first-rate people mean first-rate business."

> If I had to pick one thing that has put me where I am as far as sales are concerned, it's developing the referral system and prospecting early in the business and always getting at least three names from everyone that I sold. I would always ask the same question: "Who do you know that is as serious about their family and their future as you are?" And I would always get at least three good quality names from my client and that just mushroomed,

and I always knew where my next sale was and that made me feel good inside. If you shop in a quality store, you're going to get quality merchandise. If you prospect with quality people, you're going to have quality business. The best way to get quality people is to ask quality people for names. They'll refer you to them very readily if they're very satisfied with what you've done with them.

Phil Kessler may have raised a few eyebrows when he pointed out that there are times when being a successful business person can require courage:

One of the things I feel very, very strong about is that when you find that person you think is the perfect recruit to come into the business and you've dotted your i's and crossed your t's, don't be afraid to go ahead and gamble with that person. When I first became a general agent, I had two new agents on financing—one at $3,000 a month and one at $2,500 a month. And a lot of people told me that I was a fool to have that kind of risk outstanding. Well, both of those people are among my top four. Whatever your process is, once you've been through it and you're sure that's the person, don't all of a sudden pull in your horns because of financing or something like that. Go ahead and take the gamble.

Stan Eason reminded us of the only two criteria that should be applied in evaluating a financial commitment for the agency:

When I first became a general agent, I had two supervisors who had no limit to their telephone budget, postage, office supplies, etc. The amount of telephone calls that they could make was unbelievable. So I was forced by a situation to put in a budget. I did that and it's been very, very workable from that point on. If their agents make calls that are chargeable, then they collect them, so they do have the authority. They do have the money to work with and all I need from them is profitable production. I think it's important to recognize that a unit exists for just two basic purposes: to be of profit to the general agent and to be of profit to the company right now and/or be building. In other words, recruiting people who will make the unit of profit in a short time. Many times a unit won't be paying for itself presently. The only reason to have that unit then is if it is building people who will represent a profit in a short time in the future. Other than that you should be getting a profit on it right now. If you're not getting a profit or if you're not building to where there's going to be a profit soon, then it seems to me that it's in everybody's best interest to cease that operation. In fact, it's a crime not to.

As an "outside expert" for a Legacy of Learning unit on agency profitability, we obtained the perspective of the person we consider to be the world's greatest authority on the subject, LIMRA's Elizabeth Tovian. We end this section with these authoritative quotes from her remarks:

> We know that it costs the company somewhere in the neighborhood of $60,000 to develop one successful agent, assuming that there were 100 recruits and 30 successfully entered their fourth contract year. But that cost could skyrocket to over $150,000 per success if there are only 10 survivors instead of 30. If your rate is 20 out of 100, that is, if you have a 20 percent success rate, you're doing better than the industry but not anywhere near as good as the best quality companies and agencies.

This one may surprise you:

> I'd like to emphasize that improvements in productivity can be made by increasing certain types of

costs, that is investment costs. LIMRA studies show that higher-producing agencies spend more, mostly time, on each prospective agent, more on the training of each agent and more on management development than is spent in the smaller agencies. Their overall unit costs are lower because they have more business over which to spread those costs.

If you're concerned about the level of some of your individual expenses, you may be interested in some benchmarks from LIMRA's latest agency cost studies. The percent distributions have been quite stable. About three-quarters of an agency's expenses go out for salaries and rent—about half for salaries, and a quarter for rent. The rent tends to be a few points under 25 percent in the larger agencies and a few points over 25 percent in the smaller agencies. This is true in both the United States and Canada. The salary split is different. Canadians tend to pay a larger portion of their salary budget to the clerical staff, over 40 percent of the total agency expense, whereas in the U.S. it averages closer to 30 percent. This may be partly owing to the very strong branch administrator system in Canada where in many cases the branch administrator or branch secretary runs the business affairs and reports directly to the Home Office. Canadian managers may also be more successful in delegating activity to the branch support staff that might normally be performed by the supervisory group in the United States.

The supervisory compensation in the U.S. and Canada tends to follow the same pattern—that is, a greater percent for the supervisory staff in the larger agencies—but the level is different. In Canada, the percents go up from 16 percent in the large agencies down to nine percent in the small. In the U.S., from 23 percent in the larger agencies down to 14 percent in the small. The telephone, including terminal charges, runs five to six percent in Canada and seven to eight percent in the U.S., with the smaller percents tending to be in the larger agencies.

As a quick summary I'd just like to list four areas where quality means profitable business:

1. Agent productivity. It's definitely better to get $40,000 of premium from one agent than $20,000 each from two. But I'm not sure if it's better to get $80,000 from two rather than $160,000 from one. We haven't tried to figure that one out yet but probably should.

2. Persistency. Keep your business and your client.

3. Cost control. Make your income and expense budget from your plan and don't forget that your own time is one of the agency's most valuable resources.

4. . . . or number one for most agencies. Retention. The cost of hiring and training is so high and maintaining a revolving door is very expensive. Invest the time to select and train agents and to set them up in markets they can handle.

At the outset of this chapter we indicated that we would examine its overall subject of the Agency Head as a Business Manager under four subheads. Up to this point we have looked at what top managers and general agents have had to say about the importance of operating profitably, of being effective and efficient managers of the business units they head. Now for a look at the second area.

TIME CONTROL AND PERSONAL EFFICIENCY

If the agency is to be profitable, the agency head must set a high standard for his or her own productivity and efficiency, not only in order to adequately fulfill the many responsibilities that come with the job, but also to meet an important collateral responsibility: serving as an example to the rest of the organization.

That's asking a lot of any person! The good news, though, is that the next several pages contain the proven ideas and practices of outstandingly successful doers. Adopting and/or adapting them can pay lifelong dividends. Such worthies as Al Granum, Maurice Stewart, Jim Harding, Hank Kates, Bernie Rosen, Bob Meeker, Lew Yount, Ed Leaton, Vince Bowhers, Don Edwards, and Bob Hemmick share in a way that can provide a never-ending payoff.

Let's start with this sharing from Jim Harding:

> I feel that there is a maxim that really plays a big part in all of our lives, and that is that you must pay a price. It's just a question of when you pay it. Either you pay it up front by additional thought, effort, work, and investment, or you pay it at the other end of the line by decreased enjoyment, bit by bit maybe, but over a period of years. And if you haven't paid the price up front you're never going to be able to pay the price later and catch up unless you really take some significant risks and make big changes in your life. A four-point program can help people with the issues we're talking about.
>
> First, get in touch with your priorities. You know we're in a goal-setting business, but too often we set them at the beginning of the year and pretty soon forget about them. I think you have to make a daily project of getting away from your daily life, probably first thing in the morning, in thinking about the big picture about your priorities.

Second, be reflective so that you're able to think about the issues in your life contemporaneously rather than waiting until the end of the line and looking back and seeing you can't do much about it. I think the concept of keeping a journal, writing to yourself daily, is a vehicle to do this.

Third, make your time count. And I certainly can't suggest any better source than Alec McKenzie's work, *The Time Trap.*

The fourth thing is being willing to take risks to make changes and grow. I don't mean that everybody has to go hang-gliding, but there are things that we need to do as people, risks that we need to take. We need to run the risk of being embarrassed, of having our egos stepped on a little bit, to make some changes and grow. Otherwise we get stuck in the same ruts and we really honestly don't grow.

So get in touch with your priorities, be reflective, make your time count, and be willing to take some risks.

Vince Bowhers reminded us that systems make us more efficient when he said:

We have all learned more and more over the last few years the importance of systems. The great part of bringing someone into the business and moving them right into the marketing system (or, if you're working with your management team, establishing specific systems that they will use in recruiting and in training and in supervision) is if there's a system, then you can have confidence that if you do a certain amount of work of that type you will get a certain level of positive results. I believe that's true whether you're talking about the agent in making his calls or the person in management or the company. If we're following an operation based on systems, then the results will be predictable.

In discussing time control and priorities for his own schedule, here's how Maurice L. Stewart listed the areas of prime concern to him:

1. With associates in business less than three years.

2. Those meetings and advanced underwriting sessions for established associates.

3. Our personal conferences—some personal contact with each associate every couple of days.

4. Administrative chores.

5. Recruiting, which must be diligently planned because it doesn't force its way into your daily activity the way administrative problems do. So next in priority are these people we've been talking to about coming into the business.

6. The outside activities. This means four to six hours a week if we are going to repay our debts to our community, our industry, our society.

7. Last, but not least, is the family. We have to be flexible enough that we can move away from our plan, but it has to be pretty much of an emergency before we will move away from the priorities we have established.

He said that he monitors himself and his planned progress:

I try to take a day off every quarter, and go off and sit on a stump with my planning book and try to determine whether or not I'm working efficiently.

Jim Harding has coauthored a book that has helped many people to greater effectiveness. Here's another observation from him:

> Two other things are important to my development and efficiency. One is time management. The general agent and the manager have a more difficult time controlling their time than any other breed of businessperson. The agent feels he ought to be able to see the manager at any time. The policyholders that come in want attention from the general agent or manager and it goes on and on. Probably the whole office wants to deal through the agency head. So you often end up deep down in the pit fighting all the alligators, when your initial objective was to drain the swamp. It's critical that we deal with that issue.
>
> The other thing that was kind of interesting for me a couple of years ago was the issue of speedreading. Our CLU chapter offered a two-day seminar which the Wood people put on about speedreading. I found that in two days I was able to triple my reading speed and increase my comprehension by 50 percent. I'd strongly encourage anybody to look at that as an interesting means of both personal and business skill development.

And here are more suggestions from Jim that are both specific and practical:

> The more complex our agency operations get, the more things we have to do. So there are two factors to this. One is a to-do list. A very simple concept, just take either legal pads or printed sheets which break down the things you have to do into three categories—vital, important, and routine. Making the decisions about importance, I think, has been critical to me. And having some place where I can put everything down is important. Not on the back

of an envelope, not in my workbook, but some place where I can put it down and then take great joy in crossing it off. It's one of life's funny little satisfactions.

The other part of that is taking and internalizing it into a daily planning function. One of the biggest time wasters most of us have is ineffective planning. So the last half hour of every day for me is planned in my workbook as being two things: plans for the next day and writing in my journal. So I'm kind of being reflective on the current date. In planning for the next day, I'm going to take the time-honored idea of picking out the six most important things that I have to do, with the most important thing at the top and so on down the line. And if I never get anything done but the first thing, I'll be doing the most important thing. In addition, one of the things I've introduced because of the study group I've been in is the idea of picking the one or two most important things, the one or two most important goals for the day. And then keeping score on yourself and seeing what percentage of time you actually accomplished them in. If you can get up in the 70 to 75 percent range, you are a happy and satisfied individual. I think it's important for us to take these concepts and help our agents do them. It's important for us to practice what we preach.

Hank Kates reminds us that our efficiency is a function of the energy we have available. He walks the several (seven, as I recall) floors to his office, because he knows it's good for him to do so. The role of physical activity is important to him, for he said:

Some years ago I came to the realization that the human mind, which controls the human body, was really very similar to a windup clock. Early in the morning, when it's all wound up, it's full of energy. As it performs during the day, it exudes that energy and finds itself winding down.

I either run, play squash, play singles tennis or paddle tennis on the roof of our building. And I find that by playing that activity usually around two or three o'clock in the afternoon, my clock gets rewound immediately following the game, and I'm able to start right back in again and perform as though I had just awakened in the morning.

Al Granum is another who makes a list of things to be done tomorrow. He makes it sound not at all like a chore, but like a better way to enjoy life:

That marvelously complex brain computer of ours is working continuously, waking and sleeping. And if we will give it some input before we go to bed at night, it'll work on it all night. Sometimes when we wake up in the morning we'll have some new insight. Before going to bed at night, list everything you might conceivably like to get done tomorrow. And then with the list in front of you, prioritize it and then forget it. When you wake up tomorrow, not only will you have additional insight and enthusiasm, but you'll also have the feeling of being employed and having a place to go.

Al is smart enough to insure that he'll follow through on his plans by involving his assistant:

It's my assistant, Nancy O'Malley, who works me. We agree in cold blood when I'm full of energy and enthusiasm as to exactly what I ought to be doing and when. And then Miss O'Malley sees to it that when the time comes, I do it—even if I don't feel like doing it, and sometimes I don't. Of course, I can't try to get out from under too often, or she'd give up on me.

With regard to delegation, Mr. Granum quoted one adviser who told him:

> Ask yourself, "Does this job have to be done as well as only I can do it?" Another said, "Learn to de-skill yourself. Building an organization is a function of de-skilling one's self."
>
> There are many people who can handle complex, advanced underwriting matters better than I. By de-skilling ourselves, we release whatever nervous energy and enthusiasm and capacity and ability we have for concentration in those areas where perhaps we are more effective and can do the best job.

In a similar vein Bernie Rosen said:

> No general agent can be good at everything. He can't be the best recruiter and trainer and advanced underwriter and supervisor and Big Daddy and best financial manager. Nobody has all of these things. I've been able to find people within our agency, and I've been able then to bring them onto staff and delegate to them things that they do so much better than I do.

Few people anywhere can be any busier than Ed Leaton. Yet he conveys an impression of calmness, of confidence, of competence that must be vastly reassuring to all who work with him in his many-faceted activities. His thoughts are worth studying and applying:

> There isn't a manager alive who couldn't keep busy every minute of the day doing something. What matters is not that he's doing something, but that he's doing the right thing. You have to have some time when you can be quiet, when you can be creative, when you plan, so that you have some control over what happens to your life, your own personal performance, the performance of your

agency; otherwise, in no way are you going to be able to realize the potential that you and your agency could realize.

No time during business is too little to count. In other words, don't be easily distracted. Don't just concentrate on what's easiest or most pleasant. You have to do what's most important, or what's truly urgent. Even if just a few minutes a day go down the drain, in the course of a year, that's many, many hours. Stop to think how much money you're hoping to earn this year, and divide it by the number of truly productive hours you'll be spending. You'll be surprised that the wasting of these few minutes is a lot of dollars down the drain if you're not careful.

I'm a list-maker. I have lists of people I'm going to phone on a given day. I have lists of projects with the higher priority ones noted, the medium priority ones noted, and the lowest priority ones also indicated. I have a master date planning book that I use for long-range planning, and I have a follow-up system that my staff helps me on. When something is assigned to be done or to be followed up on at a future date, this is noted in my follow-up file that my staff keeps. And day by day, my staff gives me anything that has to be followed up on that day.

It's hard to be effective or efficient when we have health problems. We talked with Lew Yount about that:

Many of the agency heads whom I have known who developed health problems were insecure about their agencies and their associates. They were constantly making changes. I don't believe one should get into a rut, but making constant changes is not good for anyone.

So then we asked Lew if a person could just "decide" to become secure. Here is how he responded:

> Becoming secure is doing the things that develop a feeling of security. When I first became a manager, I was totally insecure. I was running around like a chicken with his head off, totally insecure and almost about to flip my lid. But when I decided that I was going to operate on a positive basis and recognize that I couldn't be everything to everyone, that I would have some failures, that I would do the things that in the long run would develop a successful agency, then I developed a feeling of security within myself.

> No matter how great the surgeon, some of his operations will be unsuccessful. Some of his patients will die. If he permitted himself to become continually involved with each person he has on the operating table, where would he be? He cannot permit this to happen. His challenge is to use all of his knowledge, training, and skill as effectively as possible. However, if some operations are unsuccessful, as they will be, he must accept a certain degree of failure and move on to the next operation without looking back.

> Well, after a lengthy think session, I decided I would manage the agency in much the same manner. I would bring new agents into the agency on a regular basis and in number, using the best selection procedures I could find, including precontract training. We would strive to give them a positive agency climate, a well-defined and administered training program with close supervision, including liberal amounts of joint work in the field. Hopefully, a higher percentage would succeed. But if they did not, I would accept the failures that occurred with no emotional involvement and continue to recruit. This was one of the most impor-

tant decisions I ever made insofar as my emotional health was concerned. I concluded that if I worked at the job consistently (and by this time I had enough experience to know what would work), I would be successful.

One Legacy interview was with Bob Meeker and his secretary, Mrs. June Baker. In the course of it we asked Bob this question: "Suppose you had a nephew who wrote and said, 'Uncle Bob, I've just been appointed manager of this agency in California. It's a small one right now. I just hired a secretary with some life insurance experience. What advice could you give us on how we could work together most effectively?' " This was Bob's reply:

> I guess I would say, "Nephew, congratulations on your appointment. The most important thing you can do is to analyze where you really want to go to really give direction to the things you want to do; and to have an exchange with your associate so that she will become aware of the things you want to do, how you want to do them, when you want to do them, and the manner in which you want to conduct your life!"

We also interviewed Al Granum's Nancy O'Malley. She said:

> Mr. Granum and I share the same appointment book, and he carries it with him every day. The only time it becomes a problem is when I don't sit down with him every single day. That's when schedules get botched up.

Bernie Rosen, too, has an effective system with his assistant. His observation is consistent with those of Al Granum and Bob Meeker:

> Far down on this list of priorities is office detail. I don't want to handle mail early in the day. There

are many days I don't want to handle the mail at all. I've a fine assistant. She is much more than a secretary. And she divides up the mail into what's important and what is not. For many of the things she can prepare her own answers for my signature. She's sort of a partner in the office detail, rather than somebody to whom I dictate or give tasks. She develops most of the tasks. Sometimes she gives me the tasks to accomplish.

June Baker, when asked how she keeps Bob Meeker's calendar, said:

Well, there are really three calendars: one for his desk, one for my desk, and one for Mrs. Meeker. We try to keep all three of them up to date, and I say "try" because occasionally one or the other of us throws something in that the other person doesn't see. But when we make travel arrangements, for instance, I always call Mrs. Meeker and let her know what plane times are, where they're going to be, and the telephone numbers for their family in case they're needed. Calendars are a very important item in the daily life.

Bob Hemmick confessed to having been a procrastinator. Then, however, he told how he solved that problem:

I suppose the greatest lesson I've learned in 15 years in management or, in fact, in life, is not to procrastinate. Procrastination is a human trait that everybody has. You do the things you enjoy, and you put off the things you don't enjoy. Procrastination has no place in management or planning. I suppose I was the worst procrastinator anybody ever was. But I learned to overcome it by one very simple method. I keep what I call a daily worksheet, and on that is everything that I have to do that day. Now instead of doing all the nice things as numbers one, two, three, four or five, all the

things that I really don't like to do become the top
of the list. Now this has a sort of magic effect on
me because I don't procrastinate about doing the
things in their order on the list. There is no tomorrow in planning. Planning is a today process because you have to meet those objectives in your
plan every day.

These words from Don Edwards provide a fitting windup
of this section on Time Control and Personal Efficiency. As
the others quoted have indicated, the rewards include better
health, peace of mind, more accomplishment. Don would
agree with all those. But he adds another:

It's been my observation over the years that the
truly successful agency men and agents are people
who get the most out of their time. I know that for
many years I was mistaken about this. I thought it
was the person who worked the hardest that got the
most done. So I tried to do it that way, and after
many years, I ended up worn out and not doing a
very good job. So to me planning is a procedure to
make better use of your time. I think planning
becomes vitally important because we either act or
we react. I never was one who liked to react. I liked
to have control of the action myself.

The big thing that's important to me is that, as a result of our planning process, my income is six times
higher than 12 years ago. That's a good payoff.

PRODUCTION STANDARDS, PRESENT AGENTS

Most people who have served in agency management,
whether as a unit head or agency head or director of agencies,
have had the experience of going over a roster of producers
with the intention of evaluating their contributions and value
to the agency. At such a time an agent of modest productivity
is likely to be defended with the statement that "he's not
costing us anything."

Today's successful agency heads would not agree. The costs that ensue from indifferent performance from an agency associate are insidious ones because they are many, varied, and often not readily evident. The quotations cited in the next pages show that successful agency heads are setting higher-than-ever standards of performance. They do so not only for economic reasons, but also to show confidence in their associates and to encourage and help them in their attainment.

This excerpt from our interview with Bob Szeyller makes it very clear how and why his agency has the kinds of standards it has:

> In this town—State College, Pennsylvania—you can live on $20,000 a year but you can't be in our agency because you're not going to be producing a sufficient amount of first-year commissions to merit the tremendous expense that we have to support you. It's hard when you're struggling to grow to make a standard which is going to cause three or four agents that may have been with you five or eight years to leave the business, but we've had to do that. We've been forced into it. We can't afford to think in terms of three or four big producers and a whole bunch of mediocre producers. Our agency can't end up looking like that. The numbers won't work. We may have to have smaller numbers than I had thought of originally, but everybody is going to be a big producer.

Burt Bauernfeind, back in the '70s, said the following:

> It's wrong to keep people in an agency just for numbers sake. They must be productive, they must be proud of their own achievements. Having drones around is expensive to everyone. We eliminated those who couldn't make a decent living.

Elliot Rothstein points out that there are ways of rewarding and helping agents raise their sights for the benefit of all:

At an agency meeting we announced what our minimum production requirements would be for housing in our agency for the balance of 1982 and for 1983. We told everybody we were going to be an agency of only winners. We have no room for losers. If a person doesn't do at least $1 million of what we call current volume with my company, which is the equivalent of $12,000 of annualized first-year commissions, he just isn't making a living. We can't afford to house such a person.

In addition, we have a study group made up of our club qualifiers. To be in the study group, which meets on a monthly basis, requires a minimum of $24,000 of first-year commissions in our company. If somebody earned only $20,000, they are not allowed to sit in, even as an observer. So people are fighting to get to a level of production so they can get the benefit of additional services, additional expertise, additional knowledge. This really affects profitability because you make each agent a more profitable unit. We have a goal that by 1990 we would like every agent in our agency to be making no less than $50,000 of first-year commissions.

Walter Vreeland was very candid when we asked if he'd made any mistakes in the area of helping agents develop. He said:

Yes, there have been times when I've preferred to be loved than to set standards of performance and then stay strong to those. I wavered sometimes in my values of the proper amount of performance or activity. In some cases if I had stayed stronger to it some of my associates might be performing at a higher level today. It's a hard thing to try to undo once you've done it. The penalty for not doing it successfully, I think, is that you devote a large part of your life to a level of mediocrity. There is no excitement in being surrounded by mashed potatoes.

We spent two days in the Al Granum agency, interviewing not only him, but also his staff and producers of various levels of experience. One of his top agents said:

> When you are brought into the agency, one of the first things that's explained to you is that success is expected. It's expected of you, and the failure to produce it will probably lead to your separation from the agency. We want an atmosphere of winning, and I've had Al say to me on several occasions that he'll sacrifice all else to keep the success atmosphere.

Irving Abramowitz did not mince words:

> I think I've learned that the marginal agency is killing the insurance company, and the marginal agent will kill an agency. It isn't true that he isn't costing you anything. That agent is costing you an awful lot. When a new agent comes in and sees that someone who is less than successful is still hanging around and can still occupy a desk and receive agency services, that doesn't provide the atmosphere that you want.

The time, effort, worry, and sleepless nights that have been devoted by so many managers to losing efforts to "save" agents could have been far better invested. Bill Allabashi is not about to make that mistake. He said:

> Many times the average agency head spends 90 percent of his time with a marginal producer. I make a conscious effort in our organization to spend 90 percent of our time and resources with the most productive forces, not with the marginal producer.

Harry Hoopis was another who was very specific when he said:

> We have an agency minimum standard. This year

every agent in our agency will have to earn at least $14,100 of first-year commissions to maintain a contract. We've indexed the minimum standard so that it will increase every year. As we move the bottom up, we know that we've improved the status of our own agents and agency.

Note: A phone call to Mr. Hoopis in May of 1984 told us that the $14,100 has now been "indexed" up to $20,700.

From the foregoing it should be evident that a practical realism characterizes the approach of leading agency heads to the need for performance standards consistent with the kind of agency they want theirs to be. Bill Millar, as usual, was forthright when he said:

If I were going to begin an agency today and walked into an organization that was a middle-of-the-road kind of an organization, I would look around thoroughly at the personalities involved. I would study them and decide whether these folks were the kind of people that I needed to build an organization or not. And then I would proceed to cull and prune more severely than most people would have the courage to do. If half of your organization is made up of seedy-looking characters, three years from now you're going to have 75 percent seedy-looking characters. And in five years they'll all be seedy-looking characters. So will you. Therefore I think the most essential thing is to cull and prune out those you don't feel will make an ample contribution, not only production-wise, but character-wise, in helping you build to the goals you have set. Once you've culled and pruned in that degree, and remember this is a difficult thing emotionally, you're now in a position to go forward and hire or select two or three people who could become your chief assistants and partners in this organization.

Don Heatherington felt he had to do the kind of "culling

and pruning" that Bill Millar talked about. After five years in charge of his company's San Francisco branch, the number of agents had "gone from" 33 to 33—but, only one was a holdover! In the same period, agency production went from $200,000 of first-year commissions to $1,000,000.

We asked Don how he'd counsel another agency head about how to increase productivity. Here was his response:

> Look at your organization and see who among your agents has the desire to be very successful. If you've got those persons already on board, sit down with them and plan with them on what they want to achieve. Find out what they want to do. Find out what they can do and what kind of support they need, and then work one-on-one with those people and build from there.
>
> If you don't have anybody like that, then I think the first step would be to go out and get somebody with that basic desire, and then work with them. Provide the backup support they need. Provide it yourself if you are technically confident and effective in advanced marketing. If not, and you have another successful agent, put them together in joint work. If you don't have that, go out in the industry, because there are successful agents with other companies happy to do joint work on advanced cases. If you can get someone in front of qualified prospects who have the ability to spend a lot of money if they have the need shown to them, then you'll be able to get the backup support to get that agent started, and then build from there. You don't have to have an elaborate operation in the beginning. Build one-on-one; then as it grows you'll get a greater team in your own agency to provide the marketing support. The big thing, I think, is creating the atmosphere and, of course, having at least one person to start the process going.

John Snow's agency is widely scattered in South Dakota, but his advice is also relevant in urban situations:

> I spend time very cautiously. I try to spend it with those who need it the most and are worthy of it. This could be a very big pitfall. It's important, especially with detached people, that you recognize failure when it's there. You don't spend a great deal of time with someone that is just not cutting it.

Bobby Yerusalim described his "winners' philosophy" this way:

> The "winners' philosophy" is that if I'm going to help people break barriers, then I've got to recognize that winners deserve more of me than guys that are just getting by. I don't mean to say that people aren't entitled to the same amount of basic training. But we've worked it out so that we can spend most of the time with those people who are dedicating more of their time and talents in the business.
>
> When I was a supervisor, it used to appall me when a man would fail and terminate in the business, and son of a gun, we'd go into his desk and find all the orphan policyholder leads that we gave him that he never even looked at. Now we give them just to the winners. The guys that are doing a good job get the orphan policyholders, the new move-ins, and any other leads we get. And by the way, it works out great for them. They *know* that we're treating them differently. We DO have favorites! That's our "winners' philosophy."

Bobby is in Cherry Hill, New Jersey. In neighboring Philadelphia, Maurey Stewart put it this way:

> I traveled to Atlanta and sat and visited all day with a very fine psychologist, Hugh Russell. Hugh

climbed all over me with the statement that "you're spending 75 percent of your time with your failures, and 25 percent of your time with your successes!" That one very simple statement after listening to Hugh for six or eight hours has changed my management operation tremendously.

How about measuring productivity by number of sales? When the automobile industry was introducing its new models for 1981 in the United States, colorful Lee Iaccoca predicted that the new model year would see the sale of 13 million cars and trucks, of which he looked forward to his organization selling 1.6 million. He did not say how many billions of dollars that would be, as we might speak of premiums. Nor did he say what the commissions would be. No, he referred to the number of sales.

Seldom, though, do we read that kind of statistic in the life insurance industry. Do you know how many people your company helped to increase their financial security last year through your company's products? Does anyone know? You won't find the answer in *Best's* nor in your company statement. Agencies are sometimes referred to as 10, 50, or 100 million dollar agencies. Some observers look forward to the time when agencies will be described as 700, 1,000, or 3,000 lives agencies.

If those 3,000 lives averaged $50,000 each, we'd have produced $150 million of volume. If the premiums were $12 a thousand, we'd have $1.8 million of new premiums and perhaps $900,000 of first-year commissions.

If, however, those totals are produced by 60 agents on 50 lives each, the overhead will be far more, and profits far less, than if the same production came from 30 agents with 100 cases each. And each agent will earn $30,000 of first-year commissions instead of half that on 50 lives!

William G. Demas, Herbert Krueger, John Pasco, and Frank Sullivan would each agree that sights need to be raised in the area of frequency of sales. Let's see why. . . .

Bill Demas asked this question:

> How can a career agent say that he is a full-time professional in our business and not have two applications a week? I find it very difficult to accept that. I think that part of the plus of the two applications a week is that it gives you a very positive mental attitude. It keeps your skills at a high level. It makes you enthusiastic; you get excited. Those victories, no matter how small or how big they are, still play an important part in the attitude which is really the foundation of our business.
>
> I think that the results you get are based on what you're compensating an individual for. And we gear most of our campaigns, our awards, any extra compensation, to applications. We have found that those individuals selling large numbers of cases are at the top of the pole in volume, premium, and commissions. Those that are selling a few cases are at the bottom.

Herbert Krueger told us earlier that the formula of 40-10-3, meaning 40 contacts about life insurance during the week resulting in 10 interviews resulting in 3 applications, is their key activity barometer. This is the quote from him:

> When persons start in our agency, we tell them right off the bat that if they take good care of this business, the business will take good care of them . . . that they will need a large number of interviews to generate sales. They have to become accustomed to the law of averages in a positive sense. The law of averages, you know, works for you or against you depending upon which way you're moving. If you don't see enough people, the law of averages works against you. You become rusty. If you see a large number of people, you have a large number of interviews. The law of averages works for you. You are sharper.

John Pasco made these comments:

> We need to be far more efficient in our work. We need to have vertical growth. There's an absolute need for increased productivity. The old application-a-week idea is far from sufficient today. The minimum goal for continued success should be 100 paid cases per year. I foresee larger agencies because bigger staffs and better support are going to be needed to accommodate the more sophisticated agencies in the future and meet their demands for better service and backup. Today's young people are not satisfied with halfway efforts. They're going to expect more of us. If we do our part then we should expect more of them.

This quote from John Pasco is in response to my question about advice he'd give to new young managers:

> I'd tell the young managers to set their standards high, set their requirements at a demanding level, and resist the temptation to make exceptions and go on hope. It has been written, "He who expecteth little shall not be disappointed." I believe that if you expect much of people and yourself you'll be rewarded far more than you'll be disappointed.

If a former MDRT chairman and company president can say the following, we'd each better think about what Frank Sullivan is saying:

> You know I have been toying with something in recent months that's sort of begun to bug me. It's always in the back of my mind. The question that I ask myself is, "Why shouldn't an agent make a sale a day?" Oh, no, I never did. I had a tough time making one a week. Never quite hit 100 sales. So I'm not saying this is what I did. But I'm asking myself and some of the consumers are asking, "What do your agents do if they only make one

sale a week?'' I don't know that my speaking of this would change the world—I know it won't—but I think every manager and every general agent (and eventually every agent) should ask themselves every morning, "If I'm not going to make a sale to-day, why am I going to work?" The only thing I can tell you to do is to make a sale, so why not a sale a day? I hope this locks in the back of your mind and rattles around as it does in mine and bothers you as much because I find that if people who can think and innovate get bothered enough by a key question, then they'll do something about it. So, each general agent and each manager should communicate this to each agent: Stick a little sign on your mirror in the morning and say, "Why not a sale a day?"

It's not true that you can't teach old dogs new tricks. In every field of endeavor, experienced people are learning new and better ways to perform in order not to be passed by and left behind. We have just cited numerous successful people to support the premise that this is a time for higher expectations and requirements of performance from experienced agents.

PRODUCTION STANDARDS, NEW AGENTS

Today's and tomorrow's new agents will earn more, and sooner, than new agents ever have in the past. This is the natural result of several factors:

1. These well-selected, top quality recruits will expect and require earnings commensurate with their abilities and what they might expect to earn elsewhere.

2. Management will expect more of them and gear financing, training, and development to those expectations.

3. Precontract work will give them a running start.

4. Joint work will accelerate their earnings rate.

Charlie Smith put the importance of this area of the manager's (and industry's) responsibility in appropriate perspective when he said:

> The pressure our present age of change places on us is that we have got to do something to reduce the time that it takes to turn the new recruit into a profit center within the agency. I believe the secret to successful recruiting in this or any other age is surviving agents, not finding agents. Regardless of the source of recruits, the selection methodology, the systems of recruiting, they all pale into the background if we're not surviving the agents that we are bringing into the organization.

Walter Vreeland reminds us, as some of his experienced people reminded him, that standards of performance for new agents, and how they are enforced, are very important to the established producers in the agency as well:

> Standards of performance are most needed by new agents. They are maintained by established agents because at one time they'd bought those values and they performed by those standards of performance. They observe them now, but not because they're mine. They have now become theirs. As a matter of fact, I am constantly reminded by some of my experienced people of the need perhaps for me to terminate an agent or two. Because of the values I have instilled in them, they are now reminding me that what is good for the goose is also good for the gander. They lean on me pretty hard to be sure that I'm remaining true to the values and the concepts that I originally committed to them.

We asked Paul Arceneaux, who has had conspicuous success in helping new agents get launched well and quickly, what happens when the agent does not get off to the good start that has been anticipated. This was his reply:

When this happens, the division manager and I map out a training plan that we feel will improve his performance. Specifically, we look first at his attitude. Is he accepting the training? Does he follow through on assignment? Second, his commitment. Does he believe in insurance? Has he bought insurance on his own life? Is he making a big effort to secure appointments? Is he really calling on a group of people he has a certain amount of influence with? Third, his plans and participation. How are his weekly plans? Do they include enough of the right kind of activity? Mainly selling interviews? Do they hold up, so to speak, under challenge? Does the agent really participate in the weekly training class as well as the individual planning sessions? If our new agent misses the first checkpoint, 10 applications, this gives us cause for concern. Now if he misses the second checkpoint, 25 cases in his first quarter, we must then look at his net annualized commissions. If it falls below our standard performance level, we know we have what you may refer to as a "slow starter." We either terminate him then or decide to work together another quarter in order to improve his results. With the closely supervised program through the second quarter we should be able to tell if he has the desire and ability to continue. His performance should have improved. The real decision, though, to terminate would come after many discussions with the agent, the division manager, and myself. We think he would have had many opportunities to demonstrate his desire to become a productive member of our agency. In most cases the agent cannot or will not do what he's asked and he removes himself from the agency.

We asked Mr. Arceneaux for some details on their new agent incentive and recognition program. He said:

The best assistance we can give our new agents is to

help them build confidence, and the biggest boost in that confidence is a fast start. He or she must begin to succeed from the very beginning. We have a recognition program that supports this. We give what we call milestone awards. For instance, on the first application, we frame it. We have a ceremony similar to the christening of a ship. He has launched his career with us. The next milestone he reaches is the agency's fast start award. This is given for 10 applications for $100,000 in his first month in the business. He then goes on to the company fast start award, which is given for 25 applications submitted during his first quarter. For the agent to do 25 paid cases for $250,000 paid we have a quarterly dinner for them, including their spouses. We also give suitable recognition for the first time he crosses $300,000 in a quarter of paid business. We have what we call a Millionaire's Award for those agents who do a million or more in their first 12 months in the business. We have a Miler Award which is given for 100 paid lives in the first year. If the agent does this again in the second year, he receives a Marathon Award. This package of awards and recognition helps to build a success image for the agent.

We asked Mr. Arceneaux what he considered a good standard of sales activity for a new agent. He replied:

Our new agent should have a standard of five calls per day for 25 calls per week, and he should shoot for eight closing calls each week. In most cases this would produce three or more applications, but most certainly will produce two and keep him on our 10 applications-a-month schedule which we feel is so important. Now our new agent really doesn't know what's expected around here. In other words, he doesn't know what's par for the course. So we've established some stretch standards. We agree that these may in some cases be high levels of sales activity, but if he doesn't know any different, he's going to adopt them, accept them, and go on—especially if he sees others around him doing the same thing.

Many of the interviewees of Legacy of Learning were introduced on tape by their senior agency officer. In the case of Bill Allabashi, that introduction was made by Mr. Howard E. Steele, who said the following:

> When a new person comes into the life insurance business, their hope, their dreams, their plan is to become a successful, full-time career agent with a stable of clients and a stream of renewals that will carry the agent through a satisfying and profitable life of insurance sales and service. Unfortunately, that stable of clients with its stream of renewals can't be ordered along with the regular office supplies. It can't be begged, bought, or borrowed. It has to be built. Whether or not that new person coming into our business will ever realize the hopes and dreams of the successful full-time career depends largely on whether or not that new agent can survive the first formative years. Can they make a living while they're building their clientele? Well, the answer is yes. And the secret is getting off to a fast start.

Mr. Allabashi said that the most important element in getting new agents off to a fast start is picking good people. He is shooting for $20,000 in first-year commissions as a minimum . . .

> . . . which as you know is an MDRT type qualifier. We've got to be careful in our selection process to attract that type of candidate, and to have training programs geared for that person so we can show that individual how to get off to a fast start. If we can't teach that agent to make a living in our business, and do it immediately, the only thing we're

going to prove is our business is tough. We have to develop that prototype agent to use in both our recruiting and training.

Ralph Brown knows what the times require. He said:

> I think we've got to be able to help the agent get to big production. Every now and then we hire someone who goes out and does three or four million in his first year. And to me that's big production in the first year. But that's really the exception rather than the rule, and yet I think that where I have an agency now where the average production is in the neighborhood of 1.8 million per agent, within the 1980s this is going to have to go to three or four million as an average. So we've got to be able to bring that new agent in, help the new agent survive through that learning period so that we can get a greater number of them up to that level of production. That's a real responsibility.

Willard Pratt would say that not only can you not fool dogs and children, you also can't fool new agents! Here is how he put it:

> You should never hire anyone that you can't have great expectations for. These expectations communicate themselves. Unless you can be very high on someone, unless you feel they're going to be greatly successful and have all the possibilities, then simply don't hire them—because that feeling communicates. It comes across in training, in everything.

Harry Hoopis was very objective and specific in our interview about their expectations for new agents. He said:

> We have a postselection program that requires $6,000 of commissions having been paid at the end of six months.

Note: In May of 1984, we called Mr. Hoopis to see if this figure had been modified. He said that the requirement for the new agent's first full calendar year is now $18,000 of first-year commissions.

After you read both of the following paragraphs from Jim Gurley, you will appreciate why his adherence to what he calls the "Newton's Law" is so relevant to the subject of performance standards for new agents:

> In an early unit of the Legacy of Learning, Al Granum verbalized what I class as the Newton's Law of our business. Ten, three, one. Ten apparently qualified suspects will result in three who will disclose adequate information and result in one sale. This formula applies anytime you start moving outside of your existing clientele. There is no point in being frightened by it. We use it. And in doing so, we feel that we allow the agent to control his or her own destiny.

> The mix of term and permanent insurance along with the reduced payments per thousand results in a consistent lowering of the commissions to the point where in our agency our trainees, those who are in their first four years in the life insurance business, last year averaged only $5.00 of commission per $1,000 of insurance that they sold. Well, it's interesting to note that this same group of agents also had an average size case of $60,000, which translates into $300 of commissions per sale. If they made 60 sales together with their training allowances, we find that their first-year earnings would run in the area of $25,000-$30,000. We really feel so comfortable and positive about these formulas (ten-three-one) that we have no hesitancy in saying to them that if they will do what we tell them to do the way we tell them to do it as often as we tell them to do it, they'll have no difficulty in achieving these kinds of earnings right from the opening gun.

And speaking of Al Granum, here's the new agent regimen he shared in our interview:

> When he shows up on the first day, I have this letter of welcome which I cover with him. And I tell him what we expect during the first 25 days and then thereafter until he's qualified for the Million Dollar Round Table.
>
> During his first 25 days, we want him at his desk, ready to work, no later than 7:45 in the morning. Number one, before he does anything else, we want him to pile up 25 cards for telephone appointment getting. He starts telephoning at 9:00 and will get no interruptions until at least 25 dialings have been made, and I let him know that my assistant, Miss O'Malley, will be in there at 10:00 to find out how many dialings he's made, how many people he's reached, and how many appointments he's made. We want him to earn at least five points a day, and if he's short, make them up over the weekend.
>
> (*Note:* "Points" are awarded at one-half point for each new "suspect" and one point for each new "facts interview" conducted and an additional one if it resulted in opening a case.)
>
> Thereafter, until he qualifies for Round Table, we want him in the office no later than 8:00 for the same duration upon arrival. We want him to earn at least 100 points a month striving for new facts at the rate of 300 the first year, 250 the second, 200 the third, and 150 thereafter. The first interview should be at 10:30, start work on CLU, participate in all agency meetings, and so forth.
>
> So in the first 25 days the four steps of progressive expectations were: (1) 125 points in the first 25 days; (2) if he doesn't make the 125 points the first time, we give him another rerun—again, with daily

supervision; (3) if he doesn't make it that time and still wants another chance, we let him try once more, but we withdraw the privilege of close super- vision, and we expect him to do it on his own; and (4) if he misses that time, it's relocation, which, I guess, is a euphemism for termination.

Al explained that for the next six months the total was 600 balanced points, with corresponding second, third, and fourth consequences for missing, with the last calling for working from his own home lest he be "contaminating the environment." Similarly the MDRT became the objective for the first full calendar year with consequences (2), (3) and (4) if missed.

Note: While preparing this unit we called Al to see if the above requirements were still in effect. He sent us a copy of the current set. It is even more requiring.

To conclude this chapter, then, *don't kid yourself.* You are not a general agent or manager because you sold a lot, be- cause you gave a great speech at the convention, or because you know the right people. You are the manager of a business and will be judged and rewarded accordingly.

Because of general awareness and acceptance of that fact of life, it is predictable that a most significant trend in agency management is the following:

> *Standards of performance in the agency will be higher and more strictly enforced than ever before.*

6 | Hey Doctor, Look At Me! I'm Not Just An Appendix

The Agency Head as a Leader/Motivator/People-Person

> **SIGNIFICANT TREND:** Agents will grow, prosper, and stay in those agencies where not only their technical needs are met, but their psychic needs are also recognized and met.

We are told that one of the biggest problems that the famed Mayo Clinic encounters is what is called "noncompliance" on the part of their patients. People spend time and money going to their physicians, and then don't heed the doctors' advice. They don't take the medicine prescribed, and not infrequently they don't even get the prescription filled! Why should this be?

Some who have searched for the answer put the blame on the seeming impersonality of medical practice today. They say that patients want to be seen as persons, as individual people, not just as charts and measurements and symptoms. In illogical frustration they often forsake competent professionals to look for someone who seems to "take more of a personal interest in me."

One of John Naisbitt's 10 "megatrends" is "High Tech-High Touch." In our technological era, people especially need to be considered and dealt with as individuals with feelings and worth.

So it is appropriate that immediately after a chapter dealing with the necessity for agency heads to be good business managers and agencies to be profit centers, for performance standards to be challenging and enforced, that we follow with this very important chapter to remind us that the life insurance business, the financial planning business, to a greater degree than any other private enterprise, is a people business. It is by, for, of, and about people.

So for this chapter we have grouped quotations from the

distinguished agency heads we were privileged to interview that bear upon these areas:

1. Motivation and leadership
2. Team-building
3. People skills.

Let's begin, then, with statements dealing with the agency head's role as a leader and motivator of others. Here is what Vincent Bowhers said:

> One thought comes across so loud and clear that it strikes me as a substantial part of the story of successful agency building. That thought is this: the need for someone to be there in the agency providing leadership. Now we either do it ourselves or we provide it through talented, equally dedicated surrogates, or both. Obviously it is best done personally, providing that we have these talents. But the point is that someone has to be there on a regular basis providing that leadership or it just doesn't happen. In operating a life insurance agency successfully, we have to have our mind on what we are doing. We have to work at it steadily and we have to be involved personally.

Our interview with Frank Friedler, Jr., was on the subject of motivation and leadership. He said:

> The essence of leadership is that you're given a job to accomplish. You're given people to accomplish that job with, and to mold those people into some sort of workable team, some sort of piece of a unit to accomplish a job. If you accomplish the job, I think you're a good leader. If you don't accomplish it, I think you're a bad leader.
>
> Remember that an agency today is many, many different things. I think an agency first is a business. And then it's a question of molding very

diverse personalities into a productive sales force. A good leader of an agency first and foremost has to be a good businessman. Because if the business of an agency is conducted on a sloppy basis, I think it's impossible to produce the sort of environment necessary to have a very good agency. He'd have to be a good business leader. He'd have to be able to conduct his finances and his affairs in such a way that sets an example for the rest of the people in his organization. I think that's the easiest part of the job, but a very critical part.

Secondly, I think he has to be one that will, by his personal example, by his strength of leadership, mold diverse personalities into a cohesive force for the purpose of the agency. You can't have leadership where you say, "Hey, look buddy, it's time to go out and sell your half a million dollars and bring back the applications by noon today." I think what you try to do is to build an atmosphere in your agency where the person wants to produce, wants to achieve the most and you provide the technical, professional leadership so that he really does maximize his own abilities.

Lastly, I think that in the '80s we're going through periods of great change. This flux in our business has created an unsettling atmosphere. I think that the agency leader of the '80s has to be a person who's very confident in himself, who by that confidence will instill in his associates that no matter what changes appear, whether we're all working on fees in the next five years, or whatever, the expertise in this shop will always be there so that we'll all make a decent living. I think that businesses have a moral character, a philosophical character. Leadership flows from the top down, not from the bottom up. And the reflection of an organization is going to be a reflection of the leadership, and the worst mistake an agency manager can make is to expect that the character of the agency is going to differ greatly from the character of the person who is running the shop.

This quote is from Aldin Porter:

> Yankelovich is reported to have said that the 1970s "was a decade of me-ism," described in words such as: "Do your own thing. Do it your way. I march to a different drummer." This attitude has, I think, spawned pessimism, and even though our new entrants into the insurance industry are better educated and they are more articulate and they do have some degree of self-assurance that's come out of their background that's different, yet somehow they are pessimistic and a little cynical. And I think that has made managing more difficult. I think we have to convince them that they are not the only generation that has grown up with peril and problems and that there is much to look forward to, and that their attitude's impact upon their success is immeasurable. So one of the principles that simply never changes is that we must watch our attitude.

We commented to Mr. Porter that it's a cliche to say that life insurance is a people business, but good life underwriters are people-people. Some will go the PPGA route and find that they truly miss being part of a team with all the personal associations that the word team connotes. Here is his response:

> There aren't many of us who want to be loners. Sometimes there's a macho image about being a loner. But in the final analysis we don't really want to be. We want to be with each other and we want to succeed with each other and we want some relationships that are permanent. Al Granum uses the phrase, if I can quote it, that "in every one of our relationships we either reduce the general level or improve the general level." Any agency I think

must seek to improve the general level and that can
only be done as each person makes a concerted effort to contribute. These things hold us together.
This is the cement. People matter. And, Bob, in
the final analysis, they're all that matter.

It was back in 1976 that we were talking with Bobby
Yerusalim about motivation and agency bulletins when he
said:

I see a lot of agency bulletins with the production
figures for all the agents. Twenty years ago when I
started in the business, I was in a 40-man agency,
and I can remember standing at the bulletin board
at the end of the year and hearing a conversation.
One guy picked his name out. He did something
like $250,000 for the whole year—even in those
days a pretty poor job. I couldn't understand the
statement he made, but it rang a bell later on when
I came into management. He said, "What the hell.
I finished in twentieth place. I was better than 19
other guys." I knew then that if I had my own
agency, nobody would ever see all the production
sheets. I don't ever want to manage by embarrass-
ment. I want to manage by showing examples. I
want people to aspire to do better things. We put
out a sheet at the end of the month on submitted
business and show only those in excess of $100,000.
Sometimes it's just 10 men and sometimes it's 25.
That's O.K.

Bobby also found another way to help motivate himself
and his people by proxy. Here is how he explained it:

When I first started as general agent, I had a
40-minute drive both ways, and I hated that non-
productive time until I started listening to tapes. So
we started building up a tape library, and we're up
to 450 tapes right now. I thought, "Gosh, if it
makes me feel good, maybe it'll make the agent

feel good,'' so we started encouraging them to buy tape recorders, not just to prepare for sales goals or to get technical knowledge, but to listen to motivational things. This led to sales training programs. We can't rely on our agents reading all the good articles in *Life Association News*, so I'll clip them out and reproduce them, and find they're more likely to read them.

Irving Abramowitz told of other methods to stimulate and encourage his associates:

Many motivational techniques can be applied to the entire team. We want our people interested in industry activities, serving on the boards of the Baltimore Life Underwriters Association, of the Baltimore CLU Chapter, and many others. We want them involved in general community work and in synagogue or church work. I think we can get people excited about industry yardsticks of success: NQA, NSAA, HIQA, MDRT, and so on. With the exception of MDRT, we now do the filing of forms for them, and now our agency has more NQA or NSAA or MDRT qualifiers than perhaps any other agency in the city. This is important as it does provide motivation for the whole team.

We have what I call an agents' council. We meet every three months or so. They tell me how they think things should be improved. I don't argue. All I do is listen. Another thing that's important to us: I take courses with my management team, where we're studying together as equals. We're listening to their ideas, and they're getting ours, and we're all better off because of the effort.

Ken Sadler reminded us that in a strict sense we can't really motivate others. But we can provide the atmosphere and conditions that will, whether you call it motivation or not, let them release the power within them. Here is his often-cited analogy:

> I have likened myself as a general agent to a farmer. The farmer selects seeds carefully. Hopefully he selects the best seed. Then he prepares the earth those seeds will be planted in. Then he makes certain that he plants them carefully—not three feet down so they'll never be able to make it up, and not on top of the ground where they'd fry in the sun, but at the right depth in properly prepared soil. He may put a little fertilizer out, and add water if nature doesn't, but there isn't much more he can do. If it's corn, it's going to come up corn. If it's cauliflower, it's going to come up cauliflower. The power—and this is the essential thing, I remind myself—the power is in the seed. It's not in the farmer. And so I'm the farmer in the analogy, and the new agent is the seed. I'm responsible to him for atmosphere and attitude and the success scene for him to live in, which is the agency. But I'm not responsible to him for his success. He's responsible for that. And he's got the power inside of himself just like the seed has the power. And I remind him continually of that—and so it's up to him.

Hugh Arrison's "10-letter philosophy" is as applicable in the U.S. as it is to his great Canadian agency:

> Our philosophy is structured around what we call a 10-letter philosophy. That is that we think the pinnacle of professionalism in our business is to be a member of the Million Dollar Round Table, which are the first four letters. The next three letters are CLU, meaning Chartered Life Underwriter, and the last three letters are NQA, perhaps the most important letters, being a qualifier for the National Quality Award of the Life Underwriters Association. So we measure everything—from acquisition

of new clients through business in force—and we publicize these achievements to our agents. And we have a number of different branch awards relative to those areas. Our 10-letter people are featured on our display in our foyer. And to get into this directory you have to do something good in the agency.

Just as the job of the professional life underwriter is to help his clients discover their needs and then do all he or she can to help them meet those needs, Key Fry indicated that the job of those in management is very analagous when he said:

The most powerful thing I'd like to convey is that you've got to go ask the agents what their needs are and hope that they can communicate them effectively. If they can't, try to ferret out of their verbiage what those needs happen to be.

Here is a longer statement from Mr. Fry, all of which warrants inclusion here:

People can get excited if they're around enthusiasm. I think people tend to limit themselves. They think of themselves maybe as being in a role, and they don't really stretch their minds and imagination. I don't believe any of us work near our capacity. If you can get some of these people stretching, then more people will stretch. I think it's one of the management laws that you're going to get 80 percent of your production or your volume from 20 percent of your people. Having heard that years ago, I set out to say, "Why can't we have 40 percent of the people reaching those levels of production?" And we began to increase our expectations, not only of the staff, but of the line and of the new recruits. And people responded. So we're trying to get these talented people operating in a creative manner, and we're doing that partly by saying we will help you be the best that you can be within our limitations. And if you have talent and expectations to go on to do other things, we'll help you find a way to get there. But our sole responsibility would be to tell you objectively and as honestly as we can what we think your limitations are.

So we're bringing people into the system and saying we don't know whether you're going to be good for line or you're going to be good for staff, but if you're leaning that way we'll help you go. If you have leanings for line and you want to go on and become district manager, we'll carve out a territory for you. If you want to be a general agent, we'll help you get there. And we'll give you everything that we know. But we would also say to the individual, you have some obligations: to be honest with us, to replace yourself, and to be loyal to us; to help us see ourselves as we are, and to help us grow. And our obligation to you is to help you go as far as you can go within your talent. And if you go past us, we won't hold you back for that. And we'll help you find what's best for you.

The whole world cries for leadership, and the leadership needed in the life insurance industry today is management. Management can't handle it if they are coasting. Management can't handle it if they are trying to do it all themselves. The general agent or the manager will not be able to handle it if they try to limit other people out of the fear of the other person outgrowing them or going on to be their own district manager or general agent. What I think I'm trying to say is that the manager in the large agency has to find the needs and effectively communicate to the agents and to the Home Office what those needs are and then hope that the Home Office will help fill that need. The agency has to fill that need if it's not profitable for the Home Office to fill that need, and then help that agent go on and grow. As long as the agent can communicate effectively with the general agent and the general agent with the Home Office, even though we may be slow, we will fill all those needs and people will know we are being very aboveboard, very honest with one another.

We asked Frank Friedler what he would say on this subject of leadership to a new manager:

I would say first to be true to himself and to follow this advice: Don't expect your agency to be anything but a reflection of yourself. Second, try to be as professionally competent as you possibly can be. For example, I think it's hard to be an agency manager without being a CLU. I think it's hard to be an agency manager without staying up on the trends in our business. He's got to make some commitment to education. I think he's got to make a commitment to staying on top of the management skills, to be exposed to change in management and the different techniques and to expose himself to the leaders in our industry. I think he has to make a total commitment to the job. This is basically an unselfish job. He's got to understand that he can't be threatened personally by the successes of the people he produces. I've seen some managers fail to really build great shops because they felt threatened by people who were perhaps growing at a rate faster than they. He's got to realize that that may happen. That he may produce people that make more money than he does, that maybe are smarter than he is. He's got to have enough confidence in himself and enough self-assurance to know that that's really the greatest tribute that anybody can pay him. If he understands those things, he will at least have the beginnings of what it takes to do the job. Of course it takes a lot of love too.

Frank wound up with these words:

> I feel a little humble trying to talk about leadership
> when I've had the great pleasure of knowing so
> many of the people whom I really do consider great
> leaders in the business. Great innovators. All I am
> is a plug. I get to work every day early. I work hard
> at the job every day. And I study every day. And I
> try to stay current every day. And I think that's the
> great message that there is. I don't think there's
> any secret component to leadership. I think that
> the best leaders are the hardest workers—the peo-
> ple who are willing to pay a price to build what they
> think is the most appropriate kind of organization
> that they're capable of building. There are no
> magical formulas. There's no book that anyone
> can read. So in summation all that I'd like to say is
> that perhaps the secret is to work hard and to be
> true to yourself. And if you do that, I think you'll
> be successful in building the kind of agency you
> want to build.

TEAM BUILDING

The other day an attorney friend of mine quoted a very
well-known judge of the Federal District Court in our area as
having confided in him, "This is a lonely job."

Under certain circumstances the job of the agency head can
be a lonely one. If he retains all responsibility for the agency's
progress unto himself, then it's going to be pretty hard for
him to involve his associates in his concerns when the going
gets rocky. Nor will his associates find a great deal of personal satisfaction in any agency accomplishments when they
have not been a part of the planning and the strategy of the
organization.

In Chapter 4 we saw that the important planning function
became really effective when the agency members partici-
pated in it and "bought" it. As Warren Bennis said of the 90

leader/achievers he interviewed, they were able to effectively communicate and then obtain from others what he called "alignment"—they were willing to *align* themselves with the leader and each other toward common goals.

Consider these quotations from our interview with Aldin Porter (we had been talking about retention of agents):

> Our solution is the climate. What is the climate in an agency? Is there an agency momentum which catches the people up in it and carries them along as they participate in developing pride in that organization? Do you have shared objectives? Is there a sharing of the agency head's dreams? First of all, does he dream and if he does, does he share it with those around him to where they want to become part of the dream?

> Money does not solve all problems. We want to be part of an organization that is successful, that's growing, that's developing. We want to see ourselves with people of successful backgrounds. We want to join in. Dreams have great power, but we must let other people in on them.

> In the final analysis, the most important of all are personal relationships. We better care about each other. We'd better be concerned, not just about production, but about families and circumstances that go on in a person's life that cause upheaval. In this agency the people care about one another. I believe that does about as much to keep us united in the midst of the wooing from other companies as anything I can think of.

Charles Fifield heads a team whose members have aligned themselves in a common cause (they would call it an uncommon, very special, cause):

> I think if you are to develop an agency of a sub-

stantial size and create a team attitude, you have to find a cause for all to participate in, in one form or another. They may only take a little piece of the cause, but I think the cause is important, whether it's the Super Bowl or whether it's achieving a certain level of production which everybody identifies as a stepping-stone to the organization we want to develop. I think a cause is important in the organization. Our cause is to develop the finest financial planning firm in the country. I think there is a great need in this country, not just for the wealthy, but for the middle-class people, for some entity that has the capacity to help them plan their financial affairs today and in the future.

J.A.C. "Cam" MacIntosh reminds us that the agency team also includes the administrative staff, the backup people. He shared his dream about their further involvement in the agency's growth when he said:

We've got 12 potentially good recruiters in the women and men who provide our administrative support. I don't think we have communicated our grand plan, what we see our agency becoming three or four years from now, in the way we should in order to get them excited. I see this will have a couple of effects. It will encourage them to see career paths for themselves within the administrative area as our agency grows. Secondly, I believe somewhere down the line it will encourage one or two of these people to say, "Hey, I would like to get into that action over there because I think it's a little more exciting than what I'm doing now." And the third thing is that I hope by our paying a little more attention to them and really sharing our dreams more with them, they're going to be more encouraged to nominate people they know, or to come into the office as salespeople, and thus be able to come up with successful candidates for us.

Great corporations today often spend much time and money in the development of a "mission statement" that purports to tell what their reason for being is in a fashion that all can understand and support. One of our interviews was with Jim Cathcart, a consultant to Joe Willard's Tulsa agency. With the whole agency participating, here is the mission statement he helped one group to hammer out:

> To effectively market the best life insurance-related products and services to selected markets through a growing organization dedicated to the development of its associates to their maximum professional potential.

He commented on the fact that the dynamics of this statement, which might sound just like a bunch of words, in reality are very profound. First of all they were the product of the group's effort. He said:

> They said "to effectively market." They didn't just say "to sell" and marketing is a much broader term than selling. And they said they were going to do it "effectively" which means profitably. It probably also implies a win/win situation where the client and the agent and the agency all are profiting from it. Then they said "the best life insurance-related products and services." That meant that they were dedicated to excellence in their product line. That if their company at that time wasn't offering what they considered the best, then they had a responsibility shown in their mission statement to go to their company and help them make it the best, to have that kind of input at the Home Office. They said "life insurance-related" because some of the things they offered were not specifically life insurance. They said "products and services" which expanded it beyond just policies, for example. And they said to effectively market these to "selected" markets, meaning there was forethought. They chose the markets

they were going to deal with ahead of time. They said they were going to do all of this through a growing organization dedicated to the development of its associates to their maximum professional potential.

It's easy to believe that the participants in that process would have no problem in "aligning" themselves with that mission statement, or in explaining its significance to new associates. After all, it was theirs; they had "ownership" of it.

A dramatic and exciting Legacy unit was entitled "Eleven Days In Houston." For it we interviewed Everett G. Lineberry and producers, staff, and assistants to get a picture of how they came together with only 11 days remaining in the production year and the agency distantly in second place for the year-to-date. The way they all committed themselves to each other and the Herculean effort that followed on the part of all was a notable example of alignment carried to the ultimate. (A year later Bill Wallace played the tape for his people as they faced a similar challenge; like Ev Lineberry and his group, they too were winners.) But we asked Ev if this kind of campaign was consistent with his being a CLU and was really professional. He said:

That's an interesting question. Maybe we ought to consider two viewpoints. I'm a professional manager. My primary responsibility is to my people, to introduce them to this great career we're in, to remove any of the roadblocks that might prevent or hinder their success, growth, or development, and then to motivate them to be as good as they can be. Considered from that viewpoint, I think the results indicate it was a pretty professional effort from the management standpoint.

From another standpoint, that of the veteran producer or CLU or whatever, I guess I have to wonder just how professional it is if you do less than you're capable of doing. And we really believe

that our policyholders and clients win right along
with us in this kind of challenge.

I don't think anyone has associates that could be
considered more professional than the people we
have in this organization, and I know they took
great pride in what happened. I wish you could
have been at the "Number One Party" when we
honored our agent of the year, because our agent
of the year spent most of his time there honoring
the guy that finished second because he pushed him
to the kind of production that he generated. He
had the number two man crying before it was
through. That kind of teamwork and that kind of
respect for one another, I think, is very professional. These people care.

One of his supervisors added:

It was worth doing, because we broke some mental
barriers.

To me it was a great example of team-building. It did not
just happen. It was the result of careful thought and planning, of involvement of all, not by accident, but on purpose.

Al Ostedgaard faced the problems in team-building that
are encountered when agents are scattered all over the large
state of Arkansas. He outlined the importance of bulletins
and the use of telephone calls to the members of his staff, and
then he made this interesting observation:

. . . and as a result I think we're in closer communication than if they were all housed in one
building in a metropolitan area. I talk to them frequently on the telephone. We've discovered something that has worked very effectively and also
does not cost very much money. All my long dis-
tance calls are made starting at seven in the morning from my home. I dial it. My cost is about 35

percent of what it would be during the day. In two to five minutes you can accomplish everything you need to accomplish, and it works out beautifully.

Peter Browne had a very different problem when he arrived in New York. He tells how he went about establishing a feeling of a shared interest with the people there:

> When I arrived here there were serious problems of communication. People didn't know who to talk to, where to turn. What I had to do was sit down with each agent, clerical management staff, second-line management people, and in a one-on-one, try and develop communication lines between the agents and myself so that they understood that if they succeeded, I would succeed. And that there was no way that they could succeed and I not succeed, or I succeed and they not succeed. What I've tried to do is to make these people feel that they became a part of something.

PEOPLE SKILLS

While more and more people may work from their homes or detached offices, connected electronically to the agency and, perhaps, to the Home Office as well, all that does is emphasize the greater-than-ever need we all have to touch and be touched by those with whom we feel a sense of community. As Aldin Porter indicated, the best defense against the proselyter is the agent's feeling of being a part of something real and important, the agency. The challenge to the agency head is a real one: The general agent or manager must continue to earn and deserve the presence and loyalty of the associates by actions that cause them to feel and believe that their best interests are served by being associated with the agency.

Doing that job calls not only for real and valuable substantive services to the members of the agency. At least as important (many would say more important) are the evidences of caring and personal regard that characterize the manager-associate relationships that are described or implied in the quotations in this section. When we use the phrase "people skills," we don't mean to suggest that we are talking about insincere or manipulative kinds of behavior. But it does little of mutual benefit for a manager to be genuinely fond of an associate and very concerned about his welfare if he doesn't overtly communicate those feelings in word and deed. And those people skills can be worked on and studied and improved and consciously used as a powerful instrument to help the agency and everyone in it.

Let's start off with this quotation from Tom O'Haren:

> I believe that every one of us—managers, agents, Home Office people, whatever, everybody in the industry, everybody in the human race, needs to be loved. And one of the common things you find in a guy moving from one agency to another, I think, is that he did not experience that love relationship between him and his manager or his general agent. I believe that the manager has to be a highly visible individual who is interested in every aspect of each of his agents' lives, whether that's social, personal, business, whatever.

Bill Wallace is one of the busiest of people. Look what he says:

> There are so many times when it seems like I have hundreds of things that have to be done, papers on the desk, dictation that has to be done, telephone calls for response—and that's exactly when someone walks in that office with a problem. And I have just forced myself to say the problem that just walked in the door is more important than any other problem I've got, because if I don't resolve it, then I'm going to have two problems: the problem he's got and the problem that's going to exist between us. And so I try to the maximum to give

top priority to those people problems. I can get to these other things later.

Another Washingtonian, Quentin C. Aanenson, gives a specific example of an important opportunity to practice the people skill of empathy:

> Bob, perhaps the most important thing we do that affects morale is to demonstrate to our associates that we really care about them and their growth and development. They sometimes carry a heavy burden. The career isn't always easy, as you well know. And they need to know we sincerely are concerned and that we'll do everything possible to help them with their problems.
>
> Be careful what you promise your agents because they'll hold you to it; they won't forget.
>
> Although the commission dollars that the agent earns on a particular case are very important to him, perhaps the most important thing to that agent is not the fact that he walked out of that office with a signed application and a check for an annual premium, and that he made a good sale, but rather that when he comes back into the agency he wants to share this story with somebody. And the logical person is his manager or supervisor or one of his peers. At that moment the manager has got to be at his very best in his human relationships and recognize that regardless of what else he has to do, the most important thing right now is to savor this victory with this field underwriter. Let him tell you about it and be vitally interested. And I am vitally interested. He's thrilled to tell me and I'm thrilled to hear it.

Cy Pick speaks of the counselor role and responsibility that comes with the job of manager:

We have a unique situation in the life insurance industry in that we get paid for helping others achieve their goals. As a result, we can achieve our goals, which to me is a very exciting part about our job. The manager is a counselor in helping those agents and must be with them in high times and low times and responsive in those areas. Only the manager can do that. In the crucial times of an agent's life, I think the manager has to be there. And in the present time where we have so many different products, so many different influences on our business, the agent really needs a great deal more counseling than he ever has before.

Vince Bowhers, like all top agency heads, is not loathe to use another's good idea:

Two quick ideas: One came originally from a Legacy of Learning tape done by Bob Meeker and I've used it ever since. It's the idea that each day be designated as the day to think about and do something with a particular member of our organization. So on that day while I'm driving or walking or whatever, I want to think about that particular member of our agency and anything that I can do to help make him or her more successful. And some way I will contact that person that day. I'll either have lunch with him or her, or perhaps make a telephone call, or if I'm away I may sit down and write a note or letter. Each day on a rotating basis, there's a day for a particular person in the agency. The other is something that is just now being put together but I'm very enthused about it. It's a schedule of having an informal lunch each month with the members of our agency organization both clerical and sales who have birthdays that month. We bring some sandwiches into the agency conference room and just visit informally about any problems they might have or any suggestions they have for the operation of the agency, and attempt just to have better communication, more open dialogue.

It is possible to do things about the physical layout of the office to enhance the opportunities for dialogue with agency associates. Bobby Yerusalim did:

> When I took over the agency, my office was in a bad spot. It was difficult for my people to get to me and for me to see other people. It took me about nine months to have a building constructed I could move into. All I said to the architect was, "You figure out how to construct the rest of this place, but one thing you've got to do is to put me right near the door where my people come in." One of the things I almost insist on when my people come in is that I want them to wave to me and say hello and I want to say hello to them. That gives me an opportunity to see what's going on in a guy's head —even, sometimes, before he wants to tell me. By gosh, you'd better continually prove to your people that you really do care for them. If you really do care, let them know it. Just don't keep it inside of yourself.

John Snow talked about those things that serve as cohesive factors in the agency:

> I believe pride and positive motivation and feeling that somebody cares are a large part of the things that pull agencies together.

Joe Gray has one of the biggest agencies in Canada, so what he says about personal contact is most relevant. He has many people with whom to maintain contact. He said:

> When you have to delegate personal contact, then you're losing something. We should do everything possible to establish proper priorities—and dele-

gate the mechanical things, the administrative things, and remember that this face-to-face contact may be our most important task.

Bernie Rosen told us about his little daily planning 3x5 card that implements his daily priority system. First it reminds him to think briefly of each member of his family, then about himself and his need for exercise, recreation, careful eating, and for study. Then he said this:

> The next priority is my present associates. I try to think about each one—again, just touching them in my mind for a second or two. A mental image comes on of them, and they're a very meaningful part of my day, even if I don't happen to see them that day. And I can talk to somebody about his children by name rather than by "How's the kids?" You know, it's bad enough not even to ask, but it's another thing just to sort of ask in a perfunctory way. This makes it more caring, more personal, and it shows people you care a lot about them.

Bob Meeker's secretary, Mrs. June Baker, made it clear that even a superb people-person like Bob tries to leave nothing in the people area to chance. She said:

> We have a list of all the important dates in our agency family, like birthdays and wedding anniversaries, the children's birthdays. Mr. Meeker sends birthday cards to both parents in a family and all the children, and each child also gets a dollar bill. On wives' birthdays we send flowers. On special wedding anniversaries like first, fifth, tenth, and so on, that means a bouquet to the home. And on special things like 25th anniversaries or anniversaries with the company, we usually plan something special like a small party or a special gift. They are all on the calendar, too, so that they're not overlooked.

John Wiener reminds us that the development of interpersonal expertise is something that can be studied formally
by the whole agency for the benefit of all. Here is what he had
to say:

> Another area that has really helped our agency has
> been the development of people skills. Our associ-
> ates attribute many sales to the people skills side of
> our ongoing training program. We have put our
> entire agency through Wilson Learning's S-4 (So-
> cial Style Sales Strategies), and eventually all speak
> to its effectiveness. Not only are the skills them-
> selves valuable, but also the feeling that our com-
> pany has taken this extra step to help make us true
> professionals in every sense of the word.

Just because an assistant manager is an employee, as opposed to an agent who may be an independent contractor,
does not mean that the employee requires or should have any
less sensitive treatment from the agency head. Dick Austin
gave us a good example:

> I think an important thing is not to make assump-
> tions about people. We all go through various
> stages of development. We all want different things
> at different times. Sometimes in a conversation
> with an individual, you're very sure that he (or she)
> is right where he wants to be and it's easy to let it
> lie, so to speak. All of a sudden you find that per-
> son very discontented and maybe even by the time
> you get around to him, he leaves simply because
> you haven't reconfirmed his position. You have as-
> sumed that because what they said a year ago or six
> months ago was true, that it's true now. Ongoing
> communication is extremely important. I've tried
> to stay in touch with my people on a daily basis. I
> want to know how they feel about what they're do-
> ing. I want to reinforce the good things they've
> done, and I want to know from them what they feel
> good about as well as what they don't feel good

about. I'll have to keep them in a proper frame of mind if they're going to be fuctioning at their best and feeling good about what they're doing.

Several years back I was working with a young assistant manager who had been doing well in the recruiting and training process, but he had reached a level of frustration. He really thought he should go back into personal production where he had been very successful before coming into management. While it would have been very easy to accept his desire to go back into personal production, and go along with it, I somehow had the feeling his frustration was temporary and that perhaps a new assignment or a new sense of direction might be meaningful. And we sent him to a new location 400 miles away where our company had never had a facility of any kind. He responded so well to that challenge that he developed it into what we call an agency office which is a satellite office. Two years later it was a full branch. Now it is one of the most successful in the country.

Dick also shared this important caveat:

We all want to be strong enough as role models to transmit those important elements that we feel must be a part of a philosophy in our organization. But because we are all unique, we're going to find different ways of doing things, and it is important that the agency head knows that he may have to bite his lip occasionally when he sees his second-line management person doing something in a way that he wouldn't do it. It is important that he allow the individual to develop and give him positive feedback for the things that are going well and not be overly critical just because of the difference in style.

In the Navy I had the opportunity of observing how differently two commanding officers comported themselves when they took over their new commands. One had many problems. He came aboard with a "this is the way it's going to be" demeanor. The other reminded me of this quote from Billy Mixon (he was far more effective):

> When you come into an established agency, everybody is worthy. You've got to believe everybody's got a story. Everybody is somebody. If you don't believe that, you'd better not start. You need to talk to them. You need to say, "Hey, really tell me what's good, tell me what's bad. I want the dog and I want all the fleas that come with it." So when you talk to everybody, you have first extended them the dignity of being someone and you've let them know that their opinion is important. And I say along with that if they've got good opinions you've got to give some evidence of having listened.

It does not seem unreasonable to suggest that the morale of an agency is likely to reflect how well the needs of its members are met. We asked David W. Smith what represents good morale to him. He said:

> I think if you were to talk about morale in terms of a sports team, you'd look at their record. If they're winning, the morale's going to be high. If they're losing, the morale is going to be low because they really don't know why. And yet they may not know why they're winning or losing. So I think in a business environment it really has a little bit to do with winning. Are we winning? How well are we doing? Are we doing a good job for our clients? Are we earning enough money? Do we have a good atmosphere in the agency? Is this a good place to work? Is it a vital place to be? Is it fun to be here? Do I dread coming to this place? Do I dread being in this business? If the answer to that is no, then that helps out morale. Trust, I think, leads to good morale. Does the agency trust me? Do they trust

each other? Are they confident in each other? How do you handle intra-agency competition? How do you work with agents? How do they feel about the staff? All these things I think go toward building a camaraderie, a commitment, and a common purpose that really leads to better agency morale.

I think a key indicator of poor morale in an agency is the role of the experienced agents in recruiting. Are they bringing people in or are they sending them down to the agency around the corner because they know they're going to get better training there? If they don't really feel confident in bringing a new person into the agency based upon what they've seen, that says there is bad morale. Another thing we don't talk about too much because it's kind of taboo, is fiscal management. Where the general agent may have a problem financially, there is going to be bad morale. It's going to become known if he's a poor financial manager. That's another factor in agency morale.

Morale comes back to the attitude of the management both at the Home Office and the field. Does the Home Office listen? Does the management of the agency listen? Are they open to hearing and implementing what the field people who are out in the trenches every day are telling them? Or do they just pay lip service and pat the guy on the head and say, "Fine, I'll consider it," and nothing happens?

We asked Dave how he felt about his agents placing business with other companies. His response may be surprising to some:

I have never been jealous and never will be of an agent doing business with other companies. I have absolutely no concern and the agents know I feel this way. The place is open to every brokerage man who wants to walk in. And we look for some new ideas from other companies and even promote it with our new agents. Because my primary goal is if I have an agent who is earning a good living and we provide him with good services here, I know that bread is going to come back. It's been cast on the water, because probably 75 percent of the business that he's going to do is eventually going to come back or be done with our company even though he may do some huge cases outside for whatever reason. Group insurance is a good example of that. We've got three or four very successful people in the agency who have entered the business by marketing group insurance, group medical, group long-term disability, this type of thing. And frankly, they haven't done a great deal of that with our company, but we have patiently waited for them to blossom and grow and I would do the same thing all over again, because it's a good way to get into the business if a person wants to get into the business insurance market. And now this is coming back to us.

One of the best examples I can think of last year is an agent who did $5 million of business with us and two or three years ago people were saying, "Why are you keeping him around?" And yet he was earning a good living at that time, but I knew if we waited and let him grow in the style in which he wanted to grow, he would do well. So we're going to continue to be interested in watching and helping people grow even though it may not be with our company's products. Let's face it. In the '80s, in the decade that appears to be so strongly inflationary, the key to morale is going to be earnings and keeping people ahead. As long as the agent knows we're there to help him with whatever products we can find for him to do a better job for his clientele, he's going to be happy with us.

The next quotation is from Warren Cappel, whom we

asked to tell us what kind of leaders he has most responded to in his career. He said:

> I think the leader that turns me on and excites me the most is the one that I know knows me and I know that he's aware of everything that I'm doing and that he takes a deep interest in me, and knowing that, he lets me alone to proceed in the direction that he is leading me and to do many things on my own, to experiment, fail, and succeed. I like the leader who isn't always telling you how much good he's doing in the community, one who doesn't publicize his do-good efforts. I don't like leaders who tell you how many clubs they belong to, who tell you how expensive all their possessions are, who are anxious to lend you money for whatever purpose. The guy who really turns me off is the guy who isn't leading, but is making an ego trip out of being the boss.

Mr. Cappel went on to say (and notice how he incorporates "alignment" when he says "gets other people to go with them in that direction"):

> Leadership to me means that we're all in this together to build and to further our careers and our enjoyment of our business lives and our personal lives. In our office, I refer to everybody as my associates. They're not my men and my women. The only things that are mine are my children. I just want to be with people. I want to be part of what they do. A leader is someone who knows where he is going or where she is going and gets other people to go with them in that direction. Some of them don't even realize they're going in that direction. We have a chance to influence people's lives more, I think, than in any other industry. When a person comes with us in the business and we lead that person toward the career objectives, we are responsible for that person, and

for that person's family, children, or what he or she gets out of a business career. If we're deeply interested in each and every one of them, they'll attain whatever goals they have. And the leader, therefore, is the one people work *with,* and not the one people work *for.*

An observation in interviewing the many splendid agency heads we had the chance to get to know was that they don't consider their involvement in the lives of their people as a chore. Important? Yes. An onerous duty? No. The right thing to do? Definitely. Always easy? No. Glad that they do? Absolutely. This from Walter Vreeland:

While I love the influence of selling life insurance in family situations, I didn't get as deeply involved in the lives of just a few human beings as an agent, compared to my situation as a manager. I am involved in terms of their personal lives. I am very much aware of what's going on with their lives, their children; I care. If I were to open up my planner and you were to take a look at it now, you'd see more people entries than what I call events. I think that might be some measure of whether one was practicing what I call a genuine caring concern for agents. If you opened it up on any given day, I think I would rather see, "So and so's birthday today," "So and so's anniversary," "Ask about Julie." These arè people entries as opposed to "Call Home Office," "Check management comp," that type of thing. It's a difference in style.

We said to Tom O'Haren: "You have 45 people on your production team counting your management folks and 40 agents. How can you have a close personal relationship with all those people?" This was his reply:

It's very difficult. And I don't mean to imply that I have a terribly personal relationship with each one of those 40 agents, but with the 25 top-producing agents I have a personal relationship. And I have an excellent staff that is charged with the responsibility of developing that same kind of relationship with the people they're working with. And as these people come to the surface, then I make it a point that Ginny and I form a personal relationship with each of these people. Husbands and wives. Now that's time-consuming. That involves one heck of a lot of socializing. Weekends, evenings, entertaining, getting to know people on a personal basis is tremendously important. They need to know that you care about them outside the agency. Ginny and I every once in a while examine ourselves and we wonder why the only real friends we seem to have are our friends in the agency. I guess I have tended to recruit and select people like ourselves that we like very, very much and we spend the majority of our time with them. I hope I don't imply that that's work because that's not work for me. We have people that we entertain every weekend and it's usually different couples. We get a wide variety. There are a number of different kinds of people, which spices up our lives and makes a great deal of fun for us. I think it helps to deepen the relationship because people know that we really do care. We're godparents to a number of kids within the agency. We have stood up at weddings for three or four people when they got married. Those are the kinds of relationships I think we have formed and that I am very proud of and wouldn't trade for anything else in the world. It's been a very big part of my compensation.

Joe Casale is a hard-nosed ex-Marine, running an agency in Manhattan. He's a black belt in judo and karate. That background is an interesting preface for Joe's statement:

Love is a very important factor in our agency. Everybody there cares about everybody else. And I care about all of them. A guy once said to me, "I was afraid you didn't like me,'' and I told him, "If I didn't like you, you wouldn't be here. How the hell am I going to work with somebody I don't like?'' There may be things about a person I don't like. That doesn't mean I don't like the person. I make it a point not to have anybody around that I can't tolerate. And that makes a happy situation. You've got to love them. If you can't love them they shouldn't be there.

Stan Eason understands the principle involved. This statement of his triggered our next question to him:

People are people. They all need to be appreciated and loved and stroked.

Then we asked Stan about stroking and appreciation, whether that was just a technique. This was his response:

Well, if it's a technique then I believe the person using the technique has a problem. I think you have to really feel it. Sometimes you have to practice something for a while to really become comfortable with it, but it can't be a phony stroke. You have to find something that you're comfortable with that the person did that you appreciate and mention that. From an unselfish personal standpoint, I enjoy it. From the business standpoint, it's probably the most productive way of motivating people. I can't motivate someone else, but it's the most productive way I know of getting people to do what I want them to do. If I want them to do "A" and they've done even a piece of "A" and I say, "Hey that was great," then my chances of getting "A" and some more of "A" in the future are greatly enhanced. So both personally and business-wise, I can think of no better way to get what I want than by complimenting somebody for doing it.

When asked to explain his analogy of the agency as a family, Irving Abramowitz said:

How do you treat your family? You trust them. You talk with them. You counsel them. You love them. You want to work closely with them. You want to give them a fair and honest shake. Well, that's how you treat your agents—in the same way you treat your family. That means, for example, that you don't want to take advantage of them. You really want them to succeed. If there's some way I can help him make money, even if it costs me money, he's going to get the benefit of that, and he knows it.

Dick Larson thinks it's essential to truly care for one's people, but he also believes that they should know how hard he is working at his job. He needs to stay mindful that one of his roles is that of a model. Dick said:

I think it was Dave Downey who said, "People don't care how much you know until they know how much you care." I think we care a lot and I think we're willing to do a lot. But our ego just stops us short of going overboard. I remember when I was an agent and an assistant manager, I didn't think the agency manager worked very hard. But now I am one. I'm realizing just how hard the job is. We'd better be real sure that the people with us, our associates, don't have the same feeling that I had. I've always made it a point to be sure that no one thought that I thought that finally being a manager was the end. You know, "Now I can go play golf and now I can drive the big car." Sometimes we can fool ourselves into how hard we're working when in fact we're really not.

Wayne LeNeave indicated his faith in this principle:

Short-range and long-range objectives are best achieved when my own personal and selfish purposes are not in any paramount position. If I put the interest of my associates, that includes the people I hope to attract to this agency, if I place their interest foremost, I know my own welfare will not suffer.

We should not conclude this section on People Skills without acknowledging that it's really not reasonable for any agent to stay with an agency just because the manager "understands me." That is a plus, of course, and can help the relationship to be more productive—IF the agent perceives that one other factor is present. Elton Brooks states it very clearly with these words (the italics are our own):

> I think sometimes when you see your job as running an organization that you can get lost in the details and forget that, particularly in a marketing organization, the organization is really people. *And those people are effective and stay around as long as they perceive you facilitating their growth.* To the extent that they don't see that, they're not going to grow and they're not going to be around.

The title of this chapter, "Hey Doctor, Look at Me, I'm Not Just an Appendix!" should remind us, then, that it could appropriately be paraphrased as, "Hey, Mr. Manager, Look at me, I'm Not Just a Unit of Production!" The significant trend that this chapter illustrates is:

> *Agents will grow, prosper, and stay in those agencies where not only their technical needs are met, but their psychic needs are also recognized and met.*

When Elton Brooks said that "people are effective and stay around as long as they perceive you facilitating their growth," he was providing a perfect lead-in to the next chapter. It bears the ominous title, "Grow or Die."

7 | Grow Or Die

The Agency Head as a Trainer

> **SIGNIFICANT TREND:** Training will become a way of life as a variety of resources from within and outside the agency are used to facilitate the growth of its members.

Our caption for this chapter has been appropriated from an esteemed friend, one George Ainsworth-Land, well-known consultant on creativity, innovation, and change, who has authored an important book with that title, *Grow or Die.* He shows how that mandate of nature, grow or die, extends to all forms of life—and to organizations as well as to individuals. It is apparent today that it most certainly applies to life insurance agencies and to the people who comprise them.

Consider some of the many reasons for saying that training and retraining in the agency will never cease:

New products—never have they come so fast and in such variety. Those who sell them must understand them and those of competitors as well.

New services and new company directions—tax shelters, financial planning, NASD, CLU, ChFC, whole companies' entry into multiple-line, all calling for training.

Changes outside the industry—changes in the demographics of our society, the age of the computer, important changes in tax law, the volatility of the economy and its impact on the market for various products—all require study to be understood and to better acquire and service clients.

In short, never have so many things come along at such an ever-accelerating rate to affect agents, managers, and general agents. The good news is that all or most of them cloak opportunities for those who pay the price in time and study to understand them.

Occasionally one encounters those who mistakenly equate the significance of the service they render with the number of dollars involved. That's why it is a special pleasure to have the first quotation in this chapter be these words from the manager of an outstanding Home Service-type agency, Mr. Charlie Cope of Andalusia, Alabama:

> On the side of my desk is a plaque that reads, "The only path to success in management is through the development of other people." Every manager has one, furnished to us by the agency department. We believe training is a continuous process, every day. We are continually training our agents to work every market: advanced underwriting, group sales, pension sales. We must plan to train. Take your agency man by man, person by person, and be specific. Joe Jones will take the estate protection course this year. Bob Brown will take the pension course this year. And then after he takes this course, you expose him to that type of field, get him in the market.
>
> There is no way the Home Service-type agent can stay in business just writing industrial insurance.

I am proud of having been one of the instruments for helping to make Wilson Learning's bicycle analogy useful and familiar to literally millions of people. In that analogy the function of the back wheel—to provide power—represents technical knowledge. The front wheel, of course, steers and directs that power to take us where we want to go. So product knowledge is back wheel; people knowledge and skills are front wheel. Mike Massad reminds us of the importance of each:

> I want the agent to feel independent as a business-man, but I also want him to feel that we are the

resource to help him become a better businessman. We suggest that he operate as the owner of a franchise. We might use this example: Let's say that I own a McDonald's hamburger franchise, and I've spent a lot of money to get that franchise operating. Now I would be a fool not to accept the help, the expertise, and the guidance of the McDonald's administrative staff on how I might do a better job in my franchise. We in the agency are here to help him. And his training involves not only his ability to sell, but also his ability to help counsel other people in financial management.

It seems to me that one of the biggest jobs a general agent has, particularly with his experienced people, is that he's got to constantly broaden their horizon with better and better training—not only the "back wheel" or technical part of the training, but also the "front wheel," the people part, because life-styles of people have changed a great deal, and people themselves are going to change as a result.

Torontonian Tony Lawes was talking about the same thing when he said:

One of the things we have found we've had to build into any plan is the training and education of our people, not just in technical matters, advanced underwriting, and study sessions; but we've instituted Counselor Selling some two years ago and the Executive Marketing Skills program and Managing Interpersonal Relationships, all of which have led to the necessity of planning the time to do all these things. It has always perturbed me when I've heard people say that they are not getting sufficient knowledge or understanding of how to market this product. I rather like to think that in our branch the biggest complaint is that there are so many things going on that a person can't attend all the sessions that are underway.

Vince Bowhers shared his discovery that one reason that training requires so much time and attention is that a "once over lightly" approach is never enough:

> If you're planning to really get a message across, it will follow this sort of a pattern. The first time you teach a principle, no one hears you. The second time you teach a principle, the people you're working with will say, "Well, I've heard that somewhere before." Then when you mention it a third time they say, "Yes, I've heard that before but I don't want to do it because I don't want to change." And the fourth time around people will say, "Yes, that's a good idea and someday I'll try it." Finally on the fifth they'll say, "That's a good idea; I'm going to give that a try today." Now I don't know if that's exactly accurate—whether it's five times or four times or seven times—but the one thing I have noticed in the operation of our agency over the last few months is that we are getting better implementation through repetition.
>
> To illustrate, our company has developed an excellent disability income product and we weren't marketing a whole lot of it even though it was really an excellent product. We started applying this kind of principle. Repeat meetings, special bulletins, discussions in our management meetings, a pattern of constant repetition. Today we're marketing a great deal of disability income coverage. Last year we quadrupled our disability income business in that single year, and we'll add a substantial additional new level of that same kind of production this year. In my mind there's nothing more involved than this idea of repetition. Now we're doing it in some other areas. It's such a simple thing and so obvious and yet we've been missing it for a good long time.

In the remainder of this chapter the many valuable quotations about training have been grouped into four areas. It will soon be recognized that some of them are relevant to more than one of these areas, but any reader who is interested in the subject of training will have no difficulty in grasping the meaning and significance of what these leaders have to say. These are the somewhat arbitrary categories that follow:

1. Precontract training
2. New agent training
3. Training through peer groups
4. Joint work as a training tool

PRECONTRACT TRAINING

In my city there is a reputable, long-established school for would-be bartenders. I called them to inquire about their program and learned that the course takes from 40 to 60 hours to complete, and that the tuition is $195. It used to be that such a program represented a larger investment than was made in fledgling potential life insurance agents who would shortly be making sales involving the commitment of thousands of dollars. Happily for the industry and those it recruits and those they serve, that situation is very different in successful agencies today. Look at what Clair Strommen said:

> I am convinced that precontract training probably won't assure the retention of unsuccessful people, but for successful ones I think it's an absolute must. More knowlege is needed in the changing marketplace. We need to minimize the risk involved in changing vocations. So we think the engagement period, as I call precontract training, is a very important period before we can even consider a marriage into the life insurance business. We must educate, teach, demonstrate, and execute. We believe it should be 90 to 120 days. This occurs while the prospective agent is still at his former job. We expect him to spend at least two to three hours per week with us, plus as many study hours as he can expend. If he can't do that we'll put him under

full-time precontract training for at least 30 days without pay. That's his investment in his business. We stress that it's mandatory.

Norbert Siegfried is not one to mince words:

> I would sooner take all of those hundreds of hours that would go into potentially terminated new field underwriters, bring it back up front, and spend two weeks a month, six weeks if I must, in precontract to make sure my attrition occurs prior to contract date.

> It's probably the single greatest mistake that we make in management. We don't recognize the necessity for doing that quality job up front prior to contract date. We want the new associate to have at least three cases with money submitted for a minimum of $50,000 ordinary life face amount, or preferably $100,000, beginning on his or her starting date. We're willing to spend a month, two months, even three months with that quality recruit, who is making $20,000 to $30,000 a year on another job, to first make sure the decision is right, but secondly, to give him or her that fast start before actually making the full-time change.

Elliot Rothstein is very specific about his agency's precontract program:

> In the last three years we have never hired any person who has not completed precontract training. I think that is a big reason that the retention has been what the company considers to be better retention than many other agencies. Our precontract training consists of field calls as well as individualized training in the office where a field underwriter must go out and get what we call six case problems. He must get fact-finders from six people, pick up their life insurance policies, and bring them back to

the office. We use the precontract as a case method of learning and then go out on the second interview, and he must sell a minimum of $50,000 of our current volume, which is the equivalent of $600 of annualized commissions and get 24 prestige recommendations so that when he actually joins the organization, he'll no longer be calling friends or relatives or anybody else that he knows. He has a nucleus of people that he didn't know existed before. It has not been difficult to sell this concept. If you are seeing the right kind of candidate, he realizes the value of field testing this business prior to actually joining your organization. It also guarantees his success the first few months, which is really the toughest time that he has in the business.

Precontract training in Jack Skalla's agency sounds like a cross between Marine boot camp and pro-football training—no place for the faint of heart! Jack said:

I would hate to be going through precontract training in our firm today. If a candidate can succeed through a 30-day period going through our precontract training, I'd say that he will know 95 percent of what all life insurance people do who've been out there for 15 or 20 years. And there is hardly a week or a month that goes by without our trying to improve upon that. We're in the process now of completely revamping it again, simply because of change. We want to bring more financial planning into our precontract training. We want to bring in more disability, more pensions, more investments. We figure that if a candidate can come in and spend 30 days with us and still think he might like to go into the life insurance business with us, then he's a candidate for us. Some go out the window within three or four days. We use the precontract training schedule not only as a training device and an organized skill training procedure, but also as an elimination device. They gain an early perspective on the business that otherwise we don't think they can get. The time is past where we think we can stick somebody in an office for six months and say learn the business and come and see us later and then we'll get you out in the field. We want them to hit the ground running. The earlier they make a solid sale the more viable the business is immediately.

Then Jack put a price tag on the precontract investment when he said:

We estimated last year that it cost us agency-wise, one way or another, about $30,000 to put a new recruit through precontract training. Just precontract training. That includes the time and the space, the books and everything else. It's a handsome figure.

To which Jack's assistant, Bill Moore, added:

When you're taking multi-million dollar producers out of the field and having them put time into this instructional and training mode, you're talking about some pretty good bucks!

Al Granum made this reference to the precontract area:

Before the new fellow's first day in the agency, he's done his homework. He's completed company educational material which has taken about 40 hours of pretty good, hard work on his own.

Harry Hoopis predicts more precontract training, and tells why:

We hear more and more about precontract training. There will probably be 50, 60, maybe 100 hours spent in the training posture in the future. It may take three or four months to prepare someone for a contract. The training will probably have to expand in its technical nature. The need-to-know-type things have increased tremendously in the last 10 years. The rate book and the pat on the back that people joke about so often is long gone in our business, and we definitely have to get into a posture of training that says they have adequate knowledge relatively early to be able to talk with people who have complex estate situations. Because if we're going to target market, we have to be able to work with people who can buy big policies. And so the training is going to be geared toward those specialized markets.

Lynn Prewitt was interviewed on the subject of agency profitability, so he was talking bottom-line when he had this to say:

These agents must produce more, faster. We have less time for getting ready to get ready. We have to have them ready to go when they start. And this means a lot of precontract. They have to have business on the books before they start. We think in terms of two sales a week as being an absolute must for our new associates. The days of producing an application a week are gone. We have to think in terms of at least two sales a week.

Al Ostedgaard succinctly reminded us of the two chief functions of precontract training when he said:

. . . another thing that we've learned the hard way over the years is that we've not been tough enough in our precontract orientation. We think that precontract training can find things that you miss in the selection process, plus be a wonderful springboard to getting a person started in higher production quicker.

Paul Sutor's company made the switch to multiple-line, so their precontract work is geared to that world. It may be foreign to what you are used to, but it works well and you should know about it. Here is how Paul explained it:

We have them come in after their work hours. They don't quit their jobs. They come in the evening. We set them up with lists, or they use their own lists. We have phone books and directories, and they just jump right in and we teach them an ex-dating approach. Something similar to: "Good evening. This is Mr. So and So with Metropolitan. I'd like to talk with you about your auto insurance. I won't bother you too much at this point in time. May I ask when you pay your auto insurance?"

The prospect usually replies with something like, "August and February each year."

"Fine. I'd like to call you back at that time and perhaps give you a quote. Maybe we can save you some money on your rates, or increase your benefits, or possibly both. Would you have any objection to that?"

Of course it's so nonthreatening to most of the people that they give us the information. We're not teaching the new associate to sell. All we're asking him to do is find out an ex-date. It sounds so simple, but if the person has some call reluctance or he's scared to talk on the phone, you find that out in this precontract training.

We go on a couple of sales appointments. I may take him on some of my own. I'll ask him to come along and get an idea of what the insurance business is really about—knocking on the door to get in the home, playing with the kids and the dog, and the things that we go through. I want him to come to work for me on Monday morning with no secrets. He knows exactly what our operation is about. I think from that standpoint we have a much better man. We have them licensed, we have their ex-dates, so when they come back from the company school they're ready to go to work. They have prospects ready and lined up for that particular Monday or Tuesday when they come to work.

We have, with considerable reluctance, resisted the temptation to cite credentials of those quoted, because all are outstanding. But only Juan Calles arrived in this country from Cuba with a wife and $100 and "a very bad accent and a strong desire to get ahead." He is doing so, in spades. About precontract training, he had this to say:

Well, when we agree that this person is a good prospective agent, and we present to him the contract and the financing arrangement, we also agree that before a starting date can be definite two things have to happen. One of them is that they must have the state license exam approved and the second is that they must have at least $2,000 of annualized premium in the Home Office. Because they are not licensed to solicit business, they must go out with a licensed agent, and that's why one of the rules about going out with a unit manager or with myself is imperative, not only on the legal side of it, but getting them on the right track from the first day. I will not ask them to even talk with their closest relative about any program that we might have discussed at the office until they have been exposed to at least 10 presentations. Sometimes if we have the right prospects and we have the proper activity, what will happen is that we will have a lot more than the minimum $2,000 before they are even licensed. But if the situation is that he has been working during that time at his prior occupation, has not had enough time to go to enough appointments, and he gets his license before he gets his

$2,000 and we have a tentative starting date and we have not reached the minimum premium requirement of $2,000, we will postpone that starting date and concentrate on making more appointments.

NEW AGENT TRAINING

Bernie Rosen was quoted earlier as saying that he liked the fact that life insurance salespeople are what he calls "decision requirers." Ken Sadler indicated that new agents must learn early that they will have that role. Here is how he put it:

> The philosophy that we put forth in the initial training process (which I do in its entirety for the new agent here) is that they are salespeople, and they need to aid people in making decisions. And so we train in that direction. We encourage our associates to pursue CLU. But, until they are secure as far as being able to sell life insurance, and make a living, and support their families, and do a first class job for their clients, I feel that we encourage them to learn the sales process and practice the sales process more than product knowledge. We are firm believers in people knowledge and sales first, and then product knowledge and CLU, and advanced underwriting, and on and on.

Terry Dunn pointed out that a rate of development that used to assume five years as par now has been accelerated to one year. The range of subjects to be covered and the costs involved combine to give new agent training top priority. Here are Terry's words:

> The subject of training is perhaps the key subject of agency building in the next five to ten years. When I first started in this business, the objective was to learn a lot about life insurance and to learn how to sell it and that's what we did. We had the luxury of time. We could mature a person over a period of years. We were looking at five years as

the period of time over which we'd hoped to develop the person into a Million Dollar Round Table producer. And then that worked its way down to three years and then two years and then one year. In the first year in the business we try to bring them up to that point. The development time continues to be a major problem that will become more of a problem as time goes on. It costs so much money to bring these people along that we've got to get them into high production much more rapidly than we had in the past. Another area is the wider variety of products. In the past we could concentrate on life insurance. Now we have to learn about a lot of different products. Right now I'm studying the American College course in wealth accumulation and working toward the new designation. Just having to learn about all those products and then trying to provide training for new agents in the wider variety of products puts enormous strain on their training capabilities.

Yankees might not think New Orleans would be the most likely place to find rigorous work schedules such as those committed to by Jack O'Brien's new associates. (*Note:* After that statement we thought about the vigor of Jack and the other top people interviewed in New Orleans for Legacy: Paul Arceneaux, Ken Sadler, Jerry Burns, Frank Friedler, Jr., and Roland Hymel, and quickly realized that energy is relatively unaffected by climate!) Look at the two promises Jack requires:

In the recruiting process we exact two promises from the individual. Based on the fact that we are entering a partnership, that he is receiving a franchise with our company, that we are going to supply him with everything he needs, he has to promise us two things: (1) he'll commit himself to 60 hours a week the first two years in the business; and (2) he will accept or swallow as best he can what we're teaching him, sort of putting on the blinders and not trying to change it until he's developed enough experience and expertise and knowledge with which to make changes. This may vary six months to a year in the business.

He's in office training six days a week his first nine months in the business on a part-time basis. This includes Saturday morning and being there until noon every Saturday. And I feel that if I can do that after 25 years in this business, a new person can. We try to break that five day a week, 40 hour a week syndrome by requiring this. Some people have said they wouldn't do it and they have not joined us. But as far as our commitment to them, in essence we tell them we'll lead them 60 percent of the way, but we won't go 90 percent. They have got to show us a positive, dedicated attitude. As long as they're willing to try and to work with us, we'll go along with them.

Vince Bowhers told us about how important the establishment and use of systems really is. Al Granum is renowned for the effectiveness of his system. Dick Larson described an activity system that he called 4-4-2-2. Here is what he said about it:

The system works like this. We ask our people to get four new names a day. I tell them, "You have to be able to accomplish that. We hope it will be four strong referrals with what we call '10' positioning, meaning that you can call these people up and they'll see you immediately. But we know that's not totally rational. We hope though that they aren't all down to a number 'one' positioning, which would be, 'Gee, I don't have any names. I'll look in the phone book.' But you see, you could do that. So from the standpoint of the first '4' in the formula, it's impossible to fail. You must be successful, because anyone could gather those four names."

The second element is that we ask them to send four letters a day. We have a number of letters that run all the way from just a cold approach to someone you don't know to a strong referral kind of letter. They are not unique. They come out of anybody's manual. They are produced on the word processor, they are numbered, and the agent turns in prospect cards with a notation to send letter number one to this person or number three or five, whichever fits the situation. We know that a person cannot fail on the second "4," because if they give us the names, the office staff will get the letters out. So again the agent has been successful.

The first "2," however, can give a little trouble. Its definition is that "I will call on the telephone until I have secured two appointments." We're not saying that when you get two appointments, go home. But we want a minimum of two. We think that's entirely possible, because if someone is giving an agent a lot of trouble, and it's late at night and you'd like to go home, you can always get an appointment with someone for next Christmas vacation or three months down the road, just so they can get rid of you. So again we think it's impossible to fail in that area.

Now if in fact a new agent goes home at the end of the day and has accomplished 4-4-2, that agent is a success. If they're brand new they can tell their spouse, "I did my job today." Because interwoven with all of this we're going to have our training sessions and all the other things that go on with new agents, so we have a success on our hands at this moment.

That last "2" is tough. It means hold two selling interviews a day. Going back to that first 4-4-2, it's obvious you can't do that the first day and expect to have interviews that day or the next, but it does build. If we do 4-4-2 every day, soon appointments will show up and sales will be made. With 4-4-2-2 we'll get the sales needed for this agent to survive. And that will give us an opportunity to move him into the affluent markets as time goes on.

After asking Dick what approach his new people used as they began in the field, he gave it to me this way:

"Bob, as I mentioned over the phone, I'd like to spend a few minutes of your time discussing our services to corporations and corporation owners like yourself—specifically those things that your company can do for you and your family more effectively than you can do them for yourself, given the current Internal Revenue Code. We think you'd like to know what other successful business people in the St. Paul area are doing to (1) increase their spendable income, and (2) increase their aftertax profits. I'd like to take just a minute of your time this morning to find out just how much information has been brought to your attention. Do you have some time that we could cover this now?"

Dick went on to say:

We make our people memorize and role-play that approach from day one. We don't care whether they're 21- or 22-year-old recent college graduates or 50-year-old ex-bank vice presidents. That's our approach.

Dick then explained when and under what circumstances the new associate goes into the field, with and without staff help:

I tell all our people when I recruit them that we're going to teach them the basic sales presentation.

We won't turn them loose until we know that they're good, until we would buy from them. We do the same thing in Financial Needs Analysis and Capital Needs Analysis areas. I say, "Once I know you know how to do it, I expect you to do it and there isn't any way that you could get me across the hall to do it for you or even to sit in and listen to you do it in front of someone. You're going to do it."

Now in the affluent market if we're dealing with a land owner, the rancher, the farmer, the business person, we're always available. It doesn't make any difference if it's Saturday morning, Sunday afternoon, evenings, midnight, I don't care. If an agent calls me and says, "I've got a person that's interested in this and this and he owns this business," that agent will have me or one of our senior people there anytime he or she wants them there. I think they know that. I think that relationship with how far we're willing to go for them is an important thing. I used to tell kids when I recruited football players, "Look, if you work half as hard to succeed as I'm going to work to make sure that you succeed, you can't miss." And I tell them that I will work just as hard and they know it.

Now that was quite a bit of Dick Larson, but I feel good about including all of it because it was specific and, I believe, useful and transferable to others.

When interviewing Joe Gray in Toronto, we reminded him that his agency produced 6,894 applications in 1981, and asked if there might be something in their training that made his people so aware of the importance of frequency of production. Joe replied this way:

I think it starts right in the hiring process. We used to start talking about 100 applications per year. We now start talking about 120. We used to be notorious in the business for being the big bad wolves who insisted that if you didn't do 20 in the first quarter, we fired you and we've stuck to this. Now the company is paying a cash bonus to the person who goes 30 apps in their first quarter. And all of a sudden we're finding that everybody is doing 30 apps. We're not crazy, we want big business too. We know that 30 apps a quarter, 10 a month will produce a happy agent. If you're trying to ride a bicycle and you keep it going, it's very easy. If you can't get the bicycle going, you're going to fall flat on your ear. Our philosophy has always been 100 apps; now we're raising that philosophy in order to survive. People have a tendency to do what you expect them to do. We have 19 or 20 in the branch that did well over 100 last year; some were over 200. So it's working.

When George W. Karr indicated they hire 35 inexperienced people per year, it was obvious that they had to have a system to follow. Here is what he said about it:

In our organization we hire 35 new people a year who do not have previous life insurance experience. Because of this we have chosen the broadest base market that we know of and that is the individual earning $25,000 or more. We teach our people to do a capital needs analysis approach to each of the people that they feel they can call on when they first go into the business. And the emphasis is to get referrals. We feel that that broad based market is something that then leads to a whole lot of other markets. But it is a market that has a short turnaround time in that you can see a person on Monday and go back on the following Monday and close a sale. You may even occasionally have a one-interview sale. But it's not the kind of selling situation that goes on and on while you move through the accountant, the lawyer, and a couple of other officers, as you would in the corporate market. That can become discouraging to the new agent versus going in and talking to a man about his own family situation and what his objectives are for his family and then showing him how to reach those objectives all in a relatively short period of time.

We have a feeling, and I think others feel the same way, that everyone in the agency can sell $3 million worth of life insurance. The question is how long it takes them to sell it. If they can sell $3 million of life insurance in a month, obviously they are doing an outstanding job. But if it takes them three years, they're only average. And if it takes them six years, they're not going to stay in the business. But the point is that they can all sell $3 million worth of life insurance. So our job is to teach them how to get into a market that has a quick turnaround time and gets them some sales under their belt. And gets them success. And gets them positive mental attitude and a feeling that this is a good business for them, a good career for them, and a place where they could look long-term for a bright future.

We asked George how the individual new agent would find those first people on whom to call:

Initially he uses people that he's had previous contact with. Whether or not he sells those people, he asks for an opportunity to at least show the kind of work that he can do. After he's done his job and evaluated a person's situation, including insurance, social security, other assets, etc., he then asks for referrals. We strongly believe that the referral system of prospecting is the only really viable system in the life insurance business. We think that if a man gets three referrals, he can make three phone calls to those referrals, get two interviews, and make one sale. If he chooses to work on a cold call basis, he probably needs 50 names and 50 phone calls or 50 cold calls to get five appointments to get one sale. In one instance he's processed 50 names. In the other he's processed three. Now obviously the numbers won't hold exactly right for every person, but they're about the relationship that we've found.

Again coming back to the fact that everyone can sell a million, or $3 million, or whatever, it's just a question of how fast you can do it, because the expenses keep coming in and if you drag it out too long, you're going to be in financial trouble. We feel that the most efficient way is the referral way. With that in mind then, we teach people to sell and we teach them to get referrals. And we emphasize that the two things are equally important. This is not just a sales business, it's a sales/prospecting business. And this is really the emphasis we teach from day one to the new people that we bring into the business.

Not only do George Karr's people learn how to get referrals, they also learn how to get better referrals. Here's how:

Our referred lead approach involves referring upwards. In other words, it has to do with finding out who the most successful people are that the particular person you've just sold knows. Who he would call on first if he were in the life insurance business as you are. Who his best friend is. Who he feels is ultimately going to be the most successful person that he knows and that kind of technique. And since we're dealing with a relatively small number of fact-finding interviews, we would try to determine as much as possible from that person who's giving us the name whether he feels that he's giving us a name that would make a good prospect. I think that ideally we would look for no more than 10 names from one individual. You can start a pretty good endless chain if you can get three and you can close one out of three. But if you try to get five or six and no more than 10, your chain will become just absolutely endless, and you'll be storehousing names of people to call on.

Walter Shields also uses a proven system to train his people to get quality referrals, acknowledging that all new agents will need prospects other than those they already know:

The agency's responsibility is first of all training our new associates in how to secure new names of individuals that they did not have heretofore. So if you go back to my definition of a market as a group of persons highly interrelated, significantly small in number, those are going to come about primarily by way of reference. In our agency we use the Al Granum one-card system. If you follow that system by using the feeding-of-a-name process, you're going to secure new persons who are likely to be highly interrelated with a person with whom you are doing business. So this is going to lead you into markets. Having said that, however, I think that we have, as agency heads, a definite responsibility to make facilities, technical assistance, whether that's at the agency level or Home Office level, available for the person who, as a result of these fact-finding interviews, uncovers a situation that leads into a specialty market.

Arthur Goldblum trains young agents in Houston in target-marketing, e.g., just dentists, or just one medical specialty!

The old system which was based on who you are, who you know, is going to give you some business. What we're trying to do today is to develop the marketplace for a man in the market and then let the man develop based on the needs of the market-place and grow along with it. It's easier to organize to a market or a profession or a group of prospects that have something in common so that we don't have to find a renaissance man who knows all things about all things at all times. We can't train a guy and give him 20 years' worth of experience when we have a financing plan that kicks off with a validation requirement in 13 weeks. It's fish or cut bait. The old ways won't work. So the answer must be: specialize! If the guy's going into the advanced, what I call the boardroom sale, he might as well do it at the age of 25, 26, or 27. Why retrain him when he's 50? I can train a man today in six weeks to sell into any professional marketplace we choose providing he'll accept direction, is presentable, owns a gray pinstriped suit or is willing to buy one, and will appear before our video screen to start training himself by himself.

In Nashville, Jerry Ezell has been very successful in hiring bright young people and training them to work in advanced markets. So what he has to say about training is interesting and authoritative:

We found that new agents fail when they don't know what to do or how to do it, so we view training as a teaching method of what to do and how to do it on the sale from A to Z. Our recruits are from 22 to 26 and generally on their first or second job after college. When they come in we assume they know nothing in relation to our business. So we pull all the strings—tell them what to do, when to do it, how to do it. If he doesn't follow directions, we know that he will not succeed. We train all our people in the advanced sales market, calling on professionals and business owners. We keep them at our training center for three and one-half to four weeks prior to making their first call for an appointment.

We can assure the new agent that if he meets the activity goal he will meet the monetary goals. We know that. He doesn't. So we have to constantly reinforce that through others that have gone before him and are meeting them. Then as soon as he gets in the field, these statistics become his statistics. We start developing his ratios with his first call. As they improve we show him the improvement and the impact it will have on future earnings, because agency ratios no longer apply. From these ratios we can often determine what performance problems may exist.

Willard Pratt in Fort Worth has a great record in the new organization area. He gets people on their mettle very quickly. He told us:

We hire what we hope are big folks. You know, grown-ups. We strongly believe that all development is self-development, and we stress that idea very quickly, because we will be very much responsible to them, but certainly not for them. They've got to be responsible for themselves, and we'll do everything we can to help.

TRAINING THROUGH PEER GROUPS

This whole book is based upon the premise that agency heads can learn more from each other than from any other resource. That's not to suggest that other resources are not useful and downright valuable. My own experience at Wilson Learning showed me that an outside company could help organizations in many industries to develop their people farther and faster than might otherwise have been the case.

But agents too can learn more from each other than from most other people or places, and wise general agents and managers encourage and facilitate that kind of learning in a variety of ways. Some of those involve interaction within the agency, and some involve going outside. In the quotations that follow we shall see examples of each.

Al Granum's "peer groups" have become well-known in

the business, for he never fails to mention their importance in his many appearances before industry audiences. He said:

> We have three peer groups going all the time—at least monthly. The first peer group is made up of those who are new in the agency, plus those who have not yet qualified for the Round Table. The second group is made up of those who are qualified as regular full-fledged Round Table members. The third group was initially made up of the nine who were life and qualifying MDRT members, plus CLU, and who had a reasonable expectation of being able to produce $100,000 of new premiums. Each group meets once a month on the first or second working day. Each person reports in a systematic way to his peers—how many times he dialed, how many people he reached, how many appointments he had, business lunches and their results, cases opened, interviews, suspects, new facts, total closes, and of course submitted and paid business. He makes any commentary he wishes, and then receives the comments and suggestions of his peers.

One of Mr. Granum's leading agents told me:

> There are many opportunities here to hear other agents talk about their operation or talk one-on-one with them. I think the agency is unique for the continuing growth it offers the people beyond the early training stage because of this rubbing shoulders with the greats.

Well, "unique" might be putting it a bit strong, for there are other outstanding agencies where similar opportunities exist. A good example lies in the nearby suburban Chicago agency headed by Jerry Urbik. Jerry explained why they had gone from an agency comprised of line units to a format consisting of a staff of specialists who serve the entire agency. This, he explained, created another kind of problem, one which the peer group concept dealt with most effectively. Here is what Jerry said:

But in going this way we did lose something. We lost the feeling of the fellows belonging to a smaller, more intimate unit. They missed the unit get-togethers and the unit meetings, unit cohesiveness. So we evolved what we now call our color group concept. The idea of the color group is to bring together those who are at like levels of production and approximate time in the business and make peer groups out of them—in a sense, artificially.

We started with the gold group, the fellows that were there at the beginning and producing then at the $2 million to $5 million range. On the other end of the spectrum it was obviously easy, the green group was the group of new people. They needed a different response, a weekly training meeting. Then we had two more groups in the middle, the red and the blue, the intermediate, the developmental groups. Last year some of the faster-moving red and blue group members said they'd like to form a new group at a higher level. They became our silver group.

I envision every year people flowing from the green group into the red and blue, some people moving faster than others, and perhaps evolving a platinum group or a bronze group or whatever. It's almost like an in-house study group.

Ken Sadler accurately calls them "mutual support groups." He described them in this way:

We've been using a concept that we call mutual support groups. My feeling is that six or eight associates meeting together can meet 90 percent of their own needs. When a peer tells another peer how he is prospecting or selling or closing, then it's heard —better than when the general agent, who's supposed to talk that way, says it. These people, at different levels, come together at intervals, set an agenda for their meeting, and go through the items that *they* want to discuss. If there are needs that the group can't meet for themselves, then they request that the needs be met, such as a session on HR 10 or IRA or whatever.

People hear the answers to questions they ask.

John Wiener described his "Prospectors Club," a 12-week Saturday morning get-together of the agents, repeated three times a year, in their earlier years (plus any veterans who might choose to join them). Each week is devoted to study of a different form of prospecting, and each participant reports to the others on total activity during the week. We asked John why he felt this program has been so effective in increasing total applications per year in the agency from 600 to 2,000 in just five years. He said:

> First of all, it really gets into the heart of the life insurance business, which is prospecting. And it's very basic. But the other thing about it is, you've got tremendous peer pressure with this, because each individual, each week for 12 weeks, gets up in front of all the people he works with and tells them exactly what he did or didn't do last week.
>
> And it's amazing, I can tell before the meeting by the looks around the table, just who wrote the applications. You know, one guy sits there eating his doughnut and says, "Let's get going. We're running a few minutes late." He probably had four or five applications last week and he can't wait to give that input!"

Jack Skalla pointed out that intra-agency help can be one-on-one, without any formal structure. As the reader looks back at those early months and years in personal production, I suspect that recollections of help, ideas, and counsel from several nonmanagement people will come to mind. Jack said:

We're lucky. We have interplay every day, almost every hour. An associate can walk out of his office door and either turn to the right or the left and walk into another associate's office and say, "Gee, you know, Jack, I've got this interview later on this afternoon and I'd really like to run it by you because I know you had a case like it last week." There's so much success there. Our associates really help each other out in our firm.

Peter Browne spoke of study groups within the agency:

Study groups can take many forms, both nonstructured and structured. We try to structure the study groups in various levels of performance. Some of the better and more sophisticated agents will meet once a month, as will those in the middle area of their career, and our newer people will also meet once a month.

Walter Downing mentioned the role of MDRT meetings and the study group affiliations they make possible when he said:

We strongly encourage our people to attend the Million Dollar Round Table meetings. We have quite a number who go to those meetings, and they create study groups so that they're meeting between MDRT meetings with Round Table study groups for additional professional know-how.

Mike Massad found that good agents often feel that it's not only more blessed to give than to receive, but it's also very rewarding to them! He said:

There are experienced agents, we found, who like to be considered THE agency expert in a certain field. So we encourage that guy to do special work in the area and assist other people in the agency in that field.

On many occasions I would find that I couldn't answer some technical question and I determined that it was important for me to admit that I didn't know the answer. I just didn't think I could bluff my way through. So there were two specific things we did. The first thing was to have that agent consult with one of our own associates who has the experience in that specific field he's interested in. The other agent is flattered when he's asked to help, and he'll nearly always do it for me. Another thing we've done that's worked very well is to bring in agents of other companies. We've found that outstanding producers with a specialty, or just outstanding producers who do a lot of business, welcome the opportunity to put on a meeting for our agency and tell us exactly how they did it. They're always delighted to do it and consider it quite an honor. We only invite salesmen who have proven they can sell in a specific market and have good credentials.

Paul Arceneaux told how a weekly sales meeting can be used in a fashion similar to some of the peer groups mentioned earlier:

Our Monday morning sales meetings help stimulate sales activity. The first ritual every Monday morning is to ask each agent for his results from the previous week. He gives us his number of appointments, his closing interviews, and number of applications. Each agent is invited and feels free to discuss any sales problems he may be having. He or she is then asked for the number of appointments for the coming week and the number of apps they expect to write. We feel that this peer pressure of sorts helps to motivate them to be productive each and every week. There's a closeness and more people are doing the applications than are not. So everyone wants to feel they belong to the group. They want to bring in something to contribute each

Monday morning. Also, our agents and wives attend agency functions about six times during the year together, so this helps promote the feeling of closeness and it spurs the friendly rivalry.

Glenn Martin learned long before he came into the life insurance business just how powerful and motivating a commitment to one's peers can be. Here's how he told about it:

When I was in school at the University of Kansas our track coach was extremely hung up, to my advantage, of course, on goal setting. We would commit every year in front of our teammates as to just what we were going to do—whether we were going to run the nine flat hundred or whether we were going to jump 25 feet or whatever. I'll never forget those sessions because you had to be awfully careful what you committed to because the whole team would be relying on you to do it. And when you would not do your workouts or you would maybe cut short a couple of wind sprints, your teammates would remind you by saying, "Martin, aren't you going to do what you said you were going to do? Aren't you going to accomplish the goals you said you had? Come on, get with it. Let's not let the team down."

I've used that same philosophy throughout the agency in respect to agents setting personal goals. We would sit down and we would talk to the agents about money needs—the normal LIMRA approach in the *Looking Ahead* book. I've used it since I came to the life insurance business. We would sit down and commit to goals, and when we did that we had a different feeling. I could say to myself that I was going to write $100,000 in premium and rationalize it all year, but if I said it in front of a group of 50 or 100 agents, they're going to remind me that that's what I said I was going to do because they're competing against each other and that is an enjoyable part of this business. We can have fun in competing and have fun playing with numbers and working with each other.

We've got agents who now even identify with another agent's goals. They'll say, "What's the problem?" I've got an agent that called me last week worried about another agent. He said, "I'm concerned. He's got half of what he had last year. I know what he's trying to get; what can I do?" That's a good feeling. He would not have known that feeling had he not been involved in that planning process with his associate in setting goals and objectives together. I think that agreement we had with our track coach in Kansas on goal setting and keeping records showed that he was really a stickler. If you ran 10 440s you would know what each one was to the tenth of a second! I was able to analyze my performance as a track man, determine my program of training, and also determine whether I had a poor performance or a bad performance. I carried that right into the life insurance business. I used it on my calls and interviews. When I went into management, I used it on my recruiting. Everything was written, everything was detailed, everything I did was documented. When I want to know what happened or why, I can just go back and find out.

JOINT WORK AS A TRAINING TOOL

I entered the business in a very successful agency headed by a charismatic general agent who was a brilliant personal producer. Only once did I ask him to go on a joint call, and never did he volunteer to do so. The one time I asked, saying I'd given him a big buildup to the prospect as one who could give him outstanding counsel, he refused to make the call with me, saying that he didn't want to make a "leaner" out of me, and that I could handle it myself. I did, and successfully, but when an offer came to go into management with another company, I was perhaps more disposed to respond than I might have been had I had the closer relationship that being on the firing line together could have engendered.

I was reminded of that forgotten experience when rereading the quotations that follow. Joint work today is a most valuable training tool, and it has many other dividends as well. They will become apparent as you review the statements of people like Cal Dings, who said:

> To move rapidly into more sophisticated markets, you must encourage more joint work between agents, and between agents and management staff. To me this is one of the most valuable training procedures that we have. You'd better be careful, because you have to recruit compatible people. You're going to have to operate within clear-cut rules and understandings, but I feel the rewards are high. What are they? Well, you get your rapid transfer of knowledge from the senior person to the junior. You have better service to the client. You have two people serving him. And you have the strengths of combined talents working with each other on a case. What one of them misses the other one saves.

> Our new people are initially trained to do simple programming; but in their fact-finding interviews we really stress that they get all the answers to all the questions. For example, we say, "Ask about whether this prospect's employer has a pension or profit-sharing plan. If not, why not? If they don't, who would be the person to see?" Then, when a good prospect appears, our younger agent teams up with an experienced one, and they go out on a joint work basis to make the call."

Bob Szeyller's agency has learned much about how to best utilize joint work. He has proven and practical suggestions to share:

If you recruit a 23-year-old who has never done anything but go to school, you're not going to invite him in to talk to a five-man medical practice with their CPA sitting there and really expect to accomplish very much. So what we've tried to do is create joint ventures among our agents. We found out that you cannot take a mediocre agent and team that mediocre agent up with a good, hard-hitting producer and expect to get good results. It just doesn't work. What does work is to take a good, hard-hitting young agent who maybe doesn't have all the expertise and knowledge to work a sophisticated market and team him or her up with the established good producer. That will work. That's one of the things we've done, and it's been very successful for us. We've identified certain good strong producers in our agency and convinced them that we could build a team of producers around them where the older agent is serving as the lead producer. He's the coach in this situation.

It's something that takes an awful lot of management involvement to make it work because you get into some difficult areas like splits and referrals and who gets what. But we found that when you're trying to penetrate a market, if you get the group together on a regular basis, say on Monday morning, and you discuss all of your efforts and who's going to do what and who's going to work with what case and you see that everybody's busy, it tends to work out. One of our agents probably has at least one additional name on every application that he writes. He's a very successful young man and he likes it that way because he feels that he's got three or four, perhaps even five or six, agents out beating the bushes for him and doing a lot of the legwork, and he's the guy who runs the seminars and comes in on the closes and has all the experience to handle the CPAs and attorneys. We're also seeing our younger agents develop much faster than I ever thought was possible in a really sophisticated, tough market area.

Bernard Mayer identified another attribute of joint work as a training tool. It provides opportunities for learning that can never be totally simulated. His observation led me to think about some of the "Aha's" I had in my early experience, and it seems that they usually took place in the field—not in a discussion in the office. The phrase Mr. Mayer uses describes perfectly those precious occasions:

> I think you can learn concepts in a class; then the concepts have to be put to work. When I say we have weekly classes, that does not mean that I don't go into the field with my managers and my men, spend time with them, watch them. Many years ago at college we had a professor, J.B. Nash, who wrote a book called *Teachable Moments.* As I developed in the life insurance business, I began to realize that there are particular moments that are best for teaching. So that in a situation when you're in the field or a situation when a supervisor is particularly troubled or confused, that's a perfect time to teach, because the chances of retaining the material are great.

Like so many others, Peter Browne recognizes the synergism that joint work generates:

> Joint work is becoming a very prominent factor in the insurance business today. If you can take the strengths of one agent and work on the weaknesses of another, you can strengthen both of them. Sources of business in the New York agency include tax-deferred annuities, pensions, estate planning. If we find that an associate wants to get involved in an area where he does not have many strengths, we will put him with one who is strong in that area.

Terry Knight points out that the synergism is really tripartite in scope, for the agency's management capacity is increased through their approach to joint work:

> One of the largest reasons for the increase in our production has been our joint work program. The philosophy behind the program is that it benefits all three parties that are involved in it. It benefits the new agent because he's getting in front of people immediately that he would not have the expertise to talk with for several years and perhaps never. Our new people are calling on business and professional people from day one (and even before that, actually, because we have an active precontract training program). Secondly, it benefits the established producers because it gets them in front of people that they would not otherwise have an opportunity to get in front of. They're being exposed to new people and the new person is doing the prospecting. It's increasing the quality of their life because they don't have to work as hard to get to see more people. And it's also increasing their income. And it's increasing the income to the agency because it's actually increasing our management capacity without proportionately increasing our costs. Joint work is a very powerful concept, and I didn't really realize all the implications of it until we began developing the program and until it came through its evolutionary process to the state that it is now.
>
> I would say 60 to 70 percent of all new applications are on a joint basis. We have guidelines for the joint work program and an experienced agent has to be able to qualify to be eligible for the program. He must produce at our "cabinet" level, which this year is about $40,000 in first-year commissions. The only exception to this is if someone else brings in the new agent other than a cabinet level producer. Then this person has the right to establish

and mentor a situation with the person that they actually brought in. But when I recruit someone or my supervisor recruits someone, then the cabinet level producer has first crack at doing joint work with him. Joint work for the senior producer is very profitable because the new person is out on a day-to-day basis contacting high-powered people. These are very high commissioned cases. Two years ago one of our senior producers experienced income well in excess of $40,000 just on joint work brought in by a new producer. The new person's primary responsibility is to contact the prospect and to motivate the prospect on the necessity of getting involved in the planning process. And at this point the experienced producer would come in and work along with him. He's introduced as the associate, not as an expert from afar. So the new person doesn't have to say, "I'm bringing in someone to bail me out," or, "I don't have enough expertise personally to handle this." The experienced person is introduced quite simply as "my associate" and that's the same way I'm introduced because I'm very active in joint field work also.

When next I talk to Terry, I'll remind him that there is also a fourth party who is well-served by their approach to joint work: the most important one of all, the client.

More and more some agencies seem to be moving to a structure not unlike that of many law firms or public accountants. Ted Santon's agency reminds me of other professional units:

Our agency is made up of seven partnerships and each partnership is at least two people. Some of them run up to as many as 10 people. The partnerships in our agency specialize, some of them in just one product line. There are partnerships with five people, each one specializing in a different product line or a different area. Our first two years is kind of a farm system and we recruit to a sales intern program. In two years we try to coordinate a move into one of these specific partnerships. It works, this combination of youth and enthusiasm on the one hand and knowledge and the good client base and the person who has specialized experience on the other hand. The older person gives the stability and adds income to both people. We're very careful not to do this to save somebody, but to make sure that $1 + 1 + 1 = 6$.

Joe Casale has formalized the joint work by assigning new agents to experienced ones for their first six months, to the benefit of each. Here's how he explains it:

It's difficult to tell a young man who's making $50,000 a year that he ought to come in and make $18,000 in management. They kind of look at you askance. And because of that now we've gotten into this senior agent system, which is something evolved from Lambert Huppeler and Dave Marks who, I think, used to require that their people have a partner for their first six months in the business. We require it for six months. That's taken a lot of the burden off my management people so they can spend more time now in the office doing technical work and follow-up and administrative work, case development, presentation planning, instead of lugging a briefcase around from door to door selling policies or talking to prospects. Under the senior agent system, each fellow is assigned someone who's been around three or four years, and he's married to that guy on a 50/50 basis for the first six months he's here. We've noticed that once a guy has been the senior agent for a year, he's a better producer on his own for the next year.

Walter Downing described two different but valuable kinds of partnerships:

I think we're going to see more agent producers getting together in different capacities so that the whole is greater than the sum of the parts. For example, we have a partnership about to be formed where the skills of the two people forming it are overlapping in no way. One is a real inside man, a walking encyclopedia on many advanced subjects; and the other has an unusual ability to open up cases, but his level of learning just isn't enough to absorb the kinds of concepts needed to solve those case problems. There's absolutely no overlap, but still they're dependent on each other for what's missing in one.

There's another kind of partnership that I feel will mature and develop. That is where the agents' skills *do* overlap. They both know the same things. They both have the same strengths. They get together because they stimulate each other personally. They keep their exhilaration levels going. They are able to provide continuity to the clients. They can take off more time. Each spells off the other. And they keep from getting bored.

As our business gets more and more sophisticated, only so much can be learned, no matter how bright or how much capacity an agent has. If he has another one of himself, that much more can be learned in the partnership.

Both Irving Abramowitz and Monroe Diefendorf have the ability to explain the joint work phenomenon in very human terms. Here is how Irving told about it:

We have what I call a joint field work concept in our agency. Obviously we have our agency management personnel who train agents, who go out in the field with agents, who work with them. But very quickly we wean them away from this and try

to teach the new person to work with the top producers. This joint work relationship between the
old and the new is certainly our very finest management tool.

We even find that our most successful salespeople
start cultivating new agents and offer their help to
make joint calls. It's also important to mention
that we get our older producers to enter into formal
arrangements with newer producers.

Informally, we talk about them working jointly;
but an older man begins to think, "You know, I'm
50 years old (or 70 years old). I've got maybe 10
years left in the business. Sometime along the way
my clientele is going to need continuing servicing.
Where are they going to get it? Maybe this young
man has the kind of integrity and knowledge that
I'd like to see developed so that he could service my
clients in the future. And along the way, I may like
to take some longer vacations. And if I have someone in the organization covering for me on an interested basis, I could enjoy life a little more."

So we put these individuals together. The older
agent ties up with the new agent, or a middle-level
experienced agent, and they all start doing better,
all start motivating each other, teaching each other
new skills.

Irving is in Baltimore, and Monroe is in New York, but the
people aren't that different. This is Mr. Diefendorf's
testimony:

I remember meeting Lambert Huppeler and having
him tell us that about 70 to 75 percent of the sales
made in his office were a result of joint work. That
made quite an impression, because I guess that his
was the first 100 million dollar agency.

A lot of agents, when they get older, are afraid to give up their clientele. They say, "Only I can deal with my clients. Nobody else can talk to them like I can." They're really afraid to let go. I've got some of them working with a new but experienced agent who's got a good record. What happens is that the older agent does more business, spends less time, and is having more fun in the business. That's a tough sale to make, but it can be made.

Joint practice is particularly successful in family situations. One of our top people, at 55, was entertaining thoughts of retiring. He was getting tired and lonely. Then his first son came in, and that gave him a boost. And then his second son came into the business two years ago. That has been like Geritol to his Dad. I've never seen a man so enthused. The business is growing. They're working together and having fun.

So, knowing that's a good family situation, I'm now getting some other family situations. A father and son or nephew. Or I've got a brother and brother combination. So I look for this. Who do I have with a son or son-in-law that might be a prospect for the business?

He also mentioned that those of Amiable social style are not likely to call on many successful businessmen who are Drivers who, in Monroe's words, "can eat them up."

So I'll say to the Amiable, "Could you dig up 10 people who are millionaires, or earn over $100,000, or both?" I'm thinking of one who'd been in the business a few years. He said, "Well, I probably could." I said, "You haven't called on them yet?" He said, "No." I said, "Could you make an appointment?" He said, "Well, I guess I could." Then I teamed him up with a Driver, who goes out as the expert, and they do a lot of business together. In that way we're taking the large reservoir of good prospects that every agency has but no one ever calls on, and opening them up. The same kind of teaming between Analyticals and Expressives, complementary social styles, is also very effective.

Norbert Siegfried says, "We've literally built our agency . . . on joint work." He calls it win-win:

One of the things we have found helpful in bringing the new recruits through to higher early production is joint work with the people in our agency, the established field underwriters who are specialists in different marketing fields. We've literally built our agency in the past few years on joint work. We have some people five to ten years in the business who really are dependent to some degree for their third million or maybe their fourth million of volume from quality interviews developed by new associates in their first year or so. So they benefit. The new associate is able to participate in large commission cases. So again, it's a win-win proposition.

Neal Campbell described how they provide incentives for senior agents to bring in new agents and how that often develops into partnerships. He said:

We have three father-son operations and they are partners. But most of the time the junior agent comes in with a senior agent assisting and counseling, promoting what he's going to do and accomplish and sometimes handing him leads of people that he doesn't want to call on. That is, the senior agent doesn't want to. But then as they move on down, it is worked out where they often work out a true partnership, maybe starting off at 70/30 with the senior agent getting 70 percent, the younger agent getting 30, and then moving gradually to a

50/50 split. We found that sons or the young agents really push the senior agents to get out and make more calls, which the senior agents are not accustomed to doing. They often feel they can make one or two calls a day and take care of all the business they need to. But because the young agent needs to get out and get the exposure, he's encouraging Daddy to get out. As a result everybody's production is up.

Jerry Gaultney explained how joint work enables his new people to work in the sophisticated markets they have chosen to serve, and to receive a variety of training experiences in the process:

Several years ago both the company and the general agency organization identified our market as being the business owner, the professional, and the highly compensated executive. By and large, we're looking for new agents who measure up in the three areas of strong financial background to be able to work with a more sophisticated client and those financial concepts that we work with. And also one who has the experience of persuading or motivating or directing people. And third are ones with a natural market that can get him or her out in the marketplace quickly and apply some of the financial concepts that we will be teaching. And they have about a six-month training process. Now currently about 80 percent of the business we do in our organization is done on a joint selling basis. We teach the new people some of the very simple basic concepts of what we do. Their first task then is to identify a prospect and/or that market in which they're willing to work, to create the client interest, the contact, and then bring that client to us whereby we will present the services that we offer to that client. It's not too much unlike what we did in the past, but it's reorganized in terms of a team concept.

I said to Jerry, "So the agent is out there giving a prospective client an awareness of the competencies of the organization and hoping to intrigue the prospect enough to let the agent bring in someone to demonstrate those competencies. Is that right?" He said:

> That's correct. The new producer is doing the client development work for the first several months while he's working with a more established supervisor-type producer and/or perhaps another personal producer in developing actual sales. The new producer would work with one or two or even three different experienced people while going through this first six months. We then tend to find people matching up. As they gain experience, they can perform each function. The experienced producer might very well be the prospector for awhile and the new producer can be the salesman or the closer for a period of time. But initially in the training process, our new producer is limited because of background and experience to some of the less technical parts of the sales process.

One unit of Legacy was called "Growing Vertically." As a guest on that unit we had the president of the Association for Advanced Underwriting, and a most outstanding personal producer, Mr. John R. Ryan. He said:

> It is my feeling that the best way to work smarter, not harder, is through joint practice. I am very fortunate to enjoy a very successful joint practice with a young man who came with me approximately 13 years ago. There is enough of an age spread between us, approximately 18 years, so our relationship is more the senior-junior partnership. I feel this business needs bright, well-educated young men to join us. To recruit these people, to induce people to come into the business, it is important to offer them proper training and a sophisticated method of operation. It seems to me that a young

man fresh out of college, 23, 24, 25 years old, is at a great disadvantage in going to the business or professional market and attempting to convince people making $50,000, $100,000, $200,000 a year that he could be their financial adviser and estate planner. I am convinced that to succeed, these young people must associate themselves with a mature agent who is doing a good job and who realizes the need for continuity in his operation.

In my particular instance, this young man came with me, and for the first year he did nothing but follow me around. I introduced him to all my clients. He sat in on all of my fact-finding interviews and my presentations. He was in effect my alter-ego. In this way he came to know my clients and my clients came to know him. He was able to observe me in action, my strengths and my weaknesses, and gradually he began to grow. Now we do very little work together. He has developed his own clientele and has taken over a number of my clients, freeing up my time to move into a more affluent market. He maintains a fine relationship with many of my clients and their children, continuing to serve this valuable business and write new business with these people and developing a clientele of his own. Four years ago my oldest son joined us and here again there was a proper age spread between the two of them. Jack is 10 years younger than Rick and is backfielding for both of us.

Martin Polhemus cites a dramatic example, and then offers himself as another:

Right now we're working on the concept of internships, joint work, and partnership team efforts. We're finding some very startling results. Two agents in our agency, neither of whom were able to earn more than about $5,000 a year a couple of years ago and were just failing, decided to pool their talents. Within a year and a half they were over $100,000 a year premium level, just because they complemented each other superbly. Each could do things and had talents that the other didn't have. And they were keen enough to perceive these and use them. We're seeing these things all over our agency. I use one (a partnership) with one of my own men who is a partner in all of my personal production. And I delegate to him the things he's good at and I go out on the things that I'm good at. Both of us have prospered as a result.

If agents would work with junior partners as they approach their peak and start to build teams, there would be a continuity of service provided to people. And this would help young men grow as they come into this business. We'd keep buyers from being left totally at sea. And we know that lapse rates increase when agents die or retire or get disabled or get shipped out to other agencies.

To me it is very significant that this section dealing with the agency head's training responsibilities should contain so many powerful testimonials to the importance and effectiveness of joint work as a training tool. After all, out of the 72 units of Legacy which were culled for this volume, there was no unit titled "Joint Work" or anything like it. Yet the references to it in this and other chapters attest most eloquently to the priority it deserves today in the plans of alert agency heads.

To wind up this section, let's summarize what has been said in the quotations cited. Joint work as a training tool is valuable to each of the following:

1. New agents

   • Through increased earnings, helped to survive
   • Can enter better markets sooner

- Learn sales skills faster
- Acquire technical expertise faster

2. Experienced agents

  - New markets opened by young associates
  - Stimulated and invigorated by energy of youth
  - Higher earnings; not just seeing old clients

3. Agency

  - More new business results
  - Better retention of new appointees
  - Lower management costs for supervisors and trainers
  - Better persistency (older agent won't permit low quality business)

4. Client

  - Better served, more expert counsel
  - More likely to be called on!
  - The ultimate service: more likely to be sold!

5. Company

  - Agency more likely to be profitable
  - Quantity and quality of business improved
  - Less turnover in agents, new and experienced

In summary, this whole chapter dealing with the training function is very appropriately titled "Grow or Die," for there is nothing static about successful agencies nor the world in which they exist today.

The significant trend that emerges in this area from not only the quotations offered here but also from so many in other chapters as well, is that:

> *Training will become a way of life as a variety of resources from within and outside the agency are used to facilitate the growth of its members.*

8 | 80-20 Isn't Good Enough

The Agency Head as a Marketer

> **SIGNIFICANT TREND:** As never before, a primary responsibility of the agency head is to facilitate and maximize the agent's presence before qualified, interested prospects.

One frequently quoted application of the 80-20 "rule" says that agents spend 80 percent of their time and efforts and energy in getting *to* their prospects, and no more than 20 percent in actual selling interviews *with* and in front of their prospects.

In Chapter Five, we dealt with the agency head's responsibilities as a business manager, and we saw that old standards of performance, such as app-a-week, just aren't good enough today. In fact, Frank Sullivan said, "Why not a sale a day?" His challenge is one that many would like to accept, but to do so with any marked degree of success means that a higher percentage of time must be spent in the selling mode.

And that, the agency heads quoted in this chapter reveal, is something that general agents and managers can and should do something about. When they put on their hats labeled "Marketing Manager," they are involved with one of their key responsibilities, one calling for creativity and imagination, often requiring a money investment, and always demanding continued attention and effort.

But the rewards are great. Recruiting is much easier when people can be helped into fruitful markets where they will work with prospects who are predisposed to talk with them. Agents sell more often when less of their time is spent finding those who are natural prospects for their services. Agents will stay with agencies that facilitate their frequent presence before such prospects on a prestigious basis.

In this chapter you will learn how agency heads with real

marketing savvy are helping their agents to knock the tar out of that 80-20 ratio!

Early in the Legacy series, guest expert Larry Wilson quoted the marketing specialist of New York City general agent Chuck Krasne as having defined a market as follows:

> "A market is a group of people, significantly small in number and significantly interrelated among themselves (that means exclusive of the agent), so that the agent can with time, effort, and planning build a reputation that will precede him or her on each and every call the agent makes."

In the pages that follow you will find a wide variety of marketing ideas and methods, as well as eloquent testimony to the necessity for continued attention to the marketing area, and specific examples of its dramatic effect on recruiting, on retention of agents, on productivity and profitability.

Gus Hansch stated the problem in very clear terms. Then he told how they are solving it:

> One of the present weights on the back of the life insurance man is the very nature of the fact that he sells a product that the other man doesn't want to talk about, to cover an eventuality he doesn't even want to contemplate, and to talk about taking money out of his money stream that he doesn't want to give up.

> So a long time ago I said, "I'm going to create a marketing plan that will get the other person, the person I select, to say, 'Hey, come tell me about it,' as opposed to selling a product which forces me to say, 'Would you please listen?' "

> What our system tries to do is exploit the strengths of each individual and get the good salesman to spend more of his time where he should spend it—

and that is talking to people he likes about things they like to talk about. That is success, not death; financial planning, rather than negative, downside, protection selling.

Our motto to our agents is, "Let us try to do for you anything that we can do better or cheaper or more efficiently than you can do." Most top-notch salesmen are terrible clerks, so we're trying to do more and more things for them—prospecting, mass marketing, follow through, case preparation —so they can spend their time where they're good, and that is in face-to-face sessions just the way you and I are now.

I think our experimentation has been very exciting in the field of seminars. Our seminars today are usually based on homogeneous groupings of people. Once we tell the story of diagnostic financial planning, and we do it completely, then it's very simple to pass out to the audience the simple form on which we have listed tax-oriented methods of buying life insurance. And some of our seminar leaders have gotten as much as 90 percent of the audience to say, in effect, "Hey, come see me and tell me about the following tax-oriented methods of buying life insurance." It's quite exciting.

A marketing concept I'm very proud of is one we call "space satellites." We have all these specialists housed in our main office at 5900 Wilshire Boulevard. In any high-rise apartment, whether in Grand Rapids or Chicago, in the very center of the high-rise is the service core. It's where the center goes up, the elevators go up, the mail goes down, and the gas is there. A lot of the high-rise building is allocated to the service. So our service core is our main office at 5900 Wilshire where our specialists, with their gray suits and their eyeglasses and pipes, sit waiting to be called into action.

Well, just like the high-rise building, we have lines going out to Riverside, Newport Beach, Tustin, and all the smaller cities (some are pretty large) in Southern California. And those are the satellite organizations. And we can bring this idea of a collective strong counseling arm to a small city out near Palm Springs by having one good man out there spending all his time selling, clear through that oxygen line to 5900 Wilshire Boulevard. He gets all of the brains and research that he requires through computers. He looks so good out there in the smaller town that he writes an inordinately larger amount of insurance than I think he would if he were right downtown in the midst of competition.

So, as a marketing agent, the financial advisory council started spreading rather rapidly as we had access to other territories. We now have 17 districts. I'd love to have 54 districts, because the specialists have a bad habit of sitting there smoking their pipes when they're not being used, and their down time costs money.

Bill Wallace, in the first volume of Legacy, made a major contribution to the literature on Marketing. Here is a quotation from that interview:

The tighter the market is (and by that I mean that the people in it share something in common; they have a common employer; they're in a common profession; they've had common training; common background; they come in contact with each other frequently; they have a common standard of living; they may have the same employee benefits as the result of having a common employer), the easier it is to apply the experience and knowledge you gain in working with one, to the other. And your reputation, if you really do a good job and build it, is being passed along among the whole group.

As you think about developing markets, don't overlook the impact this is going to have on recruiting. We have hired some good men who were turned down by other agencies because they didn't have a market. I'm interested in the man more than the market. I think a market can be developed.

Robert A. Szeyller defined marketing and its responsibilities this way:

What marketing means is developing a plan of who we're going to try to sell in the future, who it is we're going to try to approach. Once you've done that you're going to have to find out about all the necessary services, functions, products, items to handle that marketplace. You've got to develop those either by having them in-house in the agency or making some kind of an arrangement outside of the agency, so that you can control those marketplaces. Beyond that you've got to have agents who are trained to operate in that marketplace.

The following paragraph from Aldin Porter says much about the rewards for good marketing, provides a caveat for those who undertake to serve markets, and makes the prediction that life insurance people need not be too concerned about competition from outside the industry if they serve their markets well:

Agencies that identify markets and assist individuals in serving the market will retain field underwriters and will get an increasing share of the market—but they better know the market. By that I don't mean just the problems that fit it, I mean the problems that are developed in that market— the people, what their cash flow is, where their money comes from, how that is impacted by the events outside the market we're dealing with—and then of course applying our products to solving the problems in that market. I do not see a major prob-

lem in those outside our industry seeking to become life insurance people. I think it's too hard to
be good at our business for them to be good at their
business and take on ours as well.

Gordon Stovel in Mississauga, Ontario, a bedroom community outside Toronto, did a great job of planning what
kind of market his branch, his agency, should serve. When he
first became manager there, he was trying to decide in what
direction the agency was going to go and what markets they
were going to pursue when a representative from Dun and
Bradstreet called to present their sales lead service. Gordon
said:

> I asked him if through their sales lead service and
> their computers they could define for me approx-
> imately how many small closely held corporations
> there were in our specific geographical area, espe-
> cially companies employing less than 20 people
> where the president was a resident and they were
> not wholly owned subsidiaries of foreign multina-
> tionals or had any other corporate ties. We wanted
> the person that we would be talking to to have
> decision-making powers and responsibilities. He
> said that he'd get back to me on that. He did and I
> learned that within a 10-mile radius of our office,
> there were 17,000 of those businesses. So we took it
> upon ourselves to try to do everything that we
> could within the agency to aim our associates at
> that marketing opportunity. We developed a list of
> things that we perceived to be the agency challenges
> of the '80s and we've tried to match those chal-
> lenges with the marketing plans, the organizational
> structure, the support systems, the products,
> everything to capture the opportunity of those
> challenges.

I asked Gordon to tell me about those challenges:

> We think that most agents want to be associated

with an organization that has marketing direction linked to opportunities that they couldn't get anywhere else, an organization that assists them in creating credibility in the marketplace. Lots of agents go out in the marketplace on a day-by-day basis solely responsible for any credibility that they're going to capitalize on. We think that if we can get the agency assisting in that, it's going to be far more effective. We want to try and create for our associates literally an unlimited supply of prospects, because we view prospecting as being the agent's biggest problem and also his biggest concern. I'm not sure where I picked up the statistic, but I understand most agents spend about 80 percent of their time, their physical mental effort, just trying to get themselves in front of a good prospect and into a favorable situation. That tells me they've only got 20 percent left to earn 100 percent of their money. If we can somehow change that 20 percent to 30 or 40 or even 60 percent, I think the opportunities are truly unlimited.

To do that we've tried to help him create support services that help him operate in what some people perceive to be a very sophisticated marketplace. We've also been working hard to get the agent to work what he perceives as being normal business hours. I believe in family time, and I know my associates feel exactly the same way. If they can be just as effective, or more so, working between 8:00 in the morning and 6:00 at night, that's very attractive to us. And because of dramatic increases in operating costs, we simply have to get the agent working on a much higher productivity level or we and the company simply can't support him in the manner in which he has to be supported.

These are the challenges we see in the '80s, and the market plan that we've put together is designed to capture the opportunities and those challenges.

Gordon indicated that they have a small group package that has the endorsement of the Chamber of Commerce, but then he told why he feels, with Gus Hansch (and others whose testimony will follow in this chapter), that seminar marketing is so effective:

I don't think over the long-term the group package is that necessary. I think more it's how you can position your organization with respect to the target market you're going after. And what's the most effective method of getting to that target market. I believe seminar marketing's time has come. It works extremely well. For every seminar we've put on over the last three years, we can clearly identify the minimum of three million of new business that has been generated from each seminar. If we didn't have the group product, maybe it would be a little bit more difficult to get the seminars rolling, but once they're rolling, away you go. It's just a way to position the agent so that when he walks through the door with a seminar questionnaire, for example, the client knows he's coming. He's answered a questionnaire. He's been to the seminar. He knows what you're talking about. You can sit down and get right to the task. When we get to the conclusion of the seminar, out goes the questionnaire. It has a complete list of all the subjects covered. It's an attitude-type questionnaire. How do you feel on a scale of 1 to 9 towards this, that, and the other thing? Interestingly, we've discovered that if you give a group of people, 20 or 30 people, the questionnaire, probably only four of them won't do it and the rest of them will. They've given us some good input on what we're doing right at the seminars, what we're doing wrong, how they should be changed. And they also give us tremendous input into what it is they want to talk to us about. We've added a question at the bottom of the questionnaire just this past year. The question says, "Would you like an appointment with our firm, yes or no.'' And 80 percent of the people that fill in the questionnaire indicate that they want us to give them a call, so we simply turn it over to the agent. Our scheduling coordinator books the appointment for the agent and in he goes.

When I reviewed these words from Elliot Rothstein, I found myself thinking what a great job institutions such as banks and brokerage houses are doing, via ads in print and on television, of telling the public it needs financial planning —and how the competent life underwriter is the best-equipped to provide that service! Others are helping to prepare the market for alert life insurance people. Elliot said:

The world is crying out for people to come out and do financial planning. The public doesn't know where to go. The public is confused by product salesmen. It's being hit hard daily by people selling different products. They want somebody who's professional, somebody who's accepted as a professional, from whom they can get the proper advice. The industry is putting itself together now. They're setting high standards of professionalism and conveying them to the public. The CLU is long standing and now comes Chartered Financial Consultant. There are other outside groups. Certified Financial Planners and others will be coming. Whom will the public turn to to get the highly desired financial planning service? The accountant? Is he the one to do the financial planning? Probably not. Is it the typical lawyer? I don't think so. How about the man at the bank? Have you ever gone into the bank to ask a question about insurance? There is only one highly trained cohesive sales force that is already in place ready to do this business. There is only one sales force that knows how to go out and collect information on a professional basis, do the fact-finding, all of the building of the needs, and then be able to evaluate them in the light of current tax laws, current financial trends, and then plug in the proper financial products. That's the sales force in the really professional life insurance companies. I think that's where we are today.

Charlie Drimal in New York is recognized as one of the pioneers in the full services financial planning concept. He says:

Offering these other products, the fact that there's an opportunity to save on taxes and to build for the future, gives the agent a great door opener. From there on it's all downhill. Because once this person will buy a shelter of any kind, the agent can take it from there and say there are other services I can now offer to help build your security picture. Life insurance sales are made a lot easier by that method.

We asked him for an example. He said:

We have an orthopedic surgeon 68 years old who never bought insurance from our company. I could never sell him. He was a personal friend. The bottom line is my son went out to see him on a tax shelter using real estate. As a result, he bought the real estate shelter from us. He started to ask other questions. We did a study for him, an estate planning study. He ended up putting away $60,000 in life premiums on an annual basis. Secondly, we obtained a pension plan at the hospital he was president of as well as group insurance. And he has since bought a number of other products from us. All this was a result of first selling the tax-oriented investments and then the life insurance. The key to this is making the parties involved aware that life insurance is our primary goal. And the bottom line is that most of our agents' (including my own) income is about 80/20 from this source—20 percent from the tax-oriented investments and 80 percent from insurance.

Being market conscious can mean sensitivity on the part of both companies and their field forces to changes in the economy and/or legislation and their impact. Burt Herman gave examples:

> Social, economic, and governmental changes impact upon product design. Joint mortgage policies and other plans insuring both the husband and wife accelerated as more wives entered the workforce. High interest rates and inflation brought down rates and forced new current interest yield plans. One example directly related to the Economic Recovery Tax Act is a new phenomenon called the "last to die" policy used for estate-planning purposes. Another example of legislative change and industry reaction and adaptability is the new IRA. Twenty percent of all the applications in my agency in the first quarter of this year were IRAs. We didn't have that a year ago.

Several of our distinguished interviewees have added a property-casualty agency to their total operation. Examples include Ed Haldeman, Bob Szeyller, Charlie Drimal, Ted Santon, and many others, including Jerry Gaultney. Here is how Jerry rationalizes this development in terms of market control:

> Our rationale is that if we're going to be providing total financial service, we must indeed provide all of that financial service, of which property and casualty is included. Furthermore, from a defensive standpoint, property and casualty people are becoming very sophisticated also. They're expanding into financial services and into life insurance and into employee benefits. Many of them have a full-blown life insurance operation. And they're very good, we find. So if we leave ourselves or our clients exposed in that area, we open the door for the property and casualty producer to come in and do business with our client, which we prefer not to

do. So property and casualty is another major part
of our work.

Now let's look at some further testimony to the nature and
value of seminars as a marketing method. Ted Santon and
Bob Szeyller's quotations precede detailed explanations by
Wayne Swenson and Dan Anderson. This is Ted's observation:

> As an example, we have an advanced underwriting
> specialist, a lawyer. We sell him. We arrange
> seminars. We send out mailings on a particular
> subject to policyholders as well as to prospects, giv-
> ing the background of our person who will run the
> seminar that day. They are well attended—about
> 40 people at a time. At the end of the session we
> always give them a form to fill out and have them
> send it back to us, and that's worked out very well.

Bob Szeyller's agency averages more than one seminar per
week:

> What seminar selling is to us is really a way for the
> agent to be more efficient. A seminar is an open in-
> terview. When you have 15 or 25 prospects sitting
> there listening to your open interview and you pro-
> ceed only with those who are truly interested in
> whatever subject you're discussing, it's bound to
> make you more efficient. Last year we did 52
> seminars, and we hope to do more than that this
> year.

Wayne Swenson and Dan Anderson were recruited by Clair
Strommen and later succeeded him as co-general agents.
When we asked them what marketing meant to them, Wayne
replied like this:

> When you ask that, I can't help but think of a pic-
> ture we show our new agents depicting a grouchy
> man sitting in a chair. As he's glaring at you he

says, "I don't know who you are, I don't know your company, I don't know your company's product, I don't know what your company stands for, I don't know your company's reputation. Now what was it you wanted to sell me?" I guess dealing with this fellow's concern would be marketing. Actually a big part of marketing is getting in front of people to get a chance to explain what it is that we want to market, and that's really prospecting. We think a good prospecting/marketing game plan should have these qualifications (they're kind of etched in stone in our agency):

1. We try to have people maximize acceptance and minimize rejection. Instead of telling an agent to make more phone calls and then have them eaten up by the rejection process that they're bound to get, we try to make prospecting a pleasant experience.

2. We hope to take people from a "don't know" to a "do know." If you're talking to someone who knows you, it's a lot easier than a cold telephone call.

3. We try to raise the economic level of our prospects and we believe that that is very do-able.

4. We try to see people under favorable circumstances. We mean by that that we like to have all of our interviews on our home court. In our office. No TV, no kids, dogs, cats, phones, kitchen tables, and all those other things that tend to complicate the whole process.

5. Whenever it's possible, we like to see more than one prospect at a time.

Wayne described the travail he went through working the

college market one-on-one, making 30 phone calls on Monday night and getting, of course, lots of rejection. And Dan Anderson figured there must be a better way. Dan said:

> Our solution to our problem at that time was to identify a small town close to the Twin Cities where we operate. We went out of the cities because we felt there'd be less expertise available in that area and we'd have more receptiveness to what we were going to discuss. We drew a circle on the map and got the phone books for all of the towns within a 50-mile radius of this small town, and we invited all the doctors, dentists, attorneys, accountants, optometrists, veterinarians, basically all the self-employed professional people in this radius to a seminar on the topic of incentives for professionals to incorporate. At that time this was a real hot topic. All of them were anxious for information about this subject and were really looking for anybody who could give them some answers on whether it would or would not work. As a result of this, out of 300 people we invited, we got 30 of them to respond and say, "Yes, I'm interested in information on that topic." Either they said, "I'll attend your seminar," or, "I'm interested but I can't attend." We gave them either option on the form. And out of those 30, about 20 came. We had very, very good results following up on all these people as prospects later on. They in effect had taken one step forward out of a group of 300 and said, "I'm interested in information on this topic."

Next we started putting on seminars in the medical school fraternities. And instead of writing 10s and 15s back in those days, we started writing 50s and 100s and our perception of the whole business changed overnight. All of a sudden it was a fun business to be in and it was seeing these people on a favorable basis without having to make those telephone calls. And then we moved on to the hospital community and pretty soon we were making the circuit there. And from there we moved on into corporations. We've literally done this hundreds of times.

Wayne told how they have refined and extended their seminar marketing:

We've changed our philosophy now so that we go to groups that have regularly scheduled meetings and we try to have that third party sponsorship. In other words, we have a captive audience. We use their letterhead and their chief person signs the letter. Obviously if you receive a letter from me and you are a doctor at a hospital, for example, I can pretty much predict where that letter will end up, but if you get a letter from the chief of staff, or the hospital administrator inviting you to a seminar, the chances are pretty good that you will attend. That's one of our major rules. Second, we've said that we will not sell products for companies. People do not want to feel they're going to be harassed and salesmen are going to be coming out of the walls and trying to get them to buy something that very night. So we've made that commitment. Thirdly, we won't follow up with anybody in attendance unless they ask us to. And the vehicle we've used to establish that is a questionnaire that we've developed to hand out to the audience. We tell them that they can use it anyway they see fit. The seminars themselves deal with financial problems that are basic to all of us, such topics as inflation, income taxes, estate taxes, loss of earning power through death, disability, retirement, accumulating money, very basic things. And then we try to come back and show some conceptual ways to minimize, reduce, or eliminate those problems in our seminar. It's not so much an attempt to educate as it is to tantalize people or make them realize they haven't done quite the job that they probably should have been doing.

Another joint interview was with two Californians, Messrs. David White and Howard Nevonen. We also asked them for a definition of marketing. Howard said:

> For the life insurance business it might be a plan or a system to enable agents to have a satisfactory number of interviews with prospects who have some common denominator of occupational activity.

Dave was invited to add to that and he said:

> The other dimension of it, as we see it, is that if we can put an agent, through daytime activity, in front of business and professional people who have a commonality of need and to whom he has an ease of entree, it seems to me we've got a great deal to do with not only marketing, but with a positive morale effect on our associate.

Dave White explained that they marketed through associations and professional groups and went on to add:

> If an agent were simply to open up the Yellow Pages of his telephone book, he'd probably find an incredible number of associations who may have a need for one or more products or services which are in his particular area of expertise or which his carrier may represent.

He shared the kind of telephone approach one of his people might make to a member of an association. He said it went something along these lines:

> "Mr. Turner, our firm handles the ABC Association's group insurance program. And as a member of the ABC Association, you're entitled to certain benefits. My responsibility is to explain those to you. Would a morning or afternoon appointment be best?" So we've got the ease of entree through the association sponsorship. And then we meet

with the people on a one-on-one basis. At this point we do fact-finding to first of all determine whether the individual is a prospect for his association-sponsored program. And then through the relationship building and the vertical growth of that associate, we keep in touch with the individual to see what other needs he or she may have with respect to insurance and/or financial planning. In fact in the Oakland agency last year, about 70 percent of our life insurance business emanated from this source. Over 90 percent of our corporate pension and profit-sharing plans did so as well.

Howard Nevonen pointed out the following:

One of the great advantages I see is for the new agent, who can obtain interviews without the prospect being aware of his lack of experience. The typical new agent in the typical situation is asked to go out and call on his friends and relatives, and I'm not against that system. However, they know that perhaps he's been in the business for a few weeks or months and so he doesn't have any prestige with them. In our system we can give him some adequate training, place him out there in the marketplace with strangers, and they don't know but what he's been in the business for years. With any type of maturity they think he's a real professional.

We asked Mr. Nevonen how they went about selling associations in the first place, and what advantages there might be for the association. This was how he responded:

A typical association is not unlike a life underwriters association. We have membership problems, we need tangible things for our membership, we need good programs. I won't take you through all of that. We'll average probably close to a 20 percent turnover nationally for a variety of reasons. Most trade associations, whether business or professional, have similar problems. They want to offer tangible services. They want to have things that can appeal to the membership. They'd like to have qualified people going out and calling on their membership. It's one thing to control a membership with 25 or 30 people, but when you have a trade association that runs in the thousands, the leadership just never gets down to the common man and vice versa, the common man never gets up to the leadership. We offer a system whereby the word of that association, the things that are going on, the representation can be placed at the doorstep of that member, and he'll realize his association is trying to do something for him that he might not necessarily read in the bulletins.

We asked Howard what he might say to an association secretary, and to pretend that Dave was such a secretary. The following dialogue took place:

"Dave, would you like more personal contact with your members?"

"Certainly."

"Would you like to have a well-qualified representative going out to your association members discussing with them a service that was to be provided by the association that you endorsed and one for which they had a great need?"

"Well, what's the cost of it, Howard?"

"The cost would be your promotional activity. We will place a well-trained representative at the doorstep of each one of your members and potential new members explaining this service. . . ."

We asked them what level of activity was par for the course:

We have the same problems that anybody has with

> respect to finding people in. Here are some of the statistics we've experienced. We have to dial about two and one-half times to reach one individual. And we know that if we make 10 phone contacts a day (and we define a phone contact as actually reaching an individual), then we will experience three appointments. And if we have 15 appointments in a week and we see 12 people, our representative is going to end up with three or four applications.

No treatment of marketing should fail to include an area that Jerry Gaultney mentioned when he spoke of having property-casualty as a defense mechanism against the property-casualty agencies' entry into the life insurance business. Jerry Burns in New Orleans has the job of helping independent property-casualty agencies do just that (get into the selling of life insurance) through the services of his multiple-line company.

Mr. Burns described a marketing system for working with the independent property-casualty agents in which he recruited inexperienced people to his staff who, after a good two years of training and selling through property-casualty agencies, were made full-fledged staff members to work with independent property-casualty agents. They might have 35 or 40 such agents assigned to them but their objective was to get five to eight, or at most 10, of what they called "target agencies" with whom they would work quite intensively, and then be "on call" for the others.

At the time we interviewed Art Goldblum in Houston, his agency had just had its fourth consecutive "Rookie of the Year" in his company. This young man had worked as an "interne" in the agency and then started as an agent upon graduation. We asked Art to tell us about him. This was his reply (and a fervent testimonial to target marketing):

> He works an intensive five-day week. He studies what we give him. He uses all of the books. He

restricts his market to dentists, dentists, dentists—their needs and their colleagues' needs. He knows everybody; he knows who everybody's alumni buddy is, when they graduated, what their families are like, who they married from the graduating class. He knows where they're living. He knows how many children they have. He knows who's set up practice and who's practicing jointly with whom and where there's an open job. And he's equipped himself to do that in a period of four years. He is also aware of all the legislation that affects the practice of dentistry. He has practiced management and so he understands staff development. How do you find and train a dental assistant? He knows the terms of chair-side assistants. He knows the terms of collection assistants. He knows the function of the appointments girl in every office. He knows the systems—managing cash receivables, collections. He has also made good contacts with layout and design people in that field and he understands the cash flow problems with managing a double practice. If I were to be asked, I would tell a young dentist who has him as his financial and insurance adviser that he is going to get a five-year experience leap in the practice of his own profession. That's how good that young man is. Now if you ask him something about selling engineers, I don't think he could help you. If you asked him about the family market, he couldn't help you. But try him on dentists and he can help the dentist. I think that's how you make a rookie of the year. It's called commitment, intelligence, hard work, and desire. And if you start with a good man, you'll end up with a better man. The old style of recruiting a man into a Project 100 made the presumption that you worked off a natural market and radiated out from there.

The public today demands impartial, objective information. They're reading consumer reports, they don't necessarily accept friendship as sincerity, and because of the mobility of society today, very few people are living where they were born. So the way to organize a marketing effort or build a man in the market is perhaps to start with a market and then let the man grow into that and practice the development of the man as it pertains to a specific calling.

As I reviewed my interview with Art Goldblum, I couldn't help but contrast it with what Auburn Lambeth in Mississippi had said.

Art spoke of the mobility of modern society, and Houston may be the best example in the country. But Auburn wants his recruits to be native to the Mississippi communities in which they work and to have been well-known and respected there before coming into the life insurance business. Each is right for his situation. Perhaps statesman Walt Shields puts it all in perspective. Here is what he said when asked how an agency head should determine the best markets for his agency:

My own thinking is that the agency head should first of all make his own definition of a market. At a LAMP meeting one time, someone once said that a market is a group of persons significantly small in number but highly interrelated where the agent is not the connecting link among those persons. I suppose if you were to draw a profile of the primary market of this agency, it would be small business owners and professional persons. That is not to say we don't have people who are employees of corporations or people in other special markets. It seems to me that there are a couple of ways you can approach this marketing thing. We can take an idea or a concept and go find people that fit it, or we can find people and analyze their particular situation and then recommend an idea or concept to them. I think both are equally successful. One of the great things about our industry is that a person coming into it or an established agent can go either

way. Some of our agents would deem it almost un-
professional to take an idea like nonqualified
deferred compensation and take that idea around
to heads of companies and determine whether they
were interested. Other agents we have would do exactly that. So you have almost a two-pronged approach to marketing: the idea of taking an idea or
concept and finding people that might be interested
in it or, conversely, taking what is more commonly
known as a more professional approach, sitting
down and gathering the facts (we call it data) and
determining what the needs of that individual and
his company might be and then moving on from
there to make a recommendation on an idea such
as a pension plan, deferred compensation, split
dollar, what have you.

Once upon a time life insurance companies' products influenced their markets only in very limited degree, e.g., weekly
premium or industrial insurance was for the lower-income
market and "ordinary" insurance was for everyone else.
Target markets were more likely to be a function of training
methods and the kinds of recruits selected. Today, however,
companies' decisions about the markets they prefer are re-
flected in their products. Burt Herman not only has 40 career
agents, but he also has some 2,000 brokers, so he is very sensitive to developments in this area. We asked him about what
market segments he felt companies might address in the
future. He said:

Well, for example, there would be those companies
that I'm sure will continue to concentrate on the
high income business or professional prospect. In
doing so they will provide sophisticated life policies
and concepts as well as the financial services products to address that marketplace. And there are
those companies that will go out to the middle-
income market, and will develop the multiple-line
approach to reach their perceived customers.

PUBLIC RELATIONS AND MARKETING

Only a relatively small number of Legacy of Learning interviews dealt with the public relations aspects of the agency head's job. But the observations made by the eight worthies about to be quoted will readily be recognized as being rightfully included in this chapter on marketing.

After all, the objectives of good "PR" for a life insurance agency are not to glorify the company; they are not to make the agency head's ego happy. No, the purpose of public relations at the agency level relates to the agent in the same way that other aspects of marketing do: to help the agent more readily and effectively get before good prospects under optimal circumstances.

That's why Irving Abramowitz said:

We give our people ads in local weekly newspapers.

It is also why John R. Driskill of the American Society of Chartered Life Underwriters said:

I think sometimes we forget that public relations is a part of every agency development operational plan. We get so involved in recruiting and working on retention figures, productivity figures, and trying to establish the professional qualifications of our agents and agency, that we often forget that we need to have a planned ongoing program of telling this story about this agency through the various audiences and publics that we are responsible to and work with.

Steve Nager described what he called his "advisers" as being 36 leading attorneys and CPAs in Phoenix who have been responsible for many referrals not only of clients but of prospective agents as well. He said:

I have a system of sending out current best-sellers

through the company to these advisers. That's just a little four-times-a-year gentle reminder that we are very active in seeking their auspices in growing.

I asked him what he meant by best-sellers. He said:

Current best-selling novels—hardcover fiction and nonfiction. They always manage to call me and thank me and I always remind them of the purpose of my having sent that book to them. Every time we deliver a change in our process, which is frequent these days, or bring out a new product, we structure a meeting and invite this corps of advisers. So it keeps us current with them and it keeps them current with us.

Vince Ruffalo defined public relations this way:

A conscious effort to provide an image that presents the agency as one with professionalism, integrity, high performance, and competence.

When I walked into Ed Nadel's agency in New York City, there was my name up on the Welcome Board. His secretary took me immediately to a lovely parlor, explaining that Ed was tied up for a minute or two. She invited me to use the telephone while waiting. I gained an impression, before I even met Ed, that here was an agency of substance, of sincere friendliness, and of what the man on the street calls "class."

Ed does a whale of a lot of cooperative (cost-shared) advertising with his agents. About that area he said:

Every time an agent wants to do something like that, I like to help him do it. The more successful my agents are, the more successful I am.

Tony Lawes cited the importance of the office situation on both public relations and agency morale when he said:

Pick your place where you want to do business. I believe the kind of offices can help retention, too. It's a good environment where they're getting good support and are surrounded by people they're proud to be associated with. They're in a total ecology where an office looks good and feels good. And I'm a great believer in good janitors. It's essential that our place is kept clean. We spend a lot of money in just having carpets cleaned, but it has paid off handsomely.

We're right in the downtown area, and we get a lot of people who come to us. We emphasize to our new associates that we want them to bring their clients in. That's worked out very well, and some six years later we are still getting compliments on our office space.

The emphasis in this chapter has been on presenting the agency head's marketing responsibility as being dedicated to helping agents find and more readily do business with quality prospects. We said the purpose was not to exalt the agency head or the company.

But perhaps that thought should be modified a bit. Agents do like to have the agency (including its head) well-regarded in the community, and they do like their company name to be familiar to those on whom they call. And, as indicated, recruiting and retention are also affected. Ralph Brown offers concrete evidence:

The agency has gotten to a size where I need to be able to delegate some of the responsibilities to someone else so that I will have more time for the recruiting and selection phase and also for building the agency's image within the community. The importance of building the agency's image within the community comes home to you when somebody outside of the agency refers a young man or woman to you who is interested in the insurance business. This has happened several times in the last two years.

Perhaps no agency can serve as a better example of the power of effective public relations in expediting the marketing success of the agency and its producers than the agency headed by Austin Rinne in Dallas. When Mr. Rinne arrived there to start his scratch agency, his company had not been represented in the community for more than 50 years. In those days, going into Texas with a northern, midwestern company presented him with a real public relations challenge. His outstanding results speak volumes about how he met that challenge, and help to explain why he is quoted so liberally in the balance of this section. He mentioned participation of his people in industry affairs:

> I think it's important for the general agent or manager to support his local association of life underwriters, pushing for 100 percent membership in the local association and also a sponsorship of the LUPAC program. We were acknowledged as a 100 percent agency in LUPAC by the Texas Association of Life Underwriters and also we receive the 100 percent membership award presented by TALU for actual membership in the association. We've received that award every year since it's been given.

I asked him what all that really meant to him. He said:

> I guess it means our agents are acknowledged as professionals by their peers and through their membership in these organizations. So that makes them more effective in a subliminal way in their sales efforts. Also they are demonstrating leadership in those organizations through holding important offices in them. We encourage our agents to get the CLU designation and qualify for the Million Dollar Round Table. We now have 22 who are qualifying

or provisional applicants. There's a certain amount of peer pressure in the agency to qualify for the Table in order to be accepted as successful. MDRT qualification and CLU attainment naturally reflect in a very positive way from the public relations point of view. We have the pictures of our life and qualifying members of the MDRT in the lobby of the general agency office. Those who have yet to qualify see these pictures daily, and the visual form of recognition they see in these beautiful framed portraits makes them want to have their picture up there for their clients and friends to see.

Mr. Rinne pointed out that there are significant ways in which companies can contribute to meeting the public relations responsibility. He said:

It should be borne out in more than just the advertising program. It should be borne out in how the company conducts its business. The basic philosophy of the company is illustrated by its conduct. And the nature of the company's support of the industry such as sponsorship of the CLU, the Million Dollar Round Table, along with the National Quality Award and LUTC, National Sales Achievement Award, and other worthwhile agent attainment objectives all contribute to the public relations performance of the company. I believe the company must be a good citizen, not only in its Home Office community, but also in the national scene. We see a lot of companies support proposed responsible legislation which will affect policyowners as well as companies. Letting the public know of this sense of responsibility through news stories, political action committees, including LUPAC, are of prime importance for opening doors for our agents as good citizen representatives. This helps tremendously in the sales effort, although indirectly. And in an even more remote way possibly, the matching gifts program of colleges and universities that our company sponsors for all agents and Home Office personnel continues to promote that good citizen image.

We asked Mr. Rinne how much of his budget he felt an agency head should set aside for the public relations area. He said:

> In the beginning it wasn't this much, but today we are committing about eight percent of budget to our public relations and advertising program. It's about $30,000 a year, and I think it's played a significant role in our agency's present position in production.

Mr. Rinne also said that an attractive agent's office contributes to the reception by the agent's clientele. He said:

> In order to encourage our agents to furnish their own offices, we offer them a starter basic furniture allowance which we want them to match or exceed, preferably exceed, in providing basics. Some of our associates are doing a beautiful job of creating a very professional yet inviting business atmosphere into which they can invite prospective buyers and clients. The newer agents' offices are not quite as plush, but they are welcome to use our nicely furnished agency conference room for interviews. Our reception area presents a very professional image. It was designed by one of the leading interior designers in the southwest. We also have a neat menu board welcome sign out in the lobby in which we place the names of agency visitors, including prospective agents and prospects.
>
> After a couple of years of relative anonymity in the community, we finally evaluated our total agency image problem and concluded that we needed to develop our PR around the quality concept of our company and also that our PR would be as supportive as possible of our agents collectively and in-

dividually. We determined that the least expensive way in dollars and cents to build the agency image was to capitalize on our local strengths and promote the identification of our associates. I would send in news stories to the papers on every occasion on behalf of agents who had achieved an honor or given a speech in the industry or out of the industry, and made it a point to know the press people personally in Dallas. And it has helped our success in getting stories and plugs for our agency and agents into well-read columns. I joined the Dallas Press Club so I could be better known by the people in the news media. But most business stories today must be accompanied by a substantial ad or there's no assurance of publication. We developed a program of ads which featured individual agents which we called our "Portrait of a Professional" series. This was not only well received by the public, but also by our agents who were most enthusiastic about the support. We now publish an ad in the centerfold of *Scene* magazine in the Sunday edition of the Dallas Morning News the last Sunday of each year. This features all of our agents and has a capsule biography of each, noting any honors such as CLU, MDRT, NQA, NSAA, plus his or her educational background. It also notes their civic endeavors and hobbies and a bit about family in each instance, and this has a humanizing and personalizing effect. It also talks about our record and the quality individuals in the agency, and we use it as a recruiting tool in lieu of publishing a brochure about the agency which is soon out of date. We know that we will have an up-to-date brochure in the reprints of this ad which we get from the newspaper.

While still working on this book I received my highly valued copy of the magnificent volume *Managing Sales Professionals,* published by The American College as a joint project of GAMC and The College. In it there is a chapter entitled "Agency Management and Social Responsibility," written by Robert W. Verhille.

Somehow, and quite inexplicably, I never had the opportunity to interview Bob Verhille for the Legacy of Learning series. Included in that superb chapter by this industry statesman was this paragraph that clearly describes the vital role of the agency head in the very area we've been considering:

> The general agent or manager must assume the responsibility of maintaining the image of the industry within the community. Managers establish the image of the insurance companies represented by the agency and also of the agents and associates marketing their products and services. In the eyes of the entire community, the manager represents all facets of the industry and is in a position to create favorable responses in the agency's marketplace.

In winding up this chapter, I found myself remembering that over the years I've said that "you could drop a good life insurance agent by parachute into any city in the country, and before long that agent could be making a good living!"

I still believe that. But if such an agent is really smart, he or she will look for an agency in that city that is marketing-oriented, one that can expedite the agent's entry into fruitful markets whose members will not be antagonists with whom to spar, but people who will look forward to being understood and helped with their financial plans and problems. Such an agent will not be satisfied with spending 80 percent of working hours in looking for opportunities to really be productive. For him or her, "80-20 Isn't Good Enough!"

This chapter, then, reminds us of the significant trend:

> *As never before, a primary responsibility of the agency head is to facilitate and maximize the agent's presence before qualified, interested prospects.*

9 | Don't Tell Me How You Did It— Show Me How To Do It!

The Agency Head as a Salesperson

> **SIGNIFICANT TREND:** To obtain and retain the regard and continued loyalty of quality associates, agency heads will have to keep pace with the marketplace and its developments.

This very short but important chapter might well have been included with the preceding chapter that dealt with the agency head and the marketing function. It is being presented separately, however, with the intention and expectation that it will encourage the reader to give serious consideration to the value and importance to the agency of the agency head's providing leadership by example in the role of salesperson.

While some companies do not permit their field management people to do personal production, among those who do allow it, a somewhat surprising number of the successful managers and general agents interviewed for the Legacy of Learning series turned out to be very big personal producers as well as outstanding agency builders. Just a few of the names that come readily to mind are those of Sidney De Young, Jack Skalla, Norman Levine, Elton Brooks, Glenn Martin, Nick Zervos, and Bob Meeker.

We have used analogies that liken the agency head to a coach of an athletic team. This is not trying to suggest that Bobby Knight, in order to be an effective coach of the United States basketball team, needed to be a better player than his athletes. But the players, like agents, need the faith and conviction that the strategies and tactics being taught them are the right ones for the situation. They get that confidence either by seeing others succeed by following the same leadership or by experiencing its validity themselves. Every time the coach's strategy works, the confidence of his people is enhanced for the next occasion.

In a CPA firm the senior partner would be expected to

cope with the toughest problems his associates might encounter. The senior partner of the law firm deals with its leading clients when the matter is important.

Agents know they must make their living in an environment different in many aspects from the one their manager experienced when entering the business. They need to know that the products, training, sales procedures provided will work in today's markets. They need models to follow; examples to emulate. If they can't find them there, they will look elsewhere. If the agency head can't, or chooses not to be that model, the agent must fill that need in other ways.

When I interviewed Glenn Martin in Orlando in late 1981, his personal production for the two prior calendar years had averaged a million dollars of premiums and fifty million of volume, and his 1981 pace was way ahead of those. I asked him to tell me about that. He said:

> The greatest revelation to me in management came from going back into personal production. I had sold personally from '66 to '70, had done some substantial production in those days, and decided to go into agency managing. I hired a few people and from '70 to '73 I devoted most of my attention to recruiting and training and personal selling. In '73 I made the "great discovery" that I needed to be totally agency management. I decided I was going to be an agency head and that's all. I was going to refer business to agents. I was going to do all those great and grand things. Well, from '73 to '78 I got out of the life insurance business and didn't realize it. I became an administrator. I became out of contact with people. I didn't really recognize the problems that agents were having. I'd say, "No, that's not the way you solve the problem. Here's how I did it in 1971." They'd say, "Who cares about 1971?"

> So in '77 I made a decision that I was going to get back into personal production just for the fun

of it. I enjoyed it a lot; I liked selling. I was not a big advocate of going out and making calls with agents. That was not my thing. I didn't enjoy going out because I couldn't keep quiet, I couldn't stay still. I'd try to make the sale. That was not teaching agents how to sell life insurance, it was teaching myself how to do it. Fortunately, I had several people in the agency in management positions who were excellent at it, and they went out and worked real well for me. So I started spending a little more time back in personal production. All of a sudden I was saying, "My goodness, it has changed!" I'd been saying things that just weren't so anymore. In just three or four years the insurance industry had passed me in knowledge and skills and in current new tax laws. I thought I was up with it, but if you're not out there swimming in the water, you don't know whether it's cold or wet. You can stand there and put your finger in it, but it's a totally different feeling if your body is in it. And putting my whole body back into sales really helped me a lot.

I believe that caused the greatest spurt we've ever had in this agency—my personal selling, not my own business. All of a sudden they were saying, "Gosh, he can sell. All of this stuff he's been telling us all these years . . . he really can sell life insurance." I set an example because when I first started building an agency, I was recruiting people based on me as an example. In other words, "Here's what I can do in personal production and, gosh, you can do it too!" I would use that as part of my recruiting to get good people in. And consequently, I was able to do a lot more in showing them how to do it as opposed to talking about how to do it. And pretty soon our producers were saying, "How about showing me how to do this?" Before that, they weren't coming to me for help.

They were looking in other places, in other ways, because I really didn't know how and I didn't know I didn't know. But when you start hitting large production as I have in the last three or four years, you get a lot of attention in your agency. You get people saying, "Well, what are you doing? Share it with us."

In our interview with Nick Zervos in Charleston, S.C., he insisted on bringing one of his key staff people, also named Nick. While talking with this associate, Nick Zervos said:

I'd like to interrupt you. I would not like our audience to think that Nick Gavalas is a typical staff man. One of the agreements we have is that he maintain Million Dollar Round Table personal production—in fact, in excess of that, because if you can't do it, you can't teach it, in my opinion. I've maintained Million Dollar Round Table for the last 20 years, and it's not been difficult. I've had a six-figure premium total every year I've been a general agent—personally. You can still do it and run an agency if you allocate your time properly.

Earl Jordan, always a substantial personal producer, told how he extended this philosophy to his staff:

We compensate our staff strictly on salary, and we encourage them to do personal production. I feel that if a person is working with our associates and our associates know that he is capable of selling, then he can say, "Do as I do," not, "Do as I say."

The following personal production experience of Jim Craig is included here because it has helped him to sell a lot of life insurance, it has helped his people to do the same, and it is a splendid example of how the shared sales experience of one person can help many others. I'm confident that Jim Craig's people listen to his suggestions as attentively as Bobby Knight's athletes do his. Here is what Jim said:

A very successful securities broker who is a client of mine made a comment to me on my first call on him three years ago. As I walked into his office, he looked at me over his bifocals, leaning back, arms crossed, and in a very strong voice said, "I suppose it's only fair that I tell you before you sit down that I've been dribbling people like you out the door for 26 years." And it was on that basis that we started our relationship. Ultimately, approximately 90 days later, he became a client of mine. Because once I was able to get him talking, he did acknowledge the fact that he had been very successful marketing securities in the same office at the same desk for 26 years, and he was now working for his fourth securities firm. Through various failures, mergers, acquisitions, they had changed names. And most recently the merger that had occurred caused his group life insurance to go from $50,000 to $5,000. So even though he had been dribbling people like me out the door for 26 years, he was concerned that he was getting out there at the end of the road and was going to retire someday, and he did want his wife to have some degree of financial security. This individual ultimately bought a $25,000 whole life policy. Granted that's not a significant amount of life insurance, although it was a significant departure in thinking for this individual.

As he wrote the premium check when he completed the application, he looked up at me over his glasses and said, "How much commission are you going to earn on this sale?" And I looked at him and smiled and said, "Six hundred dollars." And when he quit sputtering and stammering, I said, "Bob, let me remind you of one thing before we finish this discussion. If you recall, 90 days ago your first comment to me was that you'd been dribbling people like me out the door for 26 years. Now it's time to pay the premium." Then he said to me, "Where were you 25 years ago when I was young? What about all those fellows out in the office? You should be talking to them, not to me." And I said, "Bob, all those 33-year-old fellows out in the office right now are dribbling somebody like me out the door.'' Subsequently over the next three years, Bob has personally introduced me to three of the young brokers in his office and has told them they should do what he did. They should buy their insurance while they're young, while it's a more intelligent purchase, and while they are still able to get it. And the good news behind Bob's story is that he was still insurable; he was in his mid-50s. Once you turn 40, in the words of the head of our medical underwriting department, "We are a little bit like an automobile. We start to become a maintenance problem and we may or may not be able to purchase any type of life insurance on a favorable basis."

The purpose of this chapter has been to illustrate and emphasize that just as agents want and need help in getting to profitable markets, so also do they want and need help and ideas and inspiration for the sales job itself.

If the agency head is not going to be their sales model, then that function can still be performed within the agency. But the general agent or manager should make certain that it IS performed, and that agency members know that a high standard of such performance is important to the agency head.

This chapter has shown us that general agents and managers must treat sales modeling as important, no matter how it is provided. The next chapter will extend this principle to include all the ways agency heads must "multiply" themselves in order to best serve the agency's members.

Meanwhile it's still true that today's agents are far less interested in how their elders DID it than they are concerned with how they should DO it.

So this is our significant trend:

> *To obtain and retain the regard and continued loyalty of quality associates, agency heads have to keep pace with the marketplace and its developments.*

10 | You Can't Do Everything Yourself

The Agency Head as a Chief of Staff

SIGNIFICANT TREND: An ever-larger part of the agency head's job will be finding and developing others to provide the support and services increasingly required by the agency's sales force.

Veteran agency heads today are likely to recall that during their early years in the life insurance business, the top 10 agencies in town might well have included some with less than a dozen producers. The majority might have had no more than two dozen.

While there are still profitable agencies of moderate size, a trend toward larger agencies is very apparent. In some cases agencies have been combined, with the result that many companies have fewer agencies than a few years ago. At the same time, however, productivity per agent and productivity per agency have markedly improved. It appears that these companies and their agency heads have decided that there are economies in numbers.

Two major factors have influenced this development. One has to do with the increasing costs of operating an agency in terms of rent, salaries, telephones, office equipment, postage, agent financing, etc. The other factor is the increasing sophistication of the business and the consequent need to provide backup expertise to assist producers in complex estate planning, business uses of life insurance, pension plans, and a wide range of financial planning products and services.

One person cannot do all the recruiting and training and also provide the technical expertise required for a growing agency. Today's agencies and tomorrow's, whether they market only life insurance or a broad portfolio of financial services and products, must be led by a management team. This means the agency head must find and develop others to help perform the many management functions involved in the substantial business entity we call an agency.

General agents and managers don't have to know everything about everything. Agents don't have to either. (Of course, the more they do know, the better, and the many new bearers of the new ChFC designation attest to their continuing desire to grow.) What the agent needs and what the agency head must make sure is available to the agent is access to the expertise needed to serve the agent's clientele, present and prospective.

Here is what Harry Hoopis has to say as he suggests a new connotation for the term "front-runner":

> The agent now is the person who has been selected because of his ability to go out and meet the public and present the case, find the need. I see the agent as the front-runner, and behind him a staff of people to do all the follow-up work.

Ted Santon's comments include a fascinating analogy with law firms:

> I don't think you can be all things to all people; that's the reason we specialize. You are not likely to be a tax-sheltered annuity expert and also an estate planning expert. I had a very close relationship with a very successful law firm and I often wondered what one of the partners did other than being a joiner. That is, he would go out and be in the public. I asked another partner of the senior law firm and he said, "He's able to generate more business through that method than we're able to handle. He really doesn't know all the particulars about being a lawyer, but he is a prospector." Well that's the same thing we have. We really have few people in our business who are strong prospectors and closers. As I look at our agency, our top people, their greatest ability is to find people with

money and to close a sale. We try to supply the things in between, the backup, the expertise, the in-house. You can find a lot of people to do that. The other ones are scarce.

Terry Dunn says that the "monkey is back on our shoulders." The agency head must accept responsibility for giving the agent the support needed. Terry put it this way:

In the past we brought people into the business and gave them their basic training. We encouraged them, but beyond that it was up to the agent to seek his own levels of growth. I think the monkey is back on our shoulders again and that we've got to get down into the pits and go to work again. We have to develop an in-house support system. The major skill that most successful agents have is the ability to communicate. The technical skills that are necessary to measure cash flows, to design complicated presentations to meet the critical financial eye of business owners and their advisers can be provided. For example, we have a CPA who runs our technical services department. We also have an attorney on retainer who provides us with training and legal advice and is available on a split case basis to work with agents in the development of large estate-planning cases. Now the agent who might have been somewhat reluctant to open those bigger cases feels he or she has the backup and support and they don't have to put that case together. They can use their excellent communication skills to open the cases, to get the facts, and to be there to present the facts. Our attorney will not only work with the agent in developing the case, but will also go out on the presentation. He works for the agent.

Blaine Sprout told that he looked at the agency as totally a support system. Then he said:

One example of that might be the way we approach the qualified plan business. I do have several employees who work only on pension administration and pension sales. It's our goal to have an organization which will support each agent from prospecting on through the administration, so that if even a fairly new agent comes up with a pension prospect, we can give him sales support and joint field work without his sharing the commission with us. He knows that we will walk through with him all the way, so he has no fear of the technical aspects of it. That gives him a lot of confidence in going out and doing things. We try to do that also in other fields.

When Herbert F. Gold, a former general agent, introduced Stan Eason for his participation in a Legacy interview, Mr. Gold said:

There are limits to the number any one of us can supervise efficiently at one time. Delegation is the key to expansion. Meaningful agency growth is dependent upon building and maintaining a first-class management team.

Roland Hymel found out how to move established agents from mid-five figures of premiums to double and triple that rate. Here's how he told about it:

I've studied a busy agent and what he does with his time. A good agent, just he and his secretary, can do $65,000 to $80,000 of premiums a year and be quite busy. He's a good agent. MDRT member, CLU. But in order to move that agent on a consistent basis to the $150,000 to $200,000 of premiums a year, he has to have support. Somebody's got to be doing some sophisticated proposals for him on a consistent basis in order for him to stay in front of his customers and his new prospects. Otherwise he finds himself just serving the old ones. The biggest

> problem in our business is when the agents, after 10, 12, 15 years, level off and continue maybe writing 60 to 75 percent on just their old clients each year. They are really moving out of the sales business and becoming order-takers. Al Granum pointed that out and that's why his record-keeping was so valuable. Listening to him, I couldn't understand why an agent couldn't go from $60,000 to $70,000 in premiums up to $150,000. Is he too busy? Let's see how busy he is and what he is spending his time doing. And we found the thing that takes him the longest is to be able to analyze the situation and prepare a sophisticated proposal. So now we make sure these are prepared for him.

John Meehan's many years of service to the industry must have influenced his comment about industry implications of the staff development area, when he said:

> The staff development in this agency (and the entire agency system) is the most important aspect of the entire life insurance business. We in management have a definite responsibility to develop additional management, because that's the only way career agents will be developed to their greatest potential. The large agencies that have successful field underwriters must be the place where future agency managers will come from. As you know, the industry is cutting back because of the cost of opening new agencies. So the manager going out today is going to be heading up a fairly substantial agency. He's not going to learn how to run an agency in a Home Office. He's not going to learn how to run an agency in college. He's only going to learn to run and build an agency if he has been a part of a vibrant, large agency.

You will probably read the following statement by Roland Hymel at least a couple of times, and then stop to think about its great significance:

> I found through experience that the more inde-
> pendent and successful I can make an agent, the
> more dependent he becomes on me and our sup-
> port services.

That sentence said volumes about agent retention! Now read on to see how Mr. Hymel and his staff work with the producers:

> All of my specialty people, my actuary, my em-
> ployee benefit plans specialist, my estate-planning
> department head and myself as well work in the
> field. All of us are required to work a minimum of
> two days in the field. So in my case Tuesdays and
> Thursdays I'm out in the field with my agents. We
> feel it's almost impossible in the employee benefit
> plan field to teach it in the classroom. We never ask
> any of our staff people to make notes on the inter-
> view. So when these staff people are in the field,
> it's a requirement first that the agent review the
> statistics and the fact sheet that he has already ob-
> tained before he brings the staff person in. If the
> agent cannot get the necessary facts, the staff or
> specialist does not make the call with him unless
> he's a brand new agent and we're teaching him how
> to gather the facts. Then once the facts are in, we
> can recognize the needs and what type of help he
> can offer the client. We then make the call with the
> agent and we handle the interview. We restate the
> facts as obtained by the agent. And since we are
> called in as the specialist on the case we expect the
> questions to be directed to us.

As has been pointed out, agents don't have to be experts at everything. They need, however, to be able to recognize situations when they encounter them. George Karr tells how they learn to do so in his Philadelphia organization:

> I think we've walked past as much business in a
> week as we'll sell in three or four months. What

we're doing in our classes is teaching people to recognize a potential market or a potential type of buyer, so they can come back to the agency and select someone from either our agent specialists or some of our staff specialists to go along and make a good presentation in that situation. For example, a new agent goes out and he understands a little bit about pension plans. He does a capital needs analysis for a doctor who informs him that he's just formed a professional corporation and he's interested in setting up a qualified pension plan. The agent has attended a class conducted by one of our two pension specialists and he knows enough about pensions that he then offers to have this doctor meet with one of these two specialists. They're both lawyers. One's an enrolled actuary, the other is also a CPA. The next interview would consist of the doctor, the agent, and the specialist from our office.

We will do the same thing in cross purchase buy-outs. Maybe this time he would bring in his district manager. In the publicly held corporation he might bring in my partner or he might take me with him, or one of the other agents who has had some experience in that market. What we're doing in our classes is really giving the agent the opportunity to recognize a business sale situation so that he can come back with some information at a later date with the right person who has had the experience in that market. What the agent gets from that is normally a great deal of insight into the market. The agent learns a little bit in the classroom but he's learned a lot actually in the sales situation. This is the way all of our agents really grow in the life insurance business. I can't emphasize enough, that they get the chance to grow because we use the capital needs analysis as the building block that keeps them in the business until they get these various chances to grow in the different directions.

It's not only time and energy constraints that keep the agency head from being all things to all people. Some areas are those where the manager has special strengths and likes to participate; others might better be delegated. Norman Levine explained how that is true in his case:

> . . . so I guess if you're asking for the common denominator of managers and general agents, some are extroverts, some are introverts, some are analytical, and some are expressive, but the one thing they all seem to have is an absolute faith and belief, and I'd say a transferable one. You walk into their office and you leave and you get excited. You're excited because of their technical stimulation or their motivational stimulation. It rubs off and every time your battery is run down, they're there to lift you up again. And they tend to build an organization that compensates for their weak suits. I, for example, am much more a motivator and an expressive than I am a technician. So I've learned over the years to surround myself with some darn good technicians. I've learned to define the things that I don't like, the things that are dull, the things that would conceivably slow me down because they're not exciting. And I've delegated them. I mean absolutely, totally delegated them. I've got an individual in my office that has power of attorney. He signs contracts and checks without my even participating, because I hate the administrative side. I want to spend my time on people. And that motivates me. Even if those people look down when they walk in, seeing that sparkle come back into their eye and the lightness of their step when they walk out the door turns me on.

We have seen the agency compared to a law firm. Dan Anderson compares theirs to a medical clinic:

> Many years ago our predecessor, Clair Strommen, identified and began to develop a process, as we

refer to it, of our associates being general practitioners surrounded by specialists. We compare ourselves often to a medical clinic where you may deal with an internist or general practitioner 80 or 90 percent of the time. There would, however, be situations where he would say, "Well this is a situation where we want to call in a specialist," maybe a surgeon, for example, or some other special person in the clinic.

Our agency has been developed and structured in much the same way relating to various financial specialties. Each of our associates, we feel, is a specialist in the area of the life insurance products and their applications. In addition, however, we have surrounded these general practitioners with specialty people in a variety of areas. One example, and the first one really developed, would be in the pension area. We have a pension attorney in-house. He currently heads up the pension operation within our firm that provides complete services ranging all the way from initial feasibility studies on plans to recommendations regarding funding of plans, to recommendations relating to plan design. A second specialty department would be our securities department, where we have formed a joint venture with a local well-known investment banking firm who has set up a broker dealer that enables many of our associates, those licensed to operate, to have available a wide range of securities products, such as real estate, limited partnerships, tax shelters, mutual funds, bond funds. A third specialty area would be the estate analysis area. We have a second attorney in the firm who came to us from a large local law firm. A fourth specialty and a very important one is the employee benefit department. Here again we have a joint venture with a large west coast employee benefit firm. They happen to use the same primary life insurance carrier as we.

Some of these quotations from heads of really large and very successful and very sophisticated agencies may seem less than totally relevant to agency heads whose agencies are in a far earlier point in their evolution. That's why we asked Tony Lawes how he'd counsel such a manager. Tony said:

> As a new manager my strong advice is the sooner you get an assistant, or two assistants, the faster you will grow and will achieve the things you have to achieve. In retrospect, what accelerated our branch was this concept of delegation of responsibility. They make mistakes that probably I would not, but there is no way I could have handled it all anyway.

We asked Ken Fry if he were starting out, whether he would develop first with line help or staff help. This was his response:

> I would say if I were placed down in a scratch unit that I should get the line going. Then look for the talented people, the analytical type that likes to study, that has a special interest in advanced sales or pensions. Excite them about the potential. Excite the agents about the potential of using that individual. Let everybody see they're making more money, having more fun, building a better clientele, and giving better service. And it just kind of takes over. It's a synergism. It just begins to roll and roll. Then if you can get out of the way and not stop the rolling or the growth, if you can put your own ego a little bit behind you and use these other people and give them the credit, then the thing really gets in high gear. And the general agent just has to stand there and hopefully find more needs and fill those needs with more talented people.

We have seen comparisons with law firms and medical clinics. Norbert Siegfried introduces another one:

I feel it's been my responsibility to sell individual growth through the team approach. If we want an agency of any size, we have to have a lot of people participating in management. I'm not so sure that down the road a few years we won't be operating similar to a CPA firm or a law partnership where we have three, four, or five major partners and other people assigned into those ranks.

No one who knows Walter Downing has ever accused him of not having vision. But see what he said:

Our business is fast changing, and our training has to change accordingly, just to keep pace. My dependency on staff facilities is far greater than I ever envisioned. I envision even more facilities as time goes on. The job would be impossible for a trainer to do completely on his own, to equip someone to sell in these markets without staff help.

When we talk about services to the producers, we find that these top agency heads mean much more than just expertise for sophisticated markets. They also mean modern office equipment and management, whether it be word processors, computers, high speed duplicators, or any of the other rapidly proliferating aids to administrative efficiency. Ralph Brown said:

In order to survive we're going to have to find systems to support the agents so that they can become more and more productive, ways of eliminating the paper paralysis that seems to engulf us at times. Those are some of the things that we are facing up to in terms of how to help the agent be more effective in the administrative part of his job by providing him with services and systems that can help eliminate the detail.

Those companies that have abandoned the career agency

system never found out what Elton Brooks discovered, that it's very possible to enable new agents to quickly become substantial producers in profitable markets—with help! He explained his philosophy in this area:

> We've had a philosophy for a long time that an agency head ought to find the things that he can do more effectively for the agent than the agent can do for himself and develop those areas of expertise for the agency. What are the functions that we can do and streamline and make effective in a lot of ways that the agent just can't do?
>
> In most cases that's backing the agent up with specific kinds of sales materials, specific kinds of technical information, technical field help, design help. Things that will allow him to feel comfortable in going after sophisticated markets that he would not go after if he had to develop the procedures and techniques and do the design all by himself. So we think that by providing a certain atmosphere and a certain support system, we can say even to the newest man that you can go out and get yourself involved in the most sophisticated markets that are out there and we're prepared to back you up and bring that case to fruition. It's pretty tough to push a guy into the more sophisticated markets until he really feels that he's got the backup. But if they feel the backup is in the agency, we're finding out that brand new agents will go out and write pension cases. They'll get involved very quickly in sophisticated estate plans. Because what we're teaching at the front end are concepts. "The specialists will back you up and if you understand the concept and you can discuss the concept intelligently with a sophisticated market, the technical people will back you up in terms of making a sale for you."

"Doing things for him better than he can do them

himself." Those words from Dave Smith sound much like what Elton Brooks said. Here's the quote from Dave:

> Ever since I've been in the life insurance business, particularly in management, I've been kind of convinced that it's either services or money that will keep people with an agency. And money just doesn't last because there is never going to be enough once you get into the money routine. So it's really got to be service to the agent, service to the agent's client. Doing things for him better than he can do them himself. I think it's important as an agency grows to get as many specialists, whether it be part-time or full-time, whatever the agency can afford, in all the areas that we've been working— business insurance, estate planning, group sales, disability sales, qualified and nonqualified plans, any area of specialty that a general agent perceives fits his marketplace. Either he or someone on his staff or an agent part-time ought to become a specialist in that area who can answer questions, make field calls, work with the person.

We found a wide variety of approaches to the "who-pays-how-much?" question with respect to the equally wide variety of services provided agents. This quotation is from Marvin Blair:

> "I've hired a pension consultant. He works strictly with agents on a salary plus a 25/75 split. All the agent has to do is introduce him to the client and he takes care of the rest. I am also putting heavy emphasis on disability sales. Another step that I have taken is to put together a financial planning operation. Included in this group is a CPA firm, a law firm, two investment advisers, and myself representing the insurance company. I felt this was necessary because there are a lot of businessmen these days making a lot of money and paying a lot of taxes. But their banker tells them to do one

thing, their attorney to do another, their CPA tells
them to do something else. So we put together this
team and we will sit down with a client and counsel
him and make recommendations as to how to save
taxes and solve other financial problems. We do
charge a fee for this. But there is no product involved at this stage.

Would you like to get an attorney on your staff, and
perhaps you are not sure how to go about it, and you don't
want to get in over your head financially? Here is proven and
practical advice from J.D. Surber:

We have a consulting attorney who is in our agency
all day long one day a week on retainer. I think
there are many agency managers in the country
who could perhaps get an attorney into their office
free because of the chance to meet new people and
to build a clientele. I wanted to control our situation, so I'm willing to pay a handsome sum to have
an attorney sit in our agency one day a week. He's
welcome to bring his briefcase to do his own work
when we don't keep him busy. First of all, when we
began this process, we invited a number of attorneys in to conduct a class or seminar on business
insurance or estate planning in order to really get a
feel for one who is a competent person who relates
well to us and to our industry. It's win-win all the
way and I couldn't recommend it more highly.

Having made a career of making intangibles real and
understandable, it's no wonder that life insurance people use
so many analogies so effectively. We've seen agencies likened
to law firms, CPAs, and medical clinics. Al Ostedgaard
makes a case for comparison with major football powers:

We operate very much like a major football power.
I'll compare our staff to the assistant coaches.
These people are outstanding. You can visualize an
assistant coach in charge of the quarterbacks;

another is in charge of the ends. They are experts in their fields, and they can do a better job of working with the quarterbacks and the ends than the head coach himself. A number of our staff do a much better job working with people in their unit than I could. This also gives our staff men great pride and helps them tremendously in their personal development. Two examples: one of our people is a technical expert in estate planning and pensions. He can deal with any CPA, attorney, or trust officer, and probably knows more about the subject than any professional he's dealing with. Another one is a great expert in recruiting. These staff men complement each other. They work together periodically to help each other where the strengths of one can be of help to another.

The interview with Mr. Quentin Aanensen was on the subject of "Maintaining Agency Morale." We mentioned to him that the industry's annual Survey of Agents' Opinion continues to reflect that while on the whole agents have been pretty well satisfied with their jobs, they also continue to be less than satisfied with the support and help they receive from the agency and the company. We asked Mr. Aanensen what that meant to him. He replied thus:

First, we have a tendency as managers and general agents to see things the way we want to see them. So we tend to color our thinking and feel that we're doing a good job in this area when in fact our agents might very well feel less than enthusiastic about what we are doing. There was a key factor in that survey and that was that the agents' dissatisfaction was primarily with the support and help that they felt they got from the agency. So this tells me that a good way to attack this morale problem is directly through the support systems and the marketing systems that are provided to the agents, such things as creative professional marketing systems, proposal services, adequate secretarial facilities, things of this type. Agencies that don't make significant moves in these areas, I think, face some dark days. They're going to have to solve that problem. We recognize that morale is much like momentum. It takes a lot of effort to build it, to establish it, but it can be lost very easily and very rapidly.

To build and maintain morale in our agency, here are some things that we do. We lead with our marketing competence. About everything we can do to support our people in marketing we do. We are constantly looking at new things that we can put on line that would be ahead of the field underwriter and give him an opportunity to grow at a faster rate. This contributes to the underwriter's feeling of pride. And this pride factor is an essential part of good morale in any organization. Those with management functions make every effort to stay technically competent so that we can help our associates. If our associates respect our knowledge and our skill, it creates a positive relationship. A vital part in this area of building morale is to get all of our associates involved in the agency's goals and to get ideas and input from them in the actual setting of the goals and then in the planning of how to achieve those goals. The more the people are directing the ball, the more likely they are to feel a part of the agency and enjoy the success the agency has.

The years in which the morale in our agency has been the absolute highest were those years when we were working together to reach very high goals that we had set one, two, three, or four years earlier. Of course, a key factor of this involvement on the part of the agency associates is that they must feel the direct benefit individually of the agency accomplishing its objectives. This means we must constantly and immediately recognize their successes and must do things to demonstrate that we will continue to expand agency support facilities as we achieve even greater success. The impact of all this on recruiting is just outstanding because most of our new associates in the agency join us through our present organization. This just doesn't happen if there isn't good morale, high morale. This saves my time and the time of other staff members in that quality people are being introduced to us. When an associate is able to say this is a great place to work, recruiting is off to a good start.

By now this chapter has given us overwhelming testimony to the proposition that agencies cannot grow as they must without growing in numbers of people involved in management functions. We asked several interviewees for their thoughts on how these people should be selected. Here is what John Meehan said:

I think he can start into the management when he's had at least two, and perhaps four, years of successful field underwriter experience. He should also have a varied experience . . . because he'll have to develop people in many different markets. But the real answer is more in the man himself. Does he have an inherent desire to work with people? Is he interested in seeing other people succeed even though he's not being compensated for it? I think the caring individual, the man who has something extra that he wants out of the business besides making money and building a clientele, is the true test. But he does have to have success in the field.

In introducing Frank O'Brien for a unit on this subject, his senior vice president, Mr. John C. Lipsey, said:

Picking management assistants is perhaps the most vital decision the manager must make several times in his career. Yet often these decisions are made hastily and for the wrong reasons.

When asked what were the usual circumstances when someone took the first step into management in his agency, Mr. O'Brien replied:

> Most likely I've been approached by the individual. We make it very evident to all the people in the organization that we're always interested in discussing the management opportunity with anybody. I'm not one for pushing aside a good producer just to keep that person producing and trying to keep him away from management. That's probably the reason I left my first company. At 22 years old the company thought I was a little too young for management and I found a company that didn't think I was. I really think that if you don't allow anybody and everybody to "try on" the management job, they could resent you someday for never having given them the opportunity. So we try and portray, and it's easy to do, that management is a successful and rewarding life. And through that image, hopefully, we'll attract good salesmen within our own field force to come and pursue the management opportunity. So I really wait for them to come to me.

Then we asked Frank if he used tests to help determine their aptitude for management. He said this:

> There's only one true test and that's "precontract training." We let them go in head over heels, bring in their first recruit, botch up the interview, mess up the financing plan that you just taught them and do all those things. There's only one true test and that is to help that person experience the functions, learn the job the only way it can be learned and that's through activity, and see if the shortcomings and the benefits weigh out to where they would like to make a career of it. The real problem we had was not letting enough people test the waters.

I don't mind at all bringing somebody in to "try" management. I enjoy watching them find out they're not as smart as they thought they were, and seeing the respect they gain for the difficulty of the tasks involved. It's exciting to watch it happen and it's exciting to watch them grow, because they always grow. They change for the better, one way or the other—even the ones that leave it.

Jim Luhrs told about the attributes he looked for in those who were to join him on the management team:

The top of the list has to be loyalty. It doesn't matter how terribly intelligent they are if they're undermining the overall philosophy and purpose of the agency when you're not around. We're looking for someone with above average production, a person that doesn't have to be in management to eat. We want somebody the other members of the agency can respect and feel, "Yeah, there's a leader."

Mr. Luhrs said that this kind of person was likely to have demonstrated enthusiasm about the career in the early months:

They're bringing in their policyholder and saying, "This is a great business! Why don't you take the test and see whether you can get into this business?" Finally, this person has courage and vision and faith. And if you've worked with them for two or three years, you're going to be able to determine that by their past actions.

On the same subject, here is Joe Casale:

As the agency grew, it became obvious that we needed some management people. And I started to look among the people I had. I'd had some experiences with hiring people from outside of the company before and they were not happy experiences. I was running into that same thing. You know, "With my old company we did it this way," or, "My old GA did it this way," or, "My old manager did it that way." And that may have been okay where they were but that wasn't me, and that wasn't what I wanted for my agency. Some guys hire their own clone. I didn't need a clone. In fact I was probably the opposite. I needed someone to complement me, to do those things that I don't do well, to act in a manner that I don't act naturally. What I did need was somebody at least whose thinking along the lines of agency structure and agency atmosphere and agency goals was the same as mine. And I couldn't think of anybody better to meet those qualifications than the young people I had hired. Every person I have brought into management is somebody that I've hired, who has had his first day of training in the insurance business under me.

In the following quotation from John Meehan, you will recognize that he is talking about how he starts a new management person on a line assignment. We shall soon get into line versus staff considerations. Here's Mr. Meehan:

We put them in the field with a new man who's been assigned by the agency. Remember, our field underwriter's been a good salesman. He doesn't know anything about recruiting. He has never put anybody across in the business, so when it comes to the recruiting effort, he doesn't have the confidence. He's like a brand new agent out trying to sell for the first time. So during his first year as a staff man, the agency recruits enough agents for him to work with—three or four at the most—and he'll have success at putting them across. He's able to recruit the second year without any problem at all, because he himself knows he can put that kind of guy across.

We asked Elton Brooks whether an agency starting to add management talent to assist the agency head should give priority to staff or to line personnel. His response was:

> I think it really depends a lot on where that manager sees his own strength. What he wants to do is bring on someone very quickly who can complement and supplement his own areas of strength. Now if he happens to be a very good recruiter and has good leadership skills and works well in the field with people, then he probably needs to bring on a good administrative assistant. If his strengths tend to be organizational and administrative and so on, then he probably needs very badly to bring on a good line person very quickly. But in any case, I think he needs to bring on some assistants very fast. It's pretty difficult even in a small organization for one person to be very effective in making an agency grow.

Then we asked him how, in a smaller agency situation, the agency head could move into providing the kind of staff support and services that seem to be so necessary. His response was a very practical one, based on experience:

> I can relate to the problem very well, having started a scratch agency. You don't have any models, you don't have any specialists, you don't have any of the things that are kind of nice to have around when you're trying to recruit and train. So I think what you do is find good models and bring them into the agency. We used to bring in top agents of other companies and have them speak to our organization and talk to them. If we found that someone from another agency was particularly good in the pension market or some other market, we encouraged our people to do joint work with that person. So you use outside resources until you have the money or find the right timing to bring that kind of a person into your organization. There are

lots of outside people that you can use and use very effectively.

The fact that today's circumstances seem to call so loudly for staff support, as opposed to traditional line "supervisors" and "district managers" and the like (except where there are detached units or, perhaps, very large recruiting efforts), makes the next quotations from Earl Jordan and Jack Skalla less than surprising. Not so long ago they would have surprised many. Here is Mr. Jordan:

> I do not believe in the unit system. I feel that each one of our staff has certain talents, and that if anyone in our agency wants to use the talents of any one of our staff, including my partner Steve Edwards or myself, we want them to feel free to do so rather than to feel they must work with only one unit manager.

Mr. Skalla was equally forthright:

> We operate by the staff approach as far as the management team is concerned. We do not have any line supervision. I mean any associate can go to anybody on the management staff without anybody else feeling like, "Wonder why they didn't come and see me." We have found that this works out better in the long run.

Jerry Urbik would obviously agree with Messrs. Jordan and Skalla, and he tells us why:

> The unit system is structured where a man supposedly lives, trains, and supervises a given small group of men. It's very difficult for a man to be a reasonably good producer and then one day be "ordained" a paid management man. He suddenly now has responsibilities of recruiting, training, and supervising—areas that are essentially new to him. We thrust a man into this job and tell him to do all

of them at once. And we wonder why we have such a high rate of failure.

It's been my feeling, borne out by experience, that it would be much wiser to take a man we see management potential in and let him develop into the management job from the basis of his strengths. We said, "No more units." We now have specialists.

In Chapter Six we saw many splendid examples of the awareness leading agency heads have of the importance of regarding their agents as persons and not just units of production. People take courses in interpersonal skills to make sure that they effectively meet the psychic needs of their workers. Much has been written and many speeches have been given about how to stimulate, motivate, reward, and interact with agents. But much less has been said or written about the agency head's relationship with the other members of the management team. Vince Bowhers reminds us of this responsibility:

People involved in middle management in our agencies are in many ways the unsung heroes of the life insurance industry. I've sensed recently that they don't really get the recognition that they deserve. A splendid meeting that our company had for middle-management people led me to think more about doing more in the agency to try to make sure that I put the credit where it belongs. In our agency bulletins and at agency meetings we mention our management team. We release things to our company house organs so that they will receive proper recognition there. We have always encouraged our people to be involved in industry activities, but now I find that I want to release things about them to the publications that the life underwriters association or other industry associations put out. I write more notes now and letters of congratulation or of thanks than I ever did before.

You can extend this properly to the area of entertaining to make sure that we either get together on a business basis over breakfast or lunch or perhaps on a dinner basis with a management person and his or her spouse. It's so easy to overlook these things and yet it's a very important part of the development of a really effective management team.

Then Mr. Bowhers gave some splendid counsel about a frequently fouled-up (my description) management function, the so-called appraisal interview:

In the same vein we might cover the question of an appraisal interview between the general agent and his staff manager or between the supervisor and his producing associate. The idea is to make sure that this interview is based on the performance, and it's the performance that's being reviewed in the discussion during that interview, not the performer. It is so easy to have the interview break down, and instead of discussing what is being accomplished or not being accomplished, we wind up having a psychological appraisal of the nature of the performer, and that never leads anywhere that's helpful.

One final comment in that area of staff relationship would be to maintain in the agency an atmosphere where your staff members can come to you quickly with bad news. We don't want him or her to have a feeling we're going to shoot the messenger. We want to have the philosophy that the messenger should feel welcome and should feel comfortable being able to discuss any problem in the agency openly and quickly while there's still plenty of time to deal with it on an effective basis.

Like so many big men, Martin Polhemus is frank to admit

to his own shortcomings and to share how he learned to deal with them. His problem was not unique to him, and his testimony can help others:

> I had great difficulty delegating to others. I think that this is probably one of the most common management problems in our industry because we tend to recruit our managers out of the ranks of successful agents. I believe that successful agents are mostly good do-it-yourself-ers. They have a lot of initiative, they like their own style, and they tend to reach out and act. Well, that's fine with a little agency, until you get a dozen people in it. But our current trend is to build very large agencies in many companies—super agencies if you want to call them that. We're looking now to what we have to do to operate and live with a $200 or $300 million agency with 100 agents. That's a very different problem. And if we're going to do that, we have to learn to delegate and to work through others. I was not good at that at all. I would be approached by an agent with a problem that would be under one of my district managers and I would say, "Oh gee, I'd love to help. Come on up." And we'd talk it over and arrive at a solution and I wouldn't even tell the manager what I was doing. And then I'd get feedback from him about what he was trying to do. It took a long time to learn to coordinate the work through him, not around him or against him. In order for sub-managers to lead effectively in their own units, they have to be allowed to develop their own style. If you get them to try to conform to your style, you're taking away the guy's own strengths and individualities. So if he can do the job at all well, encourage him, guide him with what little you can, and correct him, but let him run his own show. I think this has been one of our great strengths. There's nothing that we are prouder of: all three of our second line managers who have had

any experience at all are in the very top ranks of our company, out of hundreds.

As we saw earlier, Frank O'Brien feels there is nothing wrong, and much that is right, in letting would-be managers try the job for size. He indicated that even if management turns out not to be their niche, the experience can be a positive one:

> A lot of the biggest producers in the agency tried management and then returned to personal production. The appreciation they have for life underwriting after they come on into the second line management position is so much more. They had never reckoned with all the blessings they'd had as a life underwriter. And that management experience helps them and lets them understand more fully their blessings. They come out of it more organized. They come out of it more empathic towards their buyer. They come out of it more experienced with people. They can experience things in a management day that might take a week to experience as a life underwriter, as a salesman. Perhaps six people in our agency today that have "failed" at the management position have gone on to be absolutely some of our premier producers. So I think it's great training not only for a future agency manager, but I've never seen it hurt a soul. I've seen it do nothing but good.

These O'Briens tend to be forthright people. In New Orleans Jack O'Brien responded in this fashion when we asked him what he'd say to his nephew if he sought his uncle's advice upon becoming an agency manager:

> I believe like Bob Woods said many, many years ago, that your success will be in direct proportion to how well you develop a staff—and I mean a quality and permanent staff. You can't be a farm system for your company or any other company. If

you want excellence, you're going to have to pay for excellence. I've never been enchanted with the idea that the manager or general agent can go home at 3:30 every day and the staff people are going to be out there until midnight, while he earns $150-$200,000 and they're starving to death on $15-$18,000 a year. What I'm really saying is you're going to have to share the wealth.

I did open a new agency for the company. I got up to 17 men before I ever had an assistant. And I lost some very good people because I was running from one brushfire to the next, and I never did a good job with anybody. And it wasn't until I developed a staff that we started to get the kind of retention and productivity that we were all looking for. So I would say to my nephew, "The first thing you have to do is go out and hire two people right away on the staff, even if they're less than totally competent. They can at least tell the new man where the men's room is while you're doing important things on your job, so that you're not running from one brushfire to another."

I have never liked to see company announcements of a person's appointment to management responsibilities use the word "promoted." For Ben Feldman, being Chairman of the Board would be a demotion. As Jack O'Brien points out, some people rightfully enter management because there is some part of the sales role where they are deficient:

Years ago I found in our company, as in many others, when you entered management you were required to recruit your own people, train those people, supervise them, and probably personally produce on the side. Invariably it seemed to me a man that was good at all four of those functions was soon running his own agency in either my company or some other. But many, many individuals in this business are good at one or two of those things but are not good across the board. Under the typical system, unfortunately, unless a man is good at all four he's asked to return to the field or leave the business.

What we've tried to do is take advantage of that particular strength in an individual and put him in that slot. For example, I have a fellow who's probably as fine an educator as there is in this business. When he first joined me, he could not recruit. Had he stayed with the old system, I would have had to tell him to get out of the job. But he's my right arm now as far as running our advanced underwriting department and teaching our group of both advanced and new. He couldn't develop the unit. He can do every facet of business but recruit. He's a crackerjack at what he does. This is true of our recruiter. We have a man who spends 90 percent of his time just in the selection of new men. And I think something else develops. You get great continuity. You're not having to wear four hats. You get a continuous process that you upgrade through experience, through doing it every day. And it really simplifies the life of our staff members. They're not running from pillar to post. They know exactly where they're going. And they know who picks up the other side of the coin.

When I asked Jack if the company could get its managers just from those occasional ones who do show ability and interest in all of his four areas, he said:

I think so. You'll always have those individuals who feel that they must run their own office. And if our company doesn't give them that opportunity, some other company will. However, there are many, many people who can bring certain abilities though they may not be agency head caliber. I think we've all seen the CLU who's been to every school and knows the business backward and forward but is a mediocre producer. We have one in our office. He loves to teach and we use him on a part-time basis. I think many good people could be conserved and used in this business in a particular spot who are now being lost because they don't do all facets well.

This short quotation from the interview with Stan Eason really tells volumes about the agency head and management assistant relationship. Agency heads know much about working with agents, but Stan's words could be helpful to many of his peers. We had asked him about his developmental program for his managers. He said:

I'm reminded of a statement by J.B. Conway, "You can't put into a man what the good Lord left out." So I think you have to start with the raw material. The next key in my mind is to let them be aware that it is their responsibility and you're not on their shoulder every minute. They're going to make mistakes. The industry calls it delegation. And that's probably been the key in our agency. I was forced by reasons of geography to delegate when I first became a general agent. Thank heaven I was forced to. I'm not sure I would have been shrewd enough to recognize it otherwise. But with a unit 135 miles away and another one 50 or 60 miles away, I had no choice but to put faith in the sales managers in those areas. So the area of development starts by getting the right people and allowing them to develop themselves. Now they need guidance. It's kind of like the ship's captain. You have to make sure the ship's going the right way but you don't necessarily have hold of the wheel all the time. We sat down and did a job description so that they knew what needed to be done. Incidentally, I didn't give them a job description. We sat down and worked it out together, and then all it took was some coaching and some prodding once in a while and making sure that they do it. I talk with each supervisor every day; some, two or three times a day.

Not only was the late W. Harvey Rogers an extremely knowledgeable expert on management principles and practices, but his team approach was a precursor of many of the great agencies' structures and modes of operation today and tomorrow. Too often, perhaps, we have tended to think that "our business is unique" and that management concepts developed in other fields are irrelevant in the life insurance business. Not so. Today great life insurance companies are exposing their field management people to the same ideas that have proved useful in other fields, and with good reason. Here is what Harvey said:

> Over the years a picture began to clear for me. I got to the place where I could see what kind of organization I wanted. It became a matter of bringing people in around me who could share those goals with me, and there began to form a management team. I went from being a strong entrepreneur with a sort of autocratic style to a more participative kind of manager. And now it's to the point where I can see where we really can build a very large organization. In school I got by with just as little as I could to get through. But I began to work on self-improvement, and I thought if there was something out there that could help I've got to find it. I became intensely interested in reading. And what I found is that the answers are all out there if we just go and find them. We don't take the time to stop and sharpen our saw because we're too busy. So I thought, well, I'm going to do that and I began to read. And I found all kinds of answers and was able to share those with the management team and we came up with some methods of operations and systems, some standards for ourselves. We came up with a regular matrix for management by agreement. What do you do? You make an agreement. You establish controls. It was a regular procedure

that we'd follow. What we were doing was pretty much a participative kind of management.

We asked him how that worked in actual practice. He said:

It was difficult to tell who was boss if you looked in at our management meeting. I think that's probably fairly descriptive, because the team runs the show. In order to determine what we're going to talk about at the management meeting, we'd work on it ahead of time at a prior meeting. We'd brainstorm. What do we want to accomplish? Where do we want to go with our next meeting? People get up and take part, participate, and do what they want to do and it actually moves quite quickly. We come up with the ideas, the ideas flow, nothing is discouraged. Out of these ideas comes an agenda and that agenda is then prioritized and it's typed and sent out to the management team. They make additions, corrections, and changes and send it back. The secretary creates the final agenda and at the next manager's meeting that's the way we go. What I might do would be to delegate parts of that agenda to the members of the management team. But actually it's gone beyond that. I don't even have to delegate it. The team sort of delegates it to itself. I guess the key is that it would be difficult to tell who really was in charge at that meeting. That may sound fairly loose but it's not. It's very productive.

We asked Harvey what advantages he saw in this approach. He said:

It brings out the best in people. I used to try to run meetings, and they were a real burden. You talk about burnout! It would wear me out getting ready for a meeting, trying to find out what kinds of things people would like, hoping to put in as many things as I could to interest them, and it just didn't work. It became old. I became a victim of overexposure. Too many of my ideas were flowing into the meeting. They'd heard it all before. I was driving for a consensus on a decision I'd already made. My main purpose there was to get them to agree to something I'd already decided on. It just didn't feel right. Finally I heard or read somewhere that if you want to know what to do about something, why not ask the person that you're doing it with. So I took it to the management team. What they told me was, it wasn't necessary for me to do all these things. Not only was it unnecessary, but it was somewhat burdensome on them to have to sit through two hours, three hours while I did all the talking. Now that was hard for me to handle because I like to talk and I've got lots of ideas. Some of them are good, but it was too much for them.

We asked him if it didn't take a lot longer to arrive at what he called a consensus decision. He said:

Peter Drucker said that the Japanese managers make decisions very slowly and only with considerable input from the people affected by those decisions. They don't make any final moves until everybody is in final agreement. He said that Americans, on the other hand, make decisions very quickly, usually unilaterally, and then spend all their time driving for a consensus. I found that both of them actually take about the same amount of time. The American method is very quick to make decisions, and it takes a good deal of time to get consensus, to sell your ideas once the decision has been made. The Japanese system, conversely, takes a lot of time to make the decision, but the implementation is very rapid. The net difference is in the quality in the Japanese method. The result that flows from that decision is much better because people have had their chance to say what they feel and have all made their decision to back it in advance. In the American system, the quality is not as good. At first I thought it was a time factor, but it's not. It's a quality factor.

Ask any 10 agency heads to tell you what they like most about their job, and most of them will say, in one way or another, that it's the fun and satisfaction they get out of watching (and playing a part in) the growth and development of their associates.

When they invite another person to join them on the management team they are inviting that person to share in those satisfactions. In visiting these many great agencies, it became obvious to me that there is nothing else quite like these shared victories. To be able to say, "We did it!" is so very much sweeter than, "I did it!"

Uniquely, the development of your management team is the all-important activity that both results from growth in your agency and also helps to make growth possible.

Fortunately, as the title of this chapter puts it, you can't do everything yourself. "Fortunately"—because otherwise you'd be denied the rewards that ensue from helping others develop in and through management.

So the trend emphasized in this chapter is a happy one:

An ever-larger part of the agency head's job will be finding and developing others to provide the support and services increasingly required by the agency's sales force.

11 | *20 Years Behind Or 10 Years Ahead? It's Your Choice*

The Agency Head and Sex

> **SIGNIFICANT TREND:** Women will play an ever-larger role in the life insurance business in all its facets, including selling, agency management, and as buyers.

This is the shortest chapter in the book, but it may be the most important one. Greg Hagan, a wonderful Irishman, was a perennial MDRT member of my agency with a great gift for colorful description. When Greg wanted to say someone was behind the times, it often came out as, "He's still wearing high-button shoes!"

I'd have to say that the life insurance industry is not only wearing high-button shoes, but it's also dragging the feet inside them in a vitally important area, namely the recognition that there really are two sexes.

Recently my wife and I took a short European trip, and I had been brushing up on my high school German. German nouns, you know, have their gender indicated by the equivalent of the English word "the." The masculine is "der" and the feminine counterpart is "die" and the neuter version is "das." Well, in the life insurance business in North America, it's almost always "der Agent"—seldom "das Agent"—and virtually never is it "die Agent."

In conducting the Legacy of Learning interviews, I would often stop and ask the interviewee to rephrase some statement when the agent was referred to as "he" or "him," but that would seldom be effective for very long. "I have a 33-man agency, plus three assistant managers." If I asked if any of them were women, he might say, "Yes, two of them are."

Perhaps it's only natural that this industry should be one of the last to avail itself of the tremendous resource (women) that could revitalize it in the years ahead. After all, when we came in the business we were men selling to men the protection that would enable women to stay home where they belonged. How could you ask women to do that? It would be a contradiction right on the face of it!

The reference librarian whom I recently consulted told me that as of June, 1983, the percentage of female workers in the total U.S. workforce was 46.9. The life insurance industry, with only 12 percent women agents, is missing the boat!

Midway through the second year of the Legacy of Learning series, we produced a unit entitled "Women Mean Business." On it were presented an outstanding producer, Mildred Parker, a general agent, Eliza Brandt, a Home Office person, Bernice Malamud, and a general agent with five women in his agency, John V. Walsh. More recently we had the privilege and pleasure of producing the recruiting video for the GAMC New Horizons Series entitled "New Horizons for Women." An audio version of that presentation was provided to all Legacy subscribers. In my own agency in the 1950s were four fine agents named Ann Dolan, Helen Carlson, Marcella Egan, and Florence Kuhn, so this is a subject about which I can write with experience and conviction.

Here is what Liz Brandt had to say about the suitability of a life insurance career for women:

> I think it's the great opportunity for women for a number of reasons. First of all, we can obtain financial independence. We can build our business without any investment, except our time. Women can have more empathy, be better listeners. I think there are absolutely no limitations either income-wise or opportunity-wise; she can be an agent, a supervisor, can become a general agent or go to the Home Office. So many opportunities—and the opportunity for growth. When I talk to a recruit, male or female, I say, "In our business you are never going to be stale up here. You always have to be learning, studying. We're like doctors." There's

an intellectual challenge for anybody who will accept it.

Liz came to the United States from Europe, so her next observation has special meaning:

> I think our business also stands for everything this country stands for, which is freedom. We have freedom to choose our own prospects, our clients. We have freedom to choose our own hours. We have freedom to choose how much money we want to make. And we have the freedom, if we look at it as our own business, to kind of close that door whenever we feel like it.

Bernice Malamud, in her role as the gadfly to assure that her giant company gives full attention to the key role women can play in the marketing of life insurance, knows what she's talking about. Her remarks provoke thought and action:

> Let's look at some of the demographics. The baby boom has matured and is forming families. This process will continue to create new markets for our products for at least the next 20 years. Where are we going to get the agents to serve those markets unless we turn to women? New studies of life insurance ownership show that the higher income family earning over $25,000 a year has inadequate life insurance. They have not kept pace with inflation. Where are we going to get the agents to serve the high quality market unless we turn to women?

> The individual pension markets are growing in ever-increasing increments as people recognize that social security and their company pensions will not be enough to insure comfortable retirement in an inflationary economy. Where are we going to get the agents to meet these new demands, and how are we going to convince the country that the private life insurance and income protection business can

meet these demands without further intrusion from government, unless we recruit tens of thousands of new agents? And where are we going to get new agents unless we turn to women?

What creates the market also creates the resource of potential women agents. These are the younger elements of potential agents: single or married, with or without children, divorced with or without children, well-educated, whose choices of careers are not perceived to be as broad as men's choices. The life insurance business demonstrates to these younger women that their income and their ability to fulfill themselves are equal, and I don't know of many businesses that can offer that.

The more mature women have discovered that despite their high education qualifications, their ambitions, their life experiences and their energy output, most businesses penalize them because they are women. Ours does not. And we can point it out, and prove it, to this vast potential of bright, mature, and highly qualified women.

Bob Hanseen might contend that trends begin in Southern California, and then the rest of the continent gradually catches up. With 11 women agents, his agency is scarcely a laggard in this area. Mr. Hanseen shared this observation:

We've had an interesting experience in the last couple of years in the area of women agents in our agency. We have 11 women successfully selling life insurance. And of those 11 people that have been with us longer than a year, nine of them are club members, showing a substantial production. I was a little opposed to bringing women into the life insurance business because I didn't think it was a woman's world. I've certainly changed my mind in the last couple of years because I find that a dedicated woman who is knowledgeable about our business has a tremendous advantage over some of us males in selling life insurance. Because they are a little more of a rarity, they can get in and open cases that men can't even begin to open. And then if they're knowledgeable, know what they're doing, they are able to make some tremendous sales.

Both Mildred Parker and Liz Brandt said that women should be treated the same as men and should be trained the same. John Walsh, whose agency included five successful women agents he'd recruited, agreed with those observations, and added:

Some general agents have discontinued recruiting women because of one bad experience. This is very interesting. Many general agents lose many men and many thousands of dollars, and continue to hire men. Another analogy: agents send out 100 direct mail letters and get three or four replies, perhaps, and end up making the telephone calls and getting their heads knocked off and never again use direct mail because it's a poor device for attracting qualified prospects!

I think in the years to come we're going to see the female agent take her place among some of the stars and become a large part of the life insurance business.

When asked if he believed the public was ready to buy from women, Mr. Walsh said:

I don't believe there's any problem for women selling in the advanced underwriting areas. Men will buy from women. They will buy from anyone who is knowledgeable and represents himself or herself effectively. I see no problem at all in this.

Finally, he gave all males food for thought, saying:

One of my women agents handed me something the other day, and I'd like to share it with you. It reads:

"A businessman is aggressive—and a businesswoman is pushy.

He is careful about details—she is picky.

He loses his temper because he's so involved in his job—she's bitchy.

He follows through—she doesn't know when to quit.

He's firm—she's stubborn.

He makes wise judgments—she reveals her prejudices.

He is a man of the world—she's been around.

He isn't afraid to say what he thinks—she is opinionated.

He exercises authority—she's tyrannical.

He's discreet—she's secretive.

He's a stern taskmaster—she's difficult to work with."

I think this might sum up some of the prejudices we're up against today.

There have been a great many references by those quoted in this book to the fact that they have lawyers available to help their agents in the more complex areas. In producing the "New Horizons for Attorneys" video, four of the many lawyers who are finding rich rewards as life underwriters were presented.

Today the legal profession is attracting many of the brightest young women anywhere. In 1982, there were 35,334 first-year law students admitted to the full-time law schools approved by the American Bar Association, of whom 13,334, or almost 4 out of 10, were women.

From all sources we are turning out about 40,000 lawyers a

year—compared to Japan's 500! So many of the brightest and best of them will spend years as "go-fers" in giant law firms. Among them are many, male and female, who could quickly put their abilities to profitable and worthwhile use in the life insurance business today.

LIMRA tells us that we now are "up to" the 12 percent mark in total number of women agents in the U.S. Alert companies and agency heads will change that drastically and soon, for a most significant trend is this:

> *Women will play an ever-larger role in the life insurance business in all its facets, including selling, agency management, and as buyers.*

Alphabetical Index Of Individuals Quoted In This Book